WORLD PEACE AND THE DEVELOPING COUNTRIES

Annals of Pugwash 1985

Edited by

Joseph Rotblat and Ubiratan D'Ambrosio

MACMILLAN
PRESS

First published 1986

Published by
THE MACMILLAN PRESS LTD
Houndmills, Basingstoke, Hampshire RG21 2XS
and London
Companies and representatives
throughout the world

Printed in Great Britain by
Oxford University Press
Oxford

British Library Cataloguing in Publication Data
World peace and the developing countries:
annals of Pugwash 1985.
1. Peace   2. Developing countries—
Defenses
I. Rotblat, Joseph   II. D'Ambrosio,
Ubiratan   III. Pugwash (*Peace Movement*)
327.1′72′091724   JX1952
ISBN 0–333–43636–9
ISBN 0–333–43637–7 Pbk

Contents

CONTENTS

Foreword

The current year is witnessing a further deterioration of the
international scene from the low ebb already reached in 1983,
the year first covered by the series 'Annals of Pugwash'. The
hopes generated by the projected summit conference in
November 1985 were cooled considerably by the lack of any
significant progress in arms control resulting from the
meeting itself. Such ebbs and flows of international hopes,
fears and actions are no strangers to Pugwash which has been
preoccupied since 1957 with its major priorities of avoiding
wars - nuclear war in particular - and with resolving
conflicts, reducing international tensions and fostering
measures to build trust and confidence among nations.

Stopping and reversing the nuclear arms race has been a
major preoccupation of Pugwash as shown by the contents of
the Annals series. In 1985 we paid attention to the problem
of both vertical and horizontal proliferation of nuclear
weapons, the former being concerned with qualitative
refinement and the latter with spread to other countries,
especially in relation to the Non-Proliferation Treaty. Other
classes of weapons, notably chemical and conventional, were
also analysed by Pugwash study groups that continue work in
these fields.

The problems of developing countries have long been a
concern of Pugwash, not only because of the many military
conflicts in these countries since World War II which have
caused immense suffering and loss of life and wasted scarce
resources, but also because of the problems of actual
survival - food supply, health, agriculture, and population
growth. Pugwash held a Symposium on Self-Reliance in Dar es
Salaam, Tanzania, in 1975, a Symposium on Feeding Africa in
Ghana in 1978, and in 1979 prepared a code of conduct for
international scientific cooperation for development which
has been widely followed in the United Nations and other
organisations. Separate meetings on Crisis Prevention and
Control in Africa and in Latin America were organised in

vii

1985. During the intervening years many Pugwash meetings included in their agenda items on arms transfers, conflicts and other major concerns of developing countries.

Thus, through recurrent periods of détente and cold war between East and West, and the fluctuating social and economic situation of the South, Pugwash has kept open lines of communication between scientists and scholars from countries of opposing political views but joined in their common goal of avoiding wars and achieving better social and economic conditions for developing countries.

The 34th Pugwash Conference held in Campinas, Brazil, gave special attention to the interrelationships of certain aspects of peace and development. The various chapters in the present volume indicate our continuing commitment to the theme of this volume, 'World Peace and the Developing Countries'. Pugwash meetings and studies in 1986 and 1987 will continue to pursue the quest for peace and stability in the interrelationships of the North and South, leading up to the 30th Anniversary of the Pugwash Movement in 1987, when an assessment will be made of results achieved and the needs for action in the coming years. We plan to keep the public informed of these matters in the continuing series of the Annals.

Preface

This volume of the Pugwash annals, the third in the series, contains material from several Pugwash meetings held in the period November 1984 to December 1985. Most of the papers were presented and debated at the Annual Pugwash Conference that was held in Campinas, Brazil, in July 1985. Because of the location of the Conference, the emphasis was on problems of developing countries, especially those relating to the security of these countries. A discussion on the prevention of nuclear weapons spreading to the Third World was particularly topical just before the Review Conference of the Non-Proliferation Treaty. The traditional Pugwash items: containment of the nuclear arms race and methods of solving disputes without the use of force, were also debated in the above context.

A selection of relevant papers from several other Pugwash meetings is included in this volume. Thus, Chapter 2 comes from the Symposium on African Security held in Cairo, in November 1984. Chapter 5 contains the statement issued by the Pugwash Executive Committee after the Workshop on Nuclear Forces in Geneva, May 1985. Chapter 6 is another statement issued after the Symposium on Strategic Defences, held in London in December 1985. Chapter 9 comes from the Workshop on Conventional Forces in Europe, held in Pöcking, FRG, March 1985. Finally, Chapter 14 was presented at the Study Group on Crisis Prevention and Control in Africa, held in Lusaka, Zambia, in April 1985.

The material is arranged in four parts.

Part One deals with the problem of major concern to Pugwash, how to stop and reverse the nuclear arms race. The danger of horizontal proliferation of nuclear weapons has been viewed by some analysts as very real, with the possibility of some countries withdrawing from the NPT during the Review Conference in September 1985. An opposite view, that it is against the self-interest of nations to acquire nuclear weapons, is presented, and a detailed analysis of the problem

is made in relation to Africa and Latin America. The comple-
mentary aspect of the nuclear arms race, vertical proliferation, has also become acute because of new technological
developments, particularly in relation to the Strategic
Defence Initiative. The general conclusion is that should SDI
go ahead, the existing treaties such as ABM would be in
jeopardy and a further acceleration of the arms race would
ensue.

Part Two is concerned with peace-keeping. Since any
type of war carries with it the danger of escalating into a
nuclear war, finding the means of managing crises without
their developing into armed conflicts becomes of prime
importance. The conditions needed to prevent conflicts, and
to manage them peacefully should they occur, are scrutinised,
in the realistic situation resulting from the existence in
the world of basically different ideological and economic
systems. The way to deal with one specific threat, chemical
warfare, is discussed in relation to the suggestion of
creating a zone free from chemical weapons. The problem of
conventional armament - especially in relation to European
security - is debated, and new concepts are advanced to take
into account the modernisation of conventional weapons.

Part Three specifically tackles the security of the
developing countries in the context of the rivalries between
the superpowers. The dangers to world peace resulting from
the numerous conflicts and actual wars in the countries of
the Third World are discussed, as well as the role of the
industrialised countries, with their own conflicts being
transplanted into other continents, thus aggravating an
already bad situation. The two most critical regions at the
present time appear to be Southern Africa and Central
America; a detailed analysis is presented of the social,
political, economic and military problems which make the
solution of the crises in those areas so urgent and yet so
difficult to find.

Part Four, also concerned with the Third World,
discusses the economic problems of the developing countries
in the light of the evolution of new concepts and policies,
recent developments and the prospects for the near future.
Here too the issues facing the countries in the South cannot
be isolated from those in the North. Therefore, a thorough
survey is made of the status of the world economy and its
prospects. Specific factors, such as the emerging of military
industries - both for internal use and for export - the
international debt crisis, and the relation between security
expenditure and economic growth, are discussed, and their
implications for interrelationships and a peaceful future are
examined.

Since the chapters from individual authors present their personal views, a divergence of opinion on some specific issues is bound to occur. However, some points of convergence usually become discernible in the course of discussions. The Pugwash Council builds on these in its assessments of the overall situation, and in making specific recommendations. These are contained in the public statement which was issued after the Campinas Conference and is presented in this volume in the Appendix (p.249).

*   *   *   *

In editing this volume we were greatly assisted by Dr David Carlton, and we wish to express our deep gratitude to him. Technical assistance in preparing the camera-ready copy was received from Jean Egerton, Karina Gilvarry and Edith Salt, and we are very much in debt to them for their skill and devotion.

April 1986   Joseph Rotblat
                                        Ubiratan D'Ambrosio

Notes on the Contributors

Nicole Ball (USA) economics. Currently Research Associate of the Swedish Institute of International Affairs.

D. Carlton (UK) history. Senior Lecturer in Diplomatic History at the Polytechnic of North London on secondment to the Open University.

M.H. Clemmesen (Denmark) military science. Infantry Major in the Danish Army.

R.P. Dagnino (Brazil) economics. Professor of Science and Technology Policy at the University of Campinas.

E. Ezz (Egypt) nuclear and chemical defence. Retired Major General. Director of Scientific Research Branch, Cairo.

A.V. Fokin (USSR) chemistry. Director of the Institute of Inorganic Compounds of the USSR Academy of Sciences.

A. Garcia-Robles (Mexico) international relations. Peace Nobel Laureate. Head of the Mexican Delegation at the United Nations; former Minister for Foreign Affairs of Mexico.

M.M. Kaplan (USA) microbiology. Secretary-General of Pugwash; former Director of Research Promotion and Development, World Health Organisation.

I. Kende (Hungary) political science. Professor of International Relations at the Karl Marx University of Economic Sciences, Budapest.

K. Lohs (GDR) chemical toxicology. Director of the Research Department of Chemical Toxicology in Leipzig.

F.A. Long (USA) chemistry. Director of Program on Science, Technology and Society at Cornell University, Ithaca.

S.N. MacFarlane (USA) international relations. Professor of International Security at the University of Virginia.

Tommie Sue Montgomery (USA) sociology. Lecturer at the Department of Political Science, Dickinson College, Carlisle, Pennsylvania.

N. Mpwotsh (Ethiopia) political science. Head of Defence and Security Division, Organisation of African Unity, Addis Ababa.

R.R. Neild (UK) economics. Professor of Economics at the University of Cambridge; former Director of SIPRI.

L.P. Rosa (Brazil) energy physics. Professor of Physics at the Federal University of Rio de Janeiro.

J. Rotblat (UK) physics. Emeritus Professor of Physics at the University of London; Secretary-General of Pugwash 1957-73; Chairman of the British Pugwash Group.

A. Ruiz-Zuniga (Costa Rica) history and philosophy of science. Professor of Mathematics at the University of Costa Rica, San Jose.

J-P. Stroot (Belgium) physics. Head of Division at CERN Geneva.

T. Toyoda (Japan) physics. Emeritus Professor of Physics at the University of Nagoya.

M.S. Wionczek (Mexico) energy economics. Senior Research Associate in Economics at the University of Mexico.

Acronyms

ABM	anti-ballistic missile
ACP	group of countries in Africa, the Caribbean and Pacific
AINIC	arms industries of newly industrialised countries
ASAT	anti-satellite weapon
ASBM	air-to-surface ballistic missile
ASEAN	Association of South East Asian Nations
ATBM	anti-tactical ballistic missile
CBM	confidence-building measures
CBW	chemical and biological warfare
CCD	Conference of the Committee on Disarmament
CD	Committee on Disarmament (Geneva)
CDU/CSU	Christian Democrat Union/Christian Social Union (FRG)
CEP	circular error probable
C^3I	command, control, communications and intelligence
CPSU	Communist Party of the Soviet Union
CSCE	Conference on Security and Cooperation in Europe
CTB	comprehensive test ban
CW	chemical warfare
CWFZ	chemical weapon-free zone
DGB	Federation of Trade Unions (FRG)
ENUWAR	environmental effects of nuclear war
ECLA	Economic Commission in Latin America
EEC	European Economic Community
FDN	Nicaraguan Democratic Front
FDR/FMLN	Frente Democratico Revolucionario/Farabundo Mardi de Liberacion Nacional (El Salvador)
FSLN	Frente Sandinista de Liberacion Nacional (Nicaragua)
GATT	General Agreement on Tariffs and Trade
GDP	gross domestic product
GNP	gross national product
GLCM	ground-launched cruise missile

IAEA	International Atomic Energy Agency
ICBM	intercontinental ballistic missile
IEA	International Energy Agency
IISS	International Institute for Strategic Studies
IMF	International Monetary Fund
INF	intermediate nuclear forces
MAD	mutually assured destruction
MAP	Military Assistance Programme
MBFR	mutual and balanced force reduction
MIRV	multiple independently targetable re-entry vehicles
MNR	Mozambique National Resistance Movement
MPLA	Popular Liberation Movement (Angola)
NATO	North Atlantic Treaty Organisation
NORAD	North American Air Defence Command
NPT	Non-Proliferation Treaty
NGO	non-governmental organisation
NIC	newly industrialised country
OAU	Organisation of African Unity
OECD	Organisation for Economic Cooperation and Development
OPEC	Organisation of Petroleum Exporting Countries
PGM	precision-guided munitions
R&D	research and development
SALT	Strategic Arms Limitation Talks
SAM	surface-to-air missile
SATO	South Atlantic Treaty Organisation
SCOPE	Scientific Committee on Problems of Environment
SED	Socialist Unity Party (GDR)
SDI	strategic defence initiative
SIPRI	Stockholm International Peace Research Institute
SLBM	submarine-launched ballistic missile
SPD	Social Democratic Party (FRG)
TNC	transnational corporation
UNCTAD	United Nations Conference on Trade and Development
UNU	United Nations University
UNITA	National Union for the Total Independence of Africa
UNITAR	United Nations Institute for Training and Research
WTO	Warsaw Treaty Organisation (Warsaw Pact)

Glossary

Anti-ballistic missile system	Weapon system for intercepting and destroying ballistic missiles.
Anti-satellite (ASAT) system	Weapon system for destroying, damaging or disturbing the normal function of artificial satellites.
Ballistic missile	Missile which follows a ballistic trajectory when thrust is terminated.
Circular error probable (CEP)	A measure of accuracy of a weapon delivery system; the radius of a circle, centred on the target, within which 50 per cent of the weapons are expected to fall.
Chemical weapon-free zone (CWFZ)	Zone which a group of nations may establish by a treaty whereby a state of total absence of chemical weapons to which the zone shall be subject is defined, and a system of verification and control is set up to guarantee compliance.
Deterrence	The ability to prevent another nation from acting in a hostile manner.
First-strike capability	Capability to destroy within a very short period of time all or a very substantial portion of an adversary's strategic forces.

Fission

Process whereby the nucleus of a heavy atom splits into lighter nuclei with the release of substantial amounts of energy.

Fratricide effect

The destruction or degradation of the accuracy and effectiveness of an attacking nuclear weapon by a nearby explosion of another attacking nuclear weapon.

Fusion

Process whereby light atoms, especially those of the isotopes of hydrogen - deuterium and tritium - combine to form a heavy atom with the release of very substantial amounts of energy.

Gross Domestic Product (GDP)

The GNP minus transactions with other countries.

Gross National Product (GNP)

Annual total value of goods produced and services provided in a country.

Intercontinental ballistic missile (ICBM)

Ballistic missile with a range in excess of 5500 km.

Intermediate nuclear forces (INF)

US designation for long-range and possibly medium-range theatre nuclear weapons.

Kiloton

Measure of the explosive yield of a nuclear weapon equivalent to 1000 metric tonne of trinitrotoluene (TNT) high explosive.

Megaton (Mt)

Measure of the explosive yield of a nuclear weapon equivalent to one thousand kiloton.

Multiple independently targetable re-entry vehicles (MIRV)

Re-entry vehicles, carried by one missile, which can be directed to separate targets.

Mutually assured destruction (MAD)

Concept of reciprocal deterrence which rests on the ability of the nuclear weapon powers to inflict intolerable damage on one another after surviving a nuclear first strike.

Mutual reduction of forces and armaments and associated measures in Central Europe (MFB or MBFR)

Subject of negotiations between NATO and the Warsaw Treaty Organisation, which began in Vienna in 1973. Often referred to as mutual (balanced) force reduction.

National technical means (NTM)

The use of technical intelligence collection means for verifying compliance with negotiated arms control agreements. These means must be consistent with the recognised provisions of international law.

Nuclear weapon-free zone (NWFZ)

Zone which a group of nations may establish by a treaty whereby a state of total absence of nuclear weapons to which the zone shall be subject is defined, and a system of verification and control is set up to guarantee compliance.

Precision-guided munition (PGM)

Non-nuclear weapon system characterised by high accuracy achieved by in-flight remote control, usually accompanied by high explosive effects.

PUREX

Process of chemical extraction of plutonium from spent fuel in reactors.

Strategic Arms Limitation Talks (SALT)

Negotiations between the Soviet Union and the United States, initiated in 1969, which seek to limit the strategic nuclear forces, both offensive and defensive, of both sides.

Strategic Defence Initiative (SDI) (Star Wars)

A concept of defence against nuclear ballistic missiles by their interception and destruction in flight.

Strategic nuclear forces	Strategic nuclear forces ICBMs, SLBMs, ASBMs and bomber aircraft of intercontinental range.
Tactical nuclear weapons	see: Theatre nuclear weapons.
Theatre nuclear weapons	Nuclear weapons of a range less than 5500 km. Often divided into long-range (over 1000 km, for instance), medium-range, and short-range (up to 200 km, also referred to as tactical or battle-field nuclear weapons).
Warhead	The part of a missile, rocket or other munition which contains the explosive or other material intended to inflict damage.
Yield	Released nuclear explosive energy expressed as equivalent of the energy produced by a given number of metric tonne of trinitrotoluene (TNT) high explosive.

PART ONE
Containment of the Nuclear Arms Race

1 Preventing the Spread of Nuclear Weapons

Joseph Rotblat

Prevention is Better than Cure

Our prime objective in Pugwash is to eliminate the danger of nuclear war. This danger arises both from the growing intensity of the nuclear arms race between the superpowers (vertical proliferation), and from the spreading of nuclear weapons among many nations (horizontal proliferation). However, there is an important difference in the nature of the effort needed to reduce the danger from these two sources. Vertical proliferation needs to be contained and eventually eliminated; horizontal proliferation needs to be **prevented.** Because the fact is that the dreaded spread of nuclear weapons, predicted for a long time[1], has not materialised. For the past 20 years there has been no addition to the number of nuclear weapon states, at least not formally or overtly.

Prevention is certainly better than cure, but it is not necessarily easier; otherwise we would not need so many medical practitioners and hospitals. In the case of nuclear weapons the nature of the danger is such that should the disease break out it could assume epidemic proportions. The underlying pathogenesis is there, and it needs only a conducive climate to set it off.

Some analysts have pin-pointed the time of the occurrence of that climate with great precision: September 1985, at the Third NPT Review Conference. They predict that the resentment many NPT members nourished for a long time - and egged on by some non-NPT states which appear to be bent on the demise of the Treaty - will find open expression in a withdrawal from it, followed by steps towards the acquisition of nuclear weapons.

The danger of such action does not appear to me to be real; indeed, I believe that not only will this be avoided but that the occasion of the Review Conference will be used to consolidate the NPT and ensure its continuance after 1995,

3

when a conference is to be convened to determine its future.

As I will show in this paper, much of the criticism level-led at the NPT is valid; several aspects of the Treaty I always thought to be unethical. But despite all its weaknes-ses I am convinced that the NPT is a very important inter-national agreement that must be supported and strengthened. It will require a determined effort to achieve this, but it is essential to make it, because if successful it would not only prevent horizontal proliferation but would also help in reducing the danger of vertical proliferation.

A Few Facts and Figures

It is useful to start with a few numerical data about the NPT[2]. At the time of writing (April 1985) the total number of states party to the Treaty is 128, of which three (UK, USA, USSR) are officially designated as nuclear weapon states. The histogram (a) on Figure 1 shows how the NPT membership has grown, year by year, since the Treaty came into force in 1970. A remarkable feature is that the graph is steadily increasing; during the 15 years not a single country availed itself of its right to withdraw from the Treaty.

The graph shows that the NPT membership has doubled since 1970, but during that period there has also been a consider-able increase in the number of independent states in the world. This increase is indicated by the upper sets of lines: (b) gives the number of members of the United Nations, and (c) the total number of independent states. The definition of the latter is sometimes rather arbitrary.

Among the states party to the Treaty, there are nine which are not UN members. One of these is the Holy See, an un-likely candidate for the acquisition of nuclear weapons, but its membership of the NPT has probably more than symbolic significance, at least for some nations.

The difference between graphs (c) and (a), representing the number of independent states that have not signed the Treaty, has been decreasing all the time, but there seems to be a hard core of states which refuse to join the NPT, and it is at these states that our efforts need to be largely directed. A list of non-NPT states is given in Table 1. It includes two nuclear weapon states, China and France.

Table 2 contains a breakdown of the total numbers under several categories. One classification is by alliances, (NATO, Warsaw Treaty) and groups like Tlatelolco. In each class, the great majority of (but not all) members belonging to it adhere to the Treaty. Among NATO countries, Spain is an exception. Albania has not signed the Treaty, but its membership of WTO is somewhat questionable. Of the Tlatelolco

Table 1. States that have not ratified the NPT

China
France
- - - - - - - - - - - -

Albania
Algeria
Andorra
Angola
*Argentina
Bahrain
Belize
Bhutan
*Brazil
Burma
*Chile
+*Colombia
Comoros
*Cuba
*Democratic People's
  Republic of Korea
Djibouti
Guinea
Guyana
India

Israel
Kiribati
+Kuwait
Malawi
Mauritania
Monaco
Mozambique
Niger
Oman
Pakistan
People's Democratic
  Republic of Yemen
Qatar
Saudi Arabia
South Africa
Spain
+Trinidad & Tobago
United Arab Emirates
United Republic of
  Tanzania
Western Samoa
Vanuatu
+Yemen Arab Republic
Zambia
Zimbabwe

+ signed but not ratified
* accepted IAEA safeguards

Table 2. Current Status of the NPT membership

	States Party to the Treaty	States outside the Treaty
Total number	128	44
Nuclear-weapon states	3	2
Non-nuclear-weapon states	125	42
United Nations: members	116	36
non-members	9	6
Groupings:		
NATO	14	1
WTO	7	(1)
Tlatelolco	20	2
Nuclear power:		
Countries with reactors:		
working	16	6
under construction	4	1
being planned	5	1

members, two (Colombia and Trinidad & Tobago) are not in the NPT, apart from Argentina, Brazil and Chile which are not full members of Tlatelolco. Cuba is not in Tlatelolco.

Among the NATO and WTO states party to the Treaty there are those that, although classified as non-nuclear weapon states, have nuclear weapons on their territory. These are: Belgium, Denmark, FRG, Italy and Netherlands of the NATO countries, and Czechoslovakia and GDR of the WTO countries.

Among the states that refused to join the NPT, one usually distinguishes a group denoted as 'potential nuclear weapon states'. The definition of such states is to a large extent arbitrary, because it is believed that some of them are not 'potential' but actual nuclear weapon states, nevertheless they can be classified under three groups:

(1)   a nuclear weapon capability established by testing (India);

(2)   widely believed to have already a weapon capability (Israel, South Africa);

(3)   widely believed to be on the way to having a weapon capability (Argentina, Brazil, Pakistan).

Thus, out of 42 non-NPT, non-nuclear weapon states, only six are generally assumed to be potential nuclear-weapon states. On the other hand, there is a much larger number of states with a potential nuclear weapon capacity among the NPT members. This follows from their possession of considerable nuclear facilities (nuclear power stations) and trained nuclear scientists and engineers.

This leads to another classification in Table 2: nuclear facilities for peaceful purposes. Here again, the criteria are not well defined. Many countries have research reactors, but these cover a very wide range of power outputs and degree of enrichment of the uranium. It is also not always clear to what extent these reactors are used, if at all. For this reason I have chosen a criterion which is easier to define: the operation - actual or planned - of at least one reactor for the generation of electricity[3]. In Table 2, the number of countries with such programmes is sub-divided into three groups: with reactors already in operation, under construction, and being planned. Considering the time needed to build a reactor (which, on average, has increased during the last decade from six years to ten years), this may be taken as the total number of states with nuclear power generation by the year 1995, when the NPT comes to the end of its present term.

Violation of the NPT by the Nuclear-Weapon States

If the NPT is to be strengthened - as is our aim - its weaknesses need first to be exposed so that they can be dealt with. (See Annex for the text of the Treaty).

A critical evaluation of the performance of the NPT regime must begin with a severe censure of the nuclear weapon members of the Treaty for their violation, both in letter and in spirit, of their undertakings.

Article I of the Treaty obliges nuclear weapon states not to transfer nuclear weapons, or **the control over such weapons, directly or indirectly,** to other states. Yet, this is what has been practiced for a long time by NATO. The most recent example is the placing by the USA of Pershing II missiles in the FRG and cruise missiles in Belgium and Italy (and exerting pressure on Netherlands to accept such missiles). The details of the agreement about the control over these weapons are not known, but it has been alleged[4] that under the 'dual key' or 'joint decision' systems, these countries would have at least indirect control over nuclear weapons, in violation of the terms of the Treaty.

This criticism - if valid - would also apply to the stationing of cruise missiles in the United Kingdom, since Article I refers to 'any recipient whatsoever'.

The Soviet Union has recently stationed some of its SS-20 launchers in Czechoslovakia and GDR. It is not known whether some control arrangement is involved, but the same accusation would apply, if it were.

It should also be noted that under Article II, countries which accept nuclear weapons on their territory and exercise direct or indirect control over them, are also in violation of the NPT.

Article VI is the main bone of contention between many NPT members and the nuclear-weapon states party to the Treaty. Under this Article, these states undertook 'to pursue negotiations in good faith on effective measures relating to the cessation of the nuclear arms race ... and to nuclear disarmament'. The history of the nuclear arms race over the past fifteen years throws very serious doubt on the good faith, as well as on the capability of the superpowers to fulfil their obligations, caught as they are in the action-reaction syndrome. Because of this, even during the 'on-periods' of negotiations on arms control, very little progress has been achieved, and the very few measures agreed to were dwarfed by the qualitative and quantitative intensi-fication of the arms race.

This failure of the nuclear-weapon states was the chief reason for the breakdown of the Second Review Conference in

1980, and it has been suggested that the same may happen in 1985. A number of non-aligned countries are said to threaten to withdraw from the Treaty, because they can see no validity in a treaty systematically violated by its 'privileged' members. However, it is doubtful whether such threats can carry sufficient impact to induce the nuclear powers to make progress towards the reduction of nuclear arms, as long as they continue with their present policies of negotiating from a position of strength (the argument used for the need of more MX missiles and even for SDI) and - more importantly - as long as they continue to believe that the development and deployment of new offensive and defensive systems are necessary to remove the vulnerability created by the earlier systems.

Yet - quite apart from the resentment about violating an undertaking - there is a genuine and legitimate reason for the concern among the non-nuclear-weapon states, particularly from the Third World, about the lack of progress towards nuclear disarmament. They are increasingly worried about the danger of a nuclear war, which the continuing and accelerating arms race is making more probable.

In the past, many Third World countries considered a nuclear war to be an issue for the North only. As far as they were concerned it was a diversion from the real problem: the need to raise the standard of living in the poor countries. Leaders of these countries used to tell the North: 'If you want to kill each other off in a nuclear war, it is your funeral; we don't want to have anything to do with it'. This argument was never tenable, bearing in mind the interdependence of all peoples on the globe, but it was the 'nuclear winter' phenomenon that has finally put an end to this isolationist myth. It is now generally recognized that a nuclear war could affect everybody, even if all the weapons were detonated in the higher latitudes of the northern hemisphere. Indeed, the tropical zones, in which many of the Third World countries are situated, might be hit hardest, because their agriculture is much more vulnerable to a reduction of temperature.

We may, therefore, expect even stronger pressure on the nuclear-weapon states to take significant steps to reduce the danger of a nuclear war.

The Phoney Bargain in the NPT

Articles II and IV (and to some extent Article III) contain a trade-off for the non-nuclear-weapon states. Under Article II they undertake not to acquire nuclear weapons, and under Article IV they receive the reward for this undertaking: help in developing nuclear technology for peaceful purposes. The allegation that this help had not been forthcoming sufficiently free and fast, was one of the main bones of contention at the previous Review Conference.

The ethics of this bargain has always appeared dubious to me: why should one be rewarded for giving up something that is bad for one in any case? That the possession of nuclear weapons is undesirable is explicitly spelled out in the Preamble to the Treaty, which states 'that the proliferation of nuclear weapons would seriously enhance the danger of nuclear war', as well as in the text, which calls for nuclear disarmament. If so, why should a state that gives it up be entitled to demand compensation? Paradoxically, the nature of the compensation is such, as to make it easier for a country to do the very thing it undertakes not to do: to make nuclear weapons; because it could utilise for such purpose the help it had received in building up its nuclear know-how. It is as if a person who gives up smoking, is offered a cigarette-making machine as a reward.

This is not an argument against sharing of nuclear, or any technology; it is an argument against sharing being used as a bargain. That Articles II and IV are a straightforward trade-off was confirmed during an important public inquiry about a reprocessing plant to be set up in the UK; the Chairman of that Inquiry, a Judge - who has since been promoted to be a Judge of the High Court, and presumably is an authority on legal interpretation - said the following in his report[5]:

> The NPT is on its face a straightforward bargain. The essence of that bargain was that, in exchange for an undertaking from non-nuclear weapon parties to refrain from making or acquiring nuclear weapons and to submit to safeguards when provided for peaceful purposes with material which was capable of diversion, the nuclear weapon states would afford every assistance to non-nuclear weapon states "in the development of nuclear energy" ... I also find it difficult to see how a party, which has developed reprocessing technology or created reprocessing facilities, would be otherwise than in breach of the agreement, if it both refused to supply the technology to another party and refused to reprocess for it.

The Futility of the Bargain

Whatever the intentions and the legal arguments about the bargain, the facts show that in this respect the existence of the Treaty has not made any difference. The situation appears to be the same - both in relation to the non-acquisition of nuclear weapons and the acquisition of nuclear technology - in all countries, whether they have joined the Treaty or not.

Take first the undertaking not to make or acquire nuclear weapons. One might have expected that at least some of the countries that refused to sign the Treaty - and therefore gave no such undertaking - would have by now made or acquired nuclear weapons. Yet, after fifteen years, not one of the 42 non-members of the NPT has done so overtly. Even India, which detonated a nuclear 'device' in 1974, claims that the intention was to explore the peaceful applications of nuclear explosives. Israel and South Africa never admitted to having nuclear weapons. Pakistan strenuously denies that it is preparing nuclear weapons. The same applies to Argentina and Brazil. These six countries are generally described as **potential nuclear-weapon states**, but no suspicion of wishing to acquire nuclear weapons has been levelled at the great majority of the countries which refused to sign the Treaty.

On the other hand, suspicions have been levelled at some countries that did sign the Treaty, such as Libya. Except for a few such cases, I submit that even in the absence of the NPT, it is unlikely that its present adherents would have decided to embark overtly on a nuclear weapons programme. Making of nuclear weapons is simply 'not on' in the present climate and this applies both to members and non-members of the NPT.

A similar conclusion is reached in relation to the other end of the bargain, the help in the development of nuclear energy. From the data given in Table 2 it is seen that 25 of the 125 countries that have signed the Treaty, that is 20 per cent, already have, or soon will have, or plan to have nuclear power for electricity. Among the countries that have not signed the Treaty the corresponding figure is 8 out of 42, that is 19 per cent. We must therefore conclude that despite the clamour for help by some countries, membership of the Treaty has not made a significant difference in this respect.

Another part of the Treaty is also relevant to this discussion. Under Article III, parties to the Treaty agree to accept the IAEA safeguards. But submission to the IAEA safeguard system, although its exclusive purpose is verification of fulfilment of NPT obligations, is not exclusive to members of the NPT. The IAEA safeguards have wider application: a number of countries which have not signed the NPT but have nuclear power programmes, have agreed to submit to a safeguard system (they are marked with an asterisk in Table 1). The same applies to other agreements about supply of materials. So, once again, there is little difference between belonging or not belonging to the NPT. Indeed, there have been complaints that NPT members were treated worse than non-members.

It is also important to note that all five nuclear-weapon states - although not obliged by the terms of the Treaty - have voluntarily agreed to submit at least some of their civil nuclear programmes to IAEA safeguards.

The NPT is Very Important

The discussion in the previous section might lead one to conclude that the existence of the NPT did not make a significant difference to the major objectives for which it was set up, and that therefore it is unnecessary. However, one can also come to the reverse conclusion: that the NPT did play a vital role, and its continuation is most important for world security. It is this conclusion that I uphold in this chapter.

In the NPT, three-quarters of all nations have put their signature to a solemn undertaking not to acquire nuclear weapons. They have all adhered to it faithfully during the past fifteen years. In my opinion, this very fact has created a new climate in world opinion on nuclear issues, a climate hostile to the possession of nuclear weapons. As a result of this, any country - whether a member of the NPT or not - that openly declared that it has acquired, or intends to acquire, nuclear weapons would incur such an opprobrium, there would be such an outcry of public opinion, with possible economic and political repercussions, that only in extreme desperation, or due to the insanity or swashbuckling of a leader, would a country take such a step. Whatever the original motive may have been, the NPT has now become the formal expression of the instinctive feeling of people everywhere that nuclear weapons are evil and must be got rid of as soon as possible.

Even so, there is still the danger that the acquisition of nuclear weapons by one country - for whatever reason - could have a domino effect: neighbouring countries suddenly feeling threatened and compelled to take similar action, and so on. It is of the utmost importance to prevent such a situation. In this respect, an important step would be a declaration by 'potential nuclear-weapon states' - particularly Israel and South Africa, which do not discourage rumours that they already have nuclear weapons - that they do not intend to acquire such weapons. This would considerably allay fears in neighbouring countries.

Notwithstanding the initial reasons for the specific

formulation of the Articles in the Treaty - the trade-offs and compromises between the negotiating parties - I believe that there has been a genuine and fundamental change since the 1960s. We should build on that change in world opinion in proposing a new formulation of the NPT which would make it stand on its own feet; the renunciation of nuclear weapons would not have to be part of a bargain.

However strongly we may feel about the violation of Article VI, the present situation is still preferable to the alternative: no Treaty, or a weakened Treaty by the withdrawal of a significant number of its members. Such a step would signal the beginning of overt horizontal proliferation, and we shall all be in a much more dangerous situation.

Not only must this be avoided, but we must concentrate our efforts on bringing in the 42 non-nuclear weapon states that have so far refused to join the NPT. In the following sections reasons will be presented that should appeal to these states and make the Treaty truly universal. This, in turn, would make it possible to exert stronger pressure on the nuclear weapon states to fulfil their obligations, and thus to achieve the ultimate aim of the Treaty, nuclear disarmament.

A More Equitable Treaty is Now Feasible

As already indicated, the situation in 1985 is in many ways radically different from that prevailing at the time the NPT was being negotiated. In most aspects the difference is such as to make it easier to draw up a more equitable Treaty, when the matter of its extension is decided in 1995. Four of these aspects will be reviewed here.

(a) More Suppliers of Nuclear Technology

In the initial period, the nuclear weapon states were - apart from Canada - the only ones capable of supplying nuclear technology to other countries.   This ceased to be the case a long time ago. Apart from members of the NPT, such as West Germany, even non-NPT members, as for example, Argentina or Spain, are now suppliers of material, equipment and know-how[6]. The terms offered are different from those of the NPT members; they are often more attractive, and carry fewer conditions - resented by many countries as restricting their sovereignty - than those stipulated by nuclear-weapon states. Let us hope that this will not result in a lowering of standards of safeguards, but the fact is that the link between Articles II and IV is now of little relevance.

(b) Nuclear Energy - a Mirage

An even more important reason for the reduced emphasis on nuclear technology in the NPT is the changed attitude towards nuclear energy. In the earlier years, many Third World countries became convinced - to a large extent thanks to the promotional drive of the IAEA - that nuclear power would be the best solution to their energy problems. The glamour which was then attached to this new source of energy, was an additional factor; some leaders of less developed countries coveted the prestige which would accrue from the possession of the most advanced technology. And, of course, one cannot exclude the conscious or subliminal motive of having the means to convert the facilities of a peaceful nuclear power programme to military purposes, should the need for this arise.

All this has changed to a very large extent. Even industrialised countries have encountered many difficulties with their nuclear power programmes, especially since some aspects of it, such as waste disposal, are still unresolved and may remain so for a long time. The Three-Mile-Island accident - even though it did not result in a disaster - has alerted the public to the possibility of human error leading to grave consequences; the need for more protection has contributed to the considerable increase in capital costs of reactors. For developing countries this has made the economic advantages of nuclear energy even more doubtful. Furthermore, there has been an upsurge of public opinion against nuclear energy, frequently linked with the mass movements against nuclear weapons. Finally, new technologies have emerged, such as space, microcomputers, or genetic engineering, that have replaced nuclear energy as the exciting frontier of science, and in some cases offering new economic and industrial avenues for progress.

The outcome of this, plus a number of other no less important factors, was a dramatic slow down in the development of nuclear power in the whole world. The projected nuclear power programmes are now an order of magnitude lower than they were in 1970, with every projection being lower than the earlier one. As Table 2 shows, only about 22 per cent of all countries now have or plan to have nuclear power. Clearly, the need for assistance in nuclear technology can no longer serve as a general inducement to give up nuclear weapons.

(c) Peaceful Nuclear Explosions are a Non-issue

At one time, another aspect of nuclear energy, namely peaceful nuclear explosions, was blown up into great prominence as offering important benefits in a variety of fields. Article V of the Treaty is devoted to this subject: it calls for all potential benefits from peaceful applications of nuclear explosions to be made available to non-nuclear weapon states party to the Treaty. In the past, this Article may have been an obstacle to some nations to join the Treaty. For example, the 1974 nuclear explosion in India was ostensibly for peaceful purposes, but it would have been a violation of the Treaty - if India had been a member - since it was not carried out under international observation and procedure laid down in the Treaty.

As it turned out, however, peaceful nuclear explosions have very limited viable applications, and even where they have been considered the benefits turned out to be only marginal. This aspect of nuclear technology can therefore be put in cold storage.

(d) Nuclear Weapons do not offer Security

The question of security offered by nuclear weapons is paramount. If it were proved that the possession of nuclear weapons proffered greater security to a state, then no international treaty would or could stop the acquisition of such weapons. Fortunately, the evidence points in the opposite direction: the history of the nuclear arms race is a clear indication that the possession of nuclear weapons gives less, not more, security.

Even though both superpowers have long ago acquired a sufficient potential to fulfil the requirements of deterrence: to inflict unacceptable damage in retaliation for an attack, they still feel impelled to acquire new weapons.   At no time was either side satisfied with what it already had in its arsenals. The dynamics of the arms race does not allow for a standstill; technological advance keeps eroding the value of the deterrent, necessitating the introduction of new measures. President Reagan's insistence on the Strategic Defense Initiative is a clear expression of the sense of insecurity in the United States, with all its arsenal of more than 20 000 nuclear warheads.

The United Kingdom and France are also not able to rest on what they already have in their arsenals. They feel compelled to update them all the time - imposing a burden on their economies - although it is difficult to imagine a situation when these countries would use, or threaten to use, nuclear weapons without the superpowers being brought in, thereby very likely leading to an all-out nuclear war with catastrophic consequences to all.

Self-interest Dictates the Renunciation of Nuclear Weapons

The above discussion leads to the formulation of the principles on which a more equitable NPT should be based, and on measures to bring it about.

The most important principle is that the **renunciation of possession of nuclear weapons is not a sacrifice but is in the self-interest of a state.** This follows directly from the analysis in the previous section showing that the possession of nuclear weapons decreases rather than increases the security of a nation.

If this is accepted, then it becomes unnecessary to offer any compensation to a state that renounces nuclear weapons, such as help in developing a nuclear technology. The present Article IV (as well as Article V) will therefore become redundant.

Instead of the technological link between Articles II, III and IV, there should be a political link, namely a commitment by the nuclear weapon states not to use nuclear weapons to endanger the security of non-nuclear weapon states party to the Treaty. If such a guarantee were to be restricted to states that do not have nuclear weapons on their territory, it would be an incentive to states with such weapons to demand their removal.

As mentioned earlier, in an all-out nuclear war it would not make much difference in the final outcome whether a country is or is not directly attacked with nuclear weapons. Nevertheless, such a guarantee would be conducive to a more relaxed atmosphere; this by itself might contribute to the lowering of the probability of a nuclear war.

As was pointed out earlier, the main danger to the non-proliferation regime is that one nation may suddenly violate it and acquire - by one means or another - a nuclear weapon capability. A neighbouring country, that is not on friendly terms with it, may perceive this as a threat to itself and attempt to restore the balance by also acquiring nuclear weapons. It is therefore in the interest of every nation to ensure that its neighbours adhere to the NPT.

One way towards this is by establishing nuclear-free zones embracing all nations in a given zone. In view of the sensitive positions of Israel and South Africa it is most urgent to establish nuclear-free zones in the Middle East and in Africa. In Latin America, Argentina and Brazil should be persuaded to join the Tlatelolco Treaty. The recent changes in the regimes in these countries make it more possible to achieve this[7]. But the ultimate aim must be to ensure that **all** nations on the globe renounce nuclear weapons by joining the NPT.

One of the chief reasons for the persistent refusal of some states to join the Treaty is that in its present formulation it perpetuates the division of nations into haves and have-nots, the former being privileged by being allowed to have nuclear weapons. However, if we accept the premise that the self-interest of a state dictates the renunciation of nuclear weapons, then the whole situation can be viewed in an entirely different light. The nuclear weapon states, far from being privileged, may in fact be seen as victims of their own folly; they have become entangled in a web of their own making, from which they are unable to extricate themselves. They deserve pity rather than envy.

All the same, since the consequences of that folly may gravely affect all other nations, these nations have the right, and the duty, to demand of the nuclear weapon states to take steps to reduce the danger, steps stipulated in Article VI. Such a demand would carry much greater weight if it were the unanimous voice of all other nations, that is if all other nations adhered to the NPT.

This demand should initially concentrate on two steps. One is a comprehensive test ban, a step specifically named in the Preamble to the Treaty. There do not appear to be sound technological reasons why compliance with such a test ban could not be verified, down to about one kiloton. A comprehensive test ban would help to curb the nuclear arms race by preventing the development of new weapons. The second step is a freeze on the deployment of existing weapons. This would prevent a deterioration of the situation while negotiations are being conducted on arms reduction.

The NPT would be strengthened immensely if the UK, and subsequently France, gave up their independent deterrents. One may ask why not all five nuclear weapon states? Realistically, one cannot expect - nor would it be feasible - for the two superpowers to abolish their nuclear arsenals in one fell swoop. China is at the crossroads at the present time and it is difficult to see in which direction its policies might take it; for the time being it is expedient to leave China alone. But there is no such hesitation in relation to France and the UK. Both are in the Western camp and one cannot conceive any rational and likely situation in which either of these two countries might use nuclear weapons, or threaten to use them, outside their NATO involvement. The main reason why France and the UK have their own nuclear arsenals is historical and out-of-date. Charles de Gaulle said: 'No country without an atom bomb could properly consider itself independent'. For the UK, Aneurin Bevan said: ' without the bomb we would be going naked into the international conference chamber'. If these arguments were con-

sidered valid at the present time, we would now have not five
but 172 nuclear weapon states.

At the Review Conference this year, strong pressure should
be exerted on the UK and France to give up their independent
deterrents, even though such a call is unlikely to be heeded
just now. It is difficult to imagine Mrs Thatcher moving in
that direction, but the next British Government may do it, if
the anti-nuclear movements in the UK gave high priority to
this end. France is in a different situation, its insistence
on the **force de frappe** seems to be irrespective of the
political colour of its Government. But it would become
difficult for France to remain intransigent if the UK gave up
its own nuclear weapons. In any case a campaign towards this
objective should start now.

Nuclear Energy Needs Safeguarding

Nuclear power programmes are likely to continue - albeit on a
small scale - and therefore there is the need to maintain the
safeguarding of sensitive technologies by the IAEA, as stipulated in Article III of the NPT. To avoid discrimination, the
same safeguards should apply to all countries. All civil
nuclear projects, whether in nuclear or in non-nuclear weapon
states, should be subject to full-scope IAEA controls.

However, additional measures should be taken to lessen the
opportunities for the diversion of sensitive materials by
terrorist groups or irrational leaders. One such important
measure would be an agreement not to carry out the chemical
processing of spent fuel elements from reactors to extract
the plutonium from them. Instead, the fuel elements should be
kept in the cooling tanks and later in storage tanks.
Existing plutonium should be put in IAEA storage. With the
present glut of uranium these measures would not have any
adverse effect on the economy of the fuel cycle in thermal
reactors. It would of course mean that the fast breeder
reactor could not be developed on a commercial scale, but
this is in any case not envisaged for the near future, and
may not become necessary even later if the next measure
proposed here is implemented, namely the development of
alternative sources of energy.

In parallel with the many difficulties encountered by the
nuclear industry - as described earlier - there has been a
growing realisation of the initial mistake, made in the
fifties, in singling out nuclear as the only energy source
with which the family of nations should concern itself, as
expressed by the setting up of the IAEA, and the consequent
neglect of other sources of energy. It is now generally
recognised that alternative sources of energy have great

potential, and that some lend themselves to early practical application, but their development had been hampered by lack of a substantial research effort, most of which went into nuclear energy.

To remedy this, all nations should be encouraged to satisfy their energy needs from alternative sources. This would be achieved best by a coordinated international effort, for example, by setting up a World Energy Organisation under the United Nations, along lines similar to those of the World Health Organization. The need for such a measure should be expressly stated in a revised Non-Proliferation Treaty.

References

1. W. Epstein, The Last Chance (New York: The Free Press, 1976).
2. U.N. Secretariat (April 1985).
3. International Atomic Energy Agency Bulletin (Vienna, 1985), 27, No.1.
4. V.P. Pavlichenko, 'Official interpretation of the "dual control" concept' (private communication).
5. Justice Parker, - The Windscale Inquiry (London, HMSO, 1978) p.18.
6. J. Perera, 'Nuclear Power in Developing Countries', Financial Times Management Report (1984).
7. L.P. Rosa (see below, p.45).

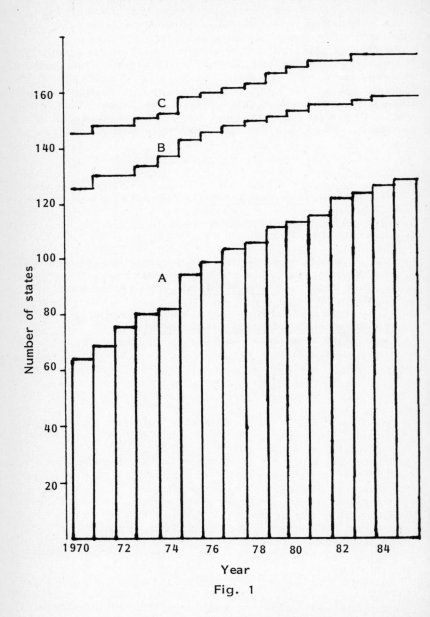

Fig. 1

Annex

Treaty on the Non-Proliferation of Nuclear Weapons (1968)

The States concluding this Treaty, hereinafter referred to as the 'Parties to the Treaty'.

Considering the devastation that would be visited upon all mankind by a nuclear war and the consequent need to make every effort to avert the danger of such a war and to take measures to safegard the securtity of peoples.

Believing that the proliferation of nuclear weapons would seriously enhance the danger of nuclear war.

In conformity with resolutions of the United Nations General Assembly calling for the conclusion of an agreement on the prevention of wider dissemination of nuclear weapons.

Undertaking to co-operate in facilitating the application of International Atomic Energy Agency safeguards on peaceful nuclear activities.

Expressing their support for research, development and other efforts to further the application, within the framework of the International Atomic Energy Agency safeguards system, of the principle of safeguarding effectively the flow of source and special fissionable materials by use of instruments and other techniques at certain strategic points.

Affirming the principle that the benefits of peaceful applications of nuclear technology, including any technological by-products which may be derived by nuclear-weapon States from the development of nuclear explosive devices, should be available for peaceful purposes to all Parties to the Treaty, whether nuclear-weapon or non-nuclear-weapon States.

Convinced that, in furtherance of this principle, all Parties to the Treaty are entitled to participate in the fullest possible exchange of scientific information for, and to contribute alone or in co-operation with other States to, the further development of the applications of atomic energy for peaceful purposes.

Declaring their intention to achieve at the earliest possible date the cessation of the nuclear arms race and to undertake effective measures in the direction of nuclear disarmament.

Urging the co-operation of all States in the attainment of this objective.

Recalling the determination expressed by the Parties to the 1963 Treaty banning nuclear weapon tests in the atmosphere, in outer space and under water in its Preamble to seek to achieve the discontinuance of all test explosions of nuclear weapons for all time and to continue negotiations to this end.

Desiring to further the easing of international tension and the strengthening of trust between States in order to facilitate the cessation of the manufacture of nuclear weapons, the liquidation of all their existing stockpiles, and the elimination from national arsenals of nuclear weapons and the means of their delivery pursuant to a Treaty on general and complete disarmament under strict and effective international control.

Recalling that, in accordance with the Charter of the United Nations, States must refrain in their international relations from the threat or use of force against the territorial integrity or political independence of any State, or in any other manner inconsistent with the Purposes of the United Nations, and that the establishment and maintenance of international peace and security are to be promoted with the least diversion for armaments of the world's human and economic resources.

Have agreed as follows:

Article I

Each nuclear-weapon State Party to the Treaty undertakes not to transfer to any recipient whatsoever nuclear weapons or other nuclear explosive devices or control over such weapons or explosive devices directly, or indirectly;   and not in any way to assist, encourage, or induce any non-nuclear-weapon State to manufacture or otherwise acquire nuclear weapons or other nuclear explosive devices, or control over such weapons or explosive devices.

Article II

Each non-nuclear weapon State Party to the Treaty under-takes not to receive the transfer from any transferor whatsoever of nuclear weapons or other nuclear explosive devices or of control over such weapons or explosive devices directly, or indirectly;   not to manufacture or otherwise acquire nuclear weapons or other nuclear explosive devices;   and not to seek or receive any assistance in the manufacture of nuclear weapons or other nuclear explosive devices.

Article III

1. Each non-nuclear-weapon State Party to the Treaty undertakes to accept safeguards, as set forth in an agreement to be negotiated and concluded with the International Atomic Energy Agency in accordance with

the Statute of the International Atomic Energy Agency
and the Agency's safeguards system, for the exclusive
purpose of verification of the fulfilment of its
obligations assumed under this Treaty with a view to
preventing diversion of nuclear energy from peaceful
uses to nuclear weapons or other nuclear explosive
devices. Procedures for the safeguards required by
this Article shall be followed with respect to source
or special fissionable material whether it is being
produced, processed or used in any principal nuclear
facility or is outside any such facility. The safeguards required by this Article shall be applied on all
source or special fissionable material in all peaceful
nuclear activities within the territory of such State,
under its jurisdiction, or carried out under its
control anywhere.

2. Each State Party to the Treaty undertakes not to
provide: (a) source or special fissionable material,
or (b) equipment or material especially designed or
prepared for the processing, use or production of
special fissionable material, to any non-nuclear-weapon
State for peaceful purposes, unless the source or
special fissionable material shall be subject to the
safeguards required by this Article.

3. The safeguards required by this Article shall be
implemented in a manner designed to comply with Article
IV of this Treaty, and to avoid hampering the economic
or technological development of the Parties or international co-operation in the field of peaceful nuclear
activities, including the international exchange of
nuclear material and equipment for the processing, use
or production of nuclear material for peaceful purposes
in accordance with the provisions of this Article and
the principle of safeguarding set forth in the Preamble
of the Treaty.

4. Non-nuclear-weapon States Party to the Treaty shall
conclude agreements with the International Atomic
Energy Agency to meet the requirements of this Article
either individually or together with other States in
accordance with the Statute of the International Atomic
Energy Agency. Negotiation of such agreements shall
commence within 180 days from the original entry into
force of this Treaty. For States depositing their
instruments of ratification or accession after the
180-day period, negotiation of such agreements shall
commence not later than the date of such deposit. Such
agreements shall enter into force not later than
eighteen months after the date of initiation of

negotiations.

Article IV

1. Nothing in this Treaty shall be interpreted as affecting the inalienable right of all the Parties to the Treaty to develop research, production and use of nuclear energy for peaceful purposes without discrimination and in conformity with Articles I and II of this Treaty.

2. All the Parties to the Treaty undertake to facilitate, and have the right to participate in, the fullest possible exchange of equipment, materials and scientific and technological information for the peaceful uses of nuclear energy. Parties to the Treaty in a position to do so shall also co-operate in contributing alone or together with other States or international organizations to the further development of the applications of nuclear energy for peaceful purposes, especially in the territories of non-nuclear-weapon States Party to the Treaty, with due consideration for the needs of the developing areas of the world.

Article V

Each Party to the Treaty undertakes to take appropriate measures to ensure that, in accordance with this Treaty, under appropriate international observation and through appropriate international procedures, potential benefits from any peaceful application of nuclear explosions will be made available to non-nuclear-weapons States Party to the Treaty on a non-discriminatory basis and that the charge to such Parties for the explosive devices used will be as low as possible and exclude any charge for research and development. Non-nuclear-weapon States Party to the Treaty shall be able to obtain such benefits, pursuant to a special international agreement or agreements, through an appropriate international body with adequate representation of non-nuclear-weapon States. Negotiations on this subject shall commence as soon as possible after the Treaty enters into force. Non-nuclear-weapon States Party to the Treaty so desiring may also obtain such benefits pursuant to bilateral agreements.

Article VI

Each of the Parties to the Treaty undertakes to pursue negotiations in good faith on effective measures relating to cessation of the nuclear arms race at an early date and to nuclear disarmament, and on a treaty on general and complete disarmament under strict and effective international control.

Article VII
Nothing in this Treaty affects the right of any group of States to conclude regional treaties in order to assure the total absence of nuclear weapons in their respective territories.

Article VIII
1. Any Party to the Treaty may propose amendments to this Treaty. The text of any proposed amendment shall be submitted to the Depositary Governments which shall circulate it to all Parties to the Treaty. Thereupon, if requested to do so by one-third or more of the Parties to the Treaty, the Depositary Governments shall convene a conference, to which they shall invite all the Parties to the Treaty, to consider such an amendment.
2. Any amendment to this Treaty must be approved by a majority of the votes of all the Parties to the Treaty, including the votes of all nuclear-weapon States Party to the Treaty and all other Parties which, on the date the amendment is circulated, are members of the Board of Governors of the International Atomic Energy Agency. The amendment shall enter into force for each Party that deposits its instruments of ratification of the amendment upon the deposit of such instruments of ratification by a majority of all the Parties, including the instruments of ratification of all nuclear-weapon States Party to the Treaty and all other Parties which, on the date the amendment is circulated, are members of the Board of Governors of the International Atomic Energy Agency. Thereafter, it shall enter into force for any other Party upon the deposit of its instrument of ratification of the amendment.
3. Five years after the entry into force of this Treaty, a conference of Parties to the Treaty shall be held in Geneva, Switzerland, in order to review the operation of this Treaty with a view to assuring that the purposes of the Preamble and the provisions of the Treaty are being realised. At intervals of five years thereafter, a majority of the Parties to the Treaty may obtain, by submitting a proposal to this effect to the Depositary Governments, the convening of further conferences with the same objective of reviewing the operation of the Treaty.

Article IX
1. This Treaty shall be open to all States for signature.
   Any State which does not sign the Treaty before its
   entry into force in accordance with paragraph 3 of this
   Article may accede to it at any time.
2. This Treaty shall be subject to ratification by
   signatory States. Instruments of ratification and
   instruments of accession shall be deposited with the
   Governments of the United Kingdom of Great Britain and
   Northern Ireland, the Union of Soviet Socialist
   Republics and the United States of America, which are
   hereby designated the Depositary Governments.
3. This Treaty shall enter into force after its
   ratification by the States, the Governments of which
   are designated Depositaries of the Treaty, and forty
   other States signatory to this Treaty and the deposit
   of their instruments of ratification. For the purposes
   of this Treaty, a nuclear-weapon State is one which has
   manufactured and exploded a nuclear weapon or other
   nuclear explosive device prior to 1 January, 1967.
4. For States whose instruments of ratification or
   accession are deposited subsequent to the entry into
   force of this Treaty, it shall enter into force on the
   date of the deposit of their instruments of ratification or accession.
5. The Depositary Governments shall promptly inform all
   signatory and acceding States of the date of each
   signature, the date of deposit of each instrument of
   ratification or of accession, the date of the entry
   into force of this Treaty, and the date of receipt of
   any requests for convening a conference or other
   notices.
6. This Treaty shall be registered by the Depositary
   Governments pursuant to Article 102 of the Charter of
   the United Nations.

Article X
1. Each Party shall in exercising its national sovereignty
   have the right to withdraw from the Treaty if it
   decides that extraordinary events, related to the
   subject matter of this Treaty, have jeopardized the
   supreme interests of its country. It shall give notice
   of such withdrawal to all other Parties to the Treaty
   and to the United Nations Security Council three months
   in advance. Such notice shall include a statement of
   the extraordinary events it regards as having jeopardized its supreme interests.
2. Twenty-five years after the entry into force of the

Treaty, a conference shall be convened to decide whether the Treaty shall continue in force indefinitely, or shall be extended for an additional fixed period or periods. This decision shall be taken by a majority of the Parties to the Treaty.

Article XI

This Treaty, the English, Russian, French, Spanish and Chinese texts of which are equally authentic, shall be deposited in the archives of the Depositary Governments. Duly certified copies of this Treaty shall be transmitted by the Depositary Governments to the Governments of the signatory and acceding states.

2 Africa and Nuclear Proliferation

Esmat Ezz

Introduction

At its 38th regular session in 1983, the General Assembly of the United Nations, passed a resolution[1], which

> Resolutely, unconditionally and for all time condemns nuclear war as being contrary to human conscience and reason, as the most monstrous crime against peoples and as violation of the foremost human right - the right to life; condemns the formulation, propounding, dissemination and propaganda of political and military doctrines and concepts intended to provide "legitimacy" for the first use of nuclear weapons and in general to justify the "admissibility" of unleashing nuclear war; calls upon all States to unite and redouble their efforts aimed at removing the threat of nuclear war, halting the nuclear arms race and reducing nuclear weapons until they are completely eliminated.

In the same session, the Assembly adopted a resolution[2] requesting the Conference on Disarmament 'to pursue its consideration of the question of adequately verified cessation and prohibition of the production of fissionable material for nuclear weapons and other nuclear explosive devices'. In another resolution[3] the Assembly recalled a previous resolution 'in which it called upon all states to consider and respect the continent of Africa and its surrounding areas as a nuclear-weapon-free zone'; condemned 'all forms of nuclear collaboration by any State, corporation, institution or individual with the racist regime (of South Africa), which enable it to frustrate the objective of the Declaration (on the Denuclearization of Africa)', and demanded 'that South Africa submit forthwith all its nuclear installations and facilities for inspection by the International Atomic Energy Agency'. The same Assembly also adopted a resolution[4] in which it requested 'the Disarmament Commission to consider substantively and as a matter of priority South Africa's nuclear capability during its session in 1984, taking into account, **inter alia,** the findings contained in the report of the Secretary-General'; and 'to take enforcement measures to prevent any racist regimes from acquiring nuclear arms or arms technology'.

Technology for Nuclear Weapon Production

According to a variety of studies, the technology necessary to construct a nuclear weapon is becoming increasingly available. It has been suggested that atomic, and even hydrogen, bombs have been designed by nuclear physics students at undergraduate level. For the construction of a Hiroshima-type atomic bomb a certain quantity of highly-enriched uranium is needed; a small amount of this material plus larger amount of plutonium are required to produce a hydrogen bomb.

But for a country to become a real nuclear power, the problem is not so simple. Apart from the political will to go nuclear, advanced technology and substantial economic resources are required. However, the spread of nuclear power technology to many semi-industrial and non-industrial countries is accelerating the rate of acquisition of skills, facilities and materials relevant to nuclear weapon development.

It is generally accepted that a modest and not very sophisticated programme could be sufficient to develop and produce a small number of simple, but militarily useful nuclear explosives. For example, a country might build a small simple reactor fuelled by natural uranium, as well as a small reprocessing plant to extract plutonium from the spent fuel. Such facilities are less difficult to construct and less costly (at least by a factor of ten) than a commercial nuclear power plant with even a small reprocessing plant[5].

Materials from commercial power reactors could be diverted to military purposes, but such materials would not normally be well suited for weapons design. Power reactors produce plutonium with significant amounts of plutonium-240 which is most troublesome for bomb design, as it raises the critical mass and undergoes fission spontaneously. There is no simple practical way of separating Pu-240 from Pu-239. (In light water reactors Pu-239 amounts to about 60 per cent of the total plutonium production, while Pu-240 contributes 21 per cent). Furthermore, international safeguard arrangements and political commitments would inhibit most countries from diverting materials from power reactors. Consequently, even countries with existing nuclear power programmes would probably build special reactors if they wanted to produce plutonium for weapons.

The other fissile material for nuclear weapons is enriched uranium. Theoretically, 10 per cent enriched uranium is weapon grade, but in practice at least 50 per cent enrichment is required. Even then the critical mass would be three times that needed in pure U-235; apparently[5], the core of uranium weapons consists of more than 90 per cent U-235.

Nuclear Capabilities of Key African Countries

Africa is rich in uranium resources. Many African countries have started nuclear programmes, but in general the technical know-how is rather limited, except in South Africa.

South Africa. The prominent status of this country in the nuclear field is due to the abundant natural uranium resources and to the generous nuclear technological aid provided by Western countries, in particular by the USA, France, FRG, the Netherlands, Israel, Taiwan and Japan.

Uranium reserves in South Africa and Namibia amount to about 300 000 tonne (about 17 per cent of the world total) and uranium production is 15 per cent of the output of the non-communist world. USA and UK helped South Africa in the technology of extraction and processing of uranium.

In 1949 a South African Atomic Energy Institute was formed which was converted in 1957 to the South Africa Atomic Energy Board. Under the US Atoms for Peace programme, South Africa concluded an agreement which ensured her progress in nuclear technology. It bought the Safari-1 20 MW light water research reactor from the USA, which went critical in 1965, and a low-enriched uranium heavy water reactor, Safari-2, which went critical in 1967. By mid-1977 more than 155 American nuclear technologists and scientists had visited South Africa to provide training and assistance, and 90 white South Africans had received training in USA (including the Argonne, Brookhaven and Oak Ridge Laboratories). South Africans were also trained in West Germany and France[6].

In 1971 South Africa set up an enrichment pilot plant at Valindaba, which is not under any safeguards. In 1974 the President of the South African Atomic Energy Board affirmed his confidence that his country would soon be marketing enriched uranium and fuel elements for power reactors, in view of its uranium resources and uranium enrichment expertise and technology.

In 1976 South Africa awarded a French consortium a contract for building two reactors (Koeborg A and Koeberg B) which were

expected to operate in 1982 and 1983. The fuel for the reactors was to be supplied by the USA. The French denied that
Koeberg would add to the nuclear weapon capability of South
Africa, on the grounds that South Africa already has the
capability[6], although the two reactors, when activated,
could produce enough plutonium for several hundred atomic
bombs annually[7]. Another source[8] estimates the number to
be 40-50 nuclear weapons a year, and also questions South
Africa's interest in nuclear power as it has plentiful
supplies of non-nuclear fuel; it suspects that South Africa's
nuclear power programme is mainly due to an interest in
acquiring nuclear weapons.

The discovery of the Kalahari test site by a Soviet
satellite, which was confirmed by Americans in 1977, and
later the possibility that the event detected by the Vela
Satellite in 1979 was a nuclear explosion in the South
Atlantic, have intensified fears that South Africa has become
a nuclear power. In their report, the United Nations Group of
Experts to study South Africa's Plan and Capability in the
Nuclear Field has concluded[9]:

> There is no doubt that South Africa has the technical capa-
> bility to make nuclear weapons and the necessary means of
> delivery. It has an unsafeguarded enrichment facility
> capable of producing weapon grade uranium and it is
> building another enrichment facility with an even higher
> capacity. Furthermore, it has access at home to the
> technical skill and expertise needed for a military nuclear
> programme. Because of its growing enrichment capacity South
> Africa's lack of access to a nuclear reactor designed to
> produce plutonium is not an obstacle.

Namibia. South Africa has been refusing to relinquish its
occupation of Namibia, despite resolutions of the United
Nations and the ruling of the International Court of Justice
that its presence in this territory is illegal. Perhaps the
most important reason for this attitude is the desire of
South Africa to retain access to the extensive mineral resources of Namibia which include extensive low-grade uranium
deposits, considered amongst the largest in the world, as
well as copper, lead, lithium, silver, tin, vanadium and
zinc. The uranium reserves are estimated as 100 000 metric
tonne of assured reserves exploitable at less than $33 per
kg. Namibia's uranium at Rossing is the only material mined,
while in South Africa it is mined as a by-product of gold
mining. The Rossing mine project has involved close collaboration between the South African Government, the British-
based Rio Tinto Zinc Corporation and its Canadian subsidiary,

Rio Algon, and the French Minatome and other transnational mining corporations. Special arrangements provide for effective control of basic Rossing policy decisions by the South African Government. The Uranium Enrichment Act of 1974 allowed the South African Government to obtain any amount of uranium for any use it required.

South Africa has surrounded Rossing with such strict secrecy and tight security that even the highest officials in Namibia require written permission from the South African Atomic Energy Board to visit the installations. This shows up the illegal character of the operations at Rossing in terms of international law, quite apart from the fact that they take place in an occupied territory.

Gabon. Independent since August 1960. Population 645 000. Armed Forces 1950 men supplemented by a French force of 750 men. The country possesses 3.2 per cent of world uranium, and produces about 1000 tonne annually. The ores are very rich in the metal (4 kg per tonne).

There is a factory for processing the ores at Mounana into yellow cake which contains 74 per cent of the metal. Despite the possession of uranium, it seems impossible for the country to embark on a programme of even the peaceful uses of atomic energy, because of lack of trained scientists and the poor socio-economic conditions.

Zaire. Although this country had a small research reactor installed by the Belgians a year before its independence in 1960, it does not have the scientific or technical base necessary for a nuclear programme. Furthermore, the financial situation emphasises the difficulty of undertaking such a programme.

In April 1982, Zaire signed an agreement with a French company (Compagnie Generale de Matiéres Nuclear) for exploration and mining of uranium. It is said that this agreement was politically motivated to prevent any collaboration between Zaire (the biggest francophone country) and Nigeria (the biggest anglophone country).

Zaire signed the NPT and concluded a safeguards agreement with IAEA.

Ghana. In 1961 Nkrumah signed an agreement with the USSR for a nuclear research reactor and research facility at Kwabenya. The facility began operating in 1964 while the reactor was still under construction. The entire research facility was closed down and the Soviet technicians were sent home after the overthrow of Nkrumah in 1966. Recently, a government committee was formed to investigate the possibility of restarting the nuclear programme, utilising the original trained personnel still available in national universities and institutes.

It is practically impossible for Ghana, with its limited financial and technical resources, to become a nuclear power. Furthermore, the country does not possess uranium. Ghana has signed the NPT and concluded an IAEA safeguards agreement.

Niger. This country is important in the nuclear field only because it ranks fifth in the production of uranium among the non-communist countries. The mines at Anlitet and Akouta are in production and a third, at Tassa N'Taglalgue, will be producing soon. In 1984 a mine at Afasto will be operated in collaboration with Nigeria and France. Niger signed an agreement with Japan for uranium exploration. Uranium metal production increased from 209 tonne in 1978 to 4129 tonne in 1980, and 4366 tonne in 1981. Niger supplies France, Libya, Spain, FRG and Iraq with uranium. But the country does not have the scientific or technical base to establish any significant activity in the nuclear field.

Libya. This country has aspirations to become a nuclear weapon state despite the unavailability of trained scientists or technologists. However, because of the extensive oil revenue, Libya is capable of investing huge amounts of money in its nuclear programme. The country brought 280 tonne of uranium from Niger in 1978, and there are major prospecting activities for uranium especially in the disputed area of north Chad. There was an agreement for peaceful uses with Argentina in 1974. Another agreement in 1977 was with the USSR to set up a nuclear research centre, including a 10 MW research reactor. A dual purpose power-desalination 440 MW(e) project was agreed upon with the Soviet Union. It was said that Finland was involved in the deal, but withdrew after one year. In 1978 there was an attempt at co-operation with India. Libya ratified the NPT in 1975 and signed a safeguards agreement with IAEA in 1980.

Egypt. Egypt's interest in the nuclear field goes back to 1956. A research centre was established in Lushas with a 2 MW Soviet research reactor which went critical in 1961. Activities were centered around peaceful uses. A small hot laboratory for isotope production was built in 1962. Some explorations for uranium have been going on in phosphate ores. Since 1974, negotiations have been going on with USA, FRG, Canada and France to obtain two or more power reactors. Egypt signed the NPT in 1968 and ratified it in 1982. It has

been supporting the estabishment of a Nuclear Weapon-Free
Zone in Africa.

Nigeria. Nigeria established an Atomic Energy Commission
in 1976 for 'the promotion and development of atomic energy
and for all matters relating to the peaceful uses of atomic
energy'[10]. The research programmes were to be at the
University of Ife and Ahmado Bello University and a National
Institute for Nuclear Studies was planned. Several students
were sent abroad, particularly to Canada and recruitment of
foreign nuclear expertise was contemplated.

A survey of uranium ore deposits was conducted and the
Nigerian Uranium Mining Company was established in partner-
ship with the French Minatome Company, in 1978. Nigeria has a
16 per cent participation share in the exploration of uranium
in Niger. Nigeria has no nuclear energy facilites at present,
but it maintained contacts with FRG and Canada for the
possible purchase of a medium sized power reactor. It is
clear that if Nigeria acquired one or two power reactors it
would be heavily dependent not only on foreign nuclear
experts but also on foreign nuclear suppliers. Since the
country is a party to the NPT, it should conclude a
'full-scope' safeguards agreement with the IAEA, including
regular inspections of all its nuclear facilities. During
the conference of the non-aligned countries in Cuba 1979,
Nigeria advocated the development of nuclear power progammes
by the Third World countries. In 1980, President Shagari
expressed Nigeria's nuclear aspiration and stated that
although Nigeria did not consider nuclear capability one of
its priorities, it 'reserved the right to do whatever she
could to protect herself if racist South Africa persisted in
acquiring nuclear weapons to threaten the continent'[7].

The Role of Africa in Nuclear Proliferation

I will consider nuclear proliferation in its broad meaning -
that is vertical proliferation, horizontal proliferation, and
deployment of nuclear weapons in non-nuclear countries, as
well as the transit of nuclear weapons in non-nuclear
countries. In this broad sense Africa has a major role in
nuclear proliferation.

Vertical Proliferation. In the cost range of $80 per kg
uranium, Africa has more than one-third of the reasonably
assured uranium resource, (534 500 tonne out of the non-
communist world total of 1 468 000 tonne). In the cost range
of $80-130 per kg uranium, Africa has in addition 149 300
tonne, out of the total of 575 000 tonne (Table 1).

Table 1. Reasonably Assured Resources
(1000 tonne uranium)

	Cost range		Total
	$80/kg	$80–130/kg	
Algeria+ c	26	–	26
Central Africa* b	18	–	18
Gabon	18.7	4.7	23.4
Namibia c	119	16	135
Niger+ a	160	–	160
Somalia* b	0	6.6	6.6
South Africa	191	122	313
Zaire+ a	1.8	–	1.8
African Total	534.5	149.3	683.8
World Total	1468	575	2043

Reported tonnages refer to quantities of uranium recoverable from mineable ore, except the following:

*   Uranium contained in-situ.
+   Uranium contained in mineable ore.

Sources
a   OECD (NEA)/IAEA: 'Uranium Resources, Production and Demand', (Paris: 1977).
b   OECD (NEA)/IAEA: 'Uranium Resources, Production and Demand', (Paris: 1979).
c   OECD (NEA)/IAEA: 'Uranium Resources, Production and Demand', (Paris: 1972).

These huge uranium resources would contribute to vertical proliferation if they became available to the nuclear powers. But if certain restrictions were imposed on these resources a limitation of vertical proliferation could be achieved. However, the difficulty is that the major nuclear powers can proceed with vertical proliferation even without African uranium.

Horizontal Proliferation. African countries with substantial uranium resources could be tempted to go nuclear if the technical know-how were developed locally or imported from abroad. South Africa is a typical example. Countries which produce uranium could also contribute to horizontal proliferation by supplying unsafeguarded uranium to other countries which are not members of NPT or have safeguards agreements with IAEA. South Africa's agreements with Israel and Taiwan are such examples.

South Africa has demonstrated its will to sell uranium outside the international safeguard system. This would become very serious if it sold enriched uranium with more immediate military applications. South Africa has made it clear that it intends to market its uranium only in accordance with its national interests, and that it will bargain over prices and supplies for political as well as economic ends.

Deployment of Nuclear Weapons. The central position of Africa is of huge strategic importance. Most of the world oil passes through the two basic African routes, either through the Suez Canal or around the Cape. Africa controls the southern flank of the NATO countries.

The proximity of the Horn of Africa to the oil rich Gulf States and the southern part of Asia shows its importance in any future East-West conflict.

Deployment of nuclear weapons in any part of Africa could trigger reactions involving deployment of such weapons in other parts of the continent. The past decade had witnessed the competition between the major powers for access to strategic spots in different parts of the African Continent.

The major military bases in Africa that could be used in a global confrontation belong to external great powers. The military communications base and tracking station in Asmara, Ethiopia, used to be operated by USA. The once secret base in Berbera was allegedly controlled by the Soviet Union. The military airfield and harbour facilities in Mahé, Seychelles, as well as the harbour facilities in Mauritius, are leased by the UK. The airfield, military base, radio station, harbour and naval and air forces in Djibouti, the Afars and the Issas, all belong to France. Speculation also has it that

China is the owner of the telemetry for missile terminal ballistics alleged to be in Zanzibar, Tanzania.

Such facilities or military bases could be of great value in any nuclear confrontation. Permission for planes or ships carrying nuclear weapons to use African air fields or ports, even in transit, would contribute to the spread of nuclear arms, and should not be granted.

Would Africa go Nuclear?

Possession of nuclear weapons has been considered as evidence of power and national prestige. Some analysts argue that China was recognised as a great power only when she went nuclear. India's nuclear power is regarded as a symbol of strength, rating her next to the five nuclear powers. Although there is some truth in this, it should be pointed out that military strength, whether nuclear or conventional, is just but one aspect of the overall strength of a country, which is basically socio-economic, moral and cultural. When it comes to prestige or overall strength, one cannot claim that nuclear India is stronger or more prestigious than non-nuclear Japan, or that West Germany being non-nuclear is weaker than nuclear China.

Nuclear weapon advocates claim that they serve as deterrents to ensure peace. The French strategist, Pierre Gallois[11], evolved a thesis that far from trying to stop the spread of nuclear weapons by signing treaties, it was more sensible to encourage the spread of nuclear weapons to let everybody who wanted them to have them. He argued that the West and Soviets had not gone to war for over twenty years largely because their nuclear weapons deterred them from doing so. They were conscious of the threat of mutual assured destruction if nuclear weapons were employed. Thus he argued that if nuclear weapons were injected into every regional conflict, the Middle East, South Asia, white versus black Africa, then a measure of nuclear deterrence would develop to ensure peace in those parts of the globe. Hedley Bull[11] argued that pursuing Gallois' thesis to its logical conclusion, was like saying that the best way to keep death off the roads was to put a small amount of nitroglycerine on every car bumper. Everybody would drive infinitely more carefully, but accidents would occur - people being human, and cars breaking down - and the results would be nastier. Gallois ignored the fact that the conflicts that had occurred in the Middle East, South Asia and Africa are not really comparable to the Cold War conflicts between the Soviets and USA in the 1950s and 1960s. These regional conflicts are qualitatively different[11].

The USSR and the USA have both deployed their nuclear weapons in a heavily protected second strike posture, with expensive reconnaissance and command-and-control systems which no country in the Third World can afford. In a conflict where a country has nuclear weapons while the other side has not, there would be always the temptation to use those weapons. In a conflict where both sides have nuclear weapons which are vulnerable to the other side's aggressive strike, each side will be tempted to strike first to destroy the other side's potential. Spence makes the analogy with two gunmen in a Western; the gunman who draws first and shoots more accurately wins[11].

In his BBC Reith lectures in 1979, Ali Mazrui[12] argued that the main African states, namely Nigeria, Zaire and, ultimately, black-run South Africa, should move towards the possession of nuclear weapons. That would be evidence of adulthood for Africa and perhaps an incentive for the present nuclear powers to become serious about disarmament. But in the same lectures, Mazrui pointed out that Africa's weakness is mainly due to three things: technological underdevelopment, organisational incompetence, and military impotence. He proceeded to say 'African countries manufacture very little themselves and are in command of only the most rudimentary technological capability. Africa's organisational incompetence is aggravated by political instability and social corruption'. One would ask, in a situation as described, would acquisition of nuclear weapons be the solution? Would it be feasible? At what cost? For what purpose? As F.O. Adisa put it[13]:

> To demand that Nigeria should divert billions of naira, as India is doing, leaving 90 per cent of the population in deprivation, is not only unjustified, it could be criminal. But the issue is not just bread and butter versus guns, for a number of reasons. Firstly, there is no plausible security threat to justify such line of action. Besides, improving the lot of the Nigerian population is a security device. Moreover, it is difficult, if not impossible, to erect any military superstructure on a weak and archaic socio-economic foundation.

Is nuclear power relevant for the survival of apartheid? Many analysts agree that the possession of nuclear power by South Africa could hardly contribute to the survival of the apartheid regime. Even the use of tactical nuclear weapons is not practical because of possible nuclear pollution. If a country is living in fear and surrounded by hatred, I do not think that nuclear weapons could guarantee its peace or survival. A policy of live and let live would be more viable.

Course of Action for Africa

Africa may proceed to make full use of the peaceful application of nuclear energy for socio-economic development if
the following steps are taken:
1. Establishment of a Nuclear Weapon-Free Zone in Africa with
   the pledges:
   a) not to acquire nuclear weapons;
   b) not to station nuclear weapons on African territory;
   c) not to grant access to airports or harbours to planes
   or ships carrying nuclear weapons.
2. Establishment of an African nuclear energy organisation
   which would cooperate in peaceful uses.
3. Cooperation with the IAEA in imposing safeguards on
   African uranium so that it is used solely for peaceful
   purposes and is not diverted to nuclear proliferation,
   vertical or horizontal.

References

1. United Nations Resolution 38/75.
2. United Nations Resolution 38/188E.
3. United Nations Resolution 38/181A.
4. United Nations Resolution 38/181B.
5. T. Greenwood, G.W. Rathjens and J. Ruina, 'Nuclear Power
   and Weapon Proliferation', Adelphi Papers (1976) No.130.
6. C.R. Mohan, 'Atomic Teeth to Apartheid: South Africa and
   Nuclear Weapons', in Nuclear Myths and Realities, (New
   Delhi: ABC Publishing House) pp.119-38.
7. T. Adeniran, 'Nuclear Proliferation and Black Africa: The
   coming crisis of choice', Third World Quarterly, Vol.13,
   No.4, (October 1981).
8. F. Barnaby, 'Nuclear South Africa', UN General Assembly
   A/Conf. 107/2/1981.
9. 'South Africa's Plan and Capability in the Nuclear Field'
   A/35/402. Report of the UN Secretary General, 1981.
10. R. D'A. Henderson, 'Nigeria: Future Nuclear Power', Orbis
    409 (Summer 1981).
11. J.E. Spence, 'International Problems of Nuclear Prolifer-
    ation and South African Position', ISBN: 0-909239-70-3
    (July 1980).
12. A. Mazrui, 'Africa's Nuclear Future', Survival Vol. XXII,
    No.2 (March/April 1980).
13. F. Adisa, 'The Nuclear Rationale in Nigeria', Traveaux et
    Documents No.3 Centre D'Etude D'Afrique Noire, 1983.

3 The Danger of a Nuclear Arms Race in Latin America involving Brazil and Argentina

Luiz Pinguelli Rosa

The Need for Joint Development of Non-Military Nuclear Technology

At the end of 1983, the nuclear bomb issue apparently became more critical in Brazil, due to the announcement, made in the last days of the Argentinian military government, that Argentina had mastered the technology of uranium enrichment. Even if the main purpose of the announcement was propaganda for the dictatorial system - a system that caused so much pain to the Argentinian people, leading it to the military adventure in the Malvinas - it indicates a technical advancement in gas diffusion enrichment. Although the production of significant quantities of uranium-235, and the continuous process necessary for an industrial scale, have clearly not yet been achieved, the technical competence of Argentina - which chose the line of heavy water and natural uranium reactors and seeks autonomy in its fuel cycle - cannot be denied. Some statements made at the time Argentina announced the enrichment technology give rise to some concern. Even within the technical sectors, a deplorable competitive and challenging atmosphere was demonstrated.

There is also concern that the previous Argentinian Government has put so much effort into enrichment rather than the development of power reactors. Enriched uranium can be used in several ways: (1) with low enrichment (3 per cent of U-235), in large quantities (dozens of tonne per reactor-year), in electro-nuclear power plants (such as Angra); (2) with medium enrichment (20 per cent of U-235), in small quantities, in research or radioisotope production reactors; (3) with high percentage of U-235, in submarine reactors; (4) with a very high percentage of U-235, in nuclear bombs.

It should also be mentioned that Argentina already owns a stock of plutonium in the irradiated fuel withdrawn from its two power reactors in operation, and is building facilities

40

for reprocessing.

If there were military intentions in these developments, the (direct) election of President Alfonsin was a step in the opposite direction. But a step is not enough; a long walk is necessary to find a solution. There is no sense in the two countries entering into a technological competition which may lead to nuclear weapons. Latin American countries should get together to solve their external debt question, and should not compete for the bomb technology which may threaten all.

Assuming the need, reached through a democratic decision process, to develop nuclear technology for non-military purposes, Brazil and Argentina should unite, complementing and aiding each other. The question of disclosure of nuclear secrets is more serious in countries under an authoritarian regime; it still remains so after the institution of a representative democratic system. There is a tendency in a civil or military technocracy to withdraw from the institutional and congressional political discussion certain specialised questions which are finally decided in government offices, with the participation of only a few (though dominant) society interests in a very exclusive manner. For this reason, it is important to continue the struggle for peace within the new democratic context. After all, it was under a representative democratic regime - namely, in the USA - that the first nuclear bomb was designed, manufactured and launched with hardly anybody knowing about it.

Reprocessing and Enrichment

The nuclear agreement between Brazil and FRG, to build reprocessing and enrichment plants, cannot be explained as being based predominantly on military objectives. These no doubt exist, but there must have been other motivations, linked to the logic of the development model, which tend to advance capital intensive technologies[1]. However, the indications of military interest are demonstrated by the obsessive form in which the nuclear programme was defended by the hardest sectors of the regime, even though there was no economic or technical argument capable of giving support to the need for nuclear energy in the face of existing abundant, and less expensive hydroelectricity.

From the technical standpoint, the reprocessing of irradiated fuel to extract plutonium and the remaining uranium is the closest phase of the Brazilian nuclear programme to military utilisation. The extracted uranium could be reutilised in the reactors, but the number of nuclear power plants which would economically justify reprocessing for this purpose is well above the scale of the Brazilian programme. Plutonium may serve for future fast breeder reactors, such as France's Phénix and Superphénix, but those are also far from being economically feasible.

However, plutonium is the raw material for the nuclear bomb. It is produced at the rate of about 100 kg per year in the Angra I reactor (purchased from Westinghouse before the Agreement with Germany) when operated at full power. Although this 0.6 GW power reactor is already working, it operated at a low power for a long time, due to technical problems. In Angra II, under construction, with 1.3 GW, plutonium generation will be more than 200 kg per year. However, this plutonium is not only dispersed in the fuel bars, needing reprocessing to separate it, but is also a mixture of several plutonium isotopes (238, 239, 240, 241, 242), only two of them being fissile. The critical mass of pure plutonium-239 is about 10 kg. With the isotope composition that normally comes out from the reactor, the critical mass is more than 15 kg. For comparison, the critical mass of uranium enriched to 95 per cent of the 235 isotope, is approximately 50 kg. These values refer to the bare material. The critical mass may be significantly reduced if a neutron reflector is used, and if we consider the increased density resulting from the implosion effect.

The reprocessing technique is simpler than that of enrichment, because it can utilise chemical processes, such as solvent extraction, which is the basis of the PUREX method. The difficulty lies in the intense radioactivity and the danger of accidentally reaching a critical mass. Reprocessing is probably the most dangerous phase of the nuclear cycle, and still presents many technical problems. Although included in the agreement, the reprocessing plant has not yet reached the industrial and demonstration phases, but is a laboratory development which is not well known to the public.

The enrichment situation is not very clear either. The jet nozzle process, imported from Germany, did not achieve the expected success, in its facility in Resende. It is known that ultracentrifugation studies are under way again in the so-called parallel nuclear programme.

Nuclear Technology in Brazil

There is concern about nuclear technology activities in Brazil, not only those of NUCLEBRAS linked to the agreement with FRG, and under the control of the International Atomic Energy Agency, but also in the so-called 'parallel nuclear programme'. Part of this parallel programme is the construction of a small reactor, primarily for the production of radioisotopes, but also to acquire technological practice, from the project phase to the construction. It is coordinated by the National Commission of Nuclear Energy, and involves several other institutions. It would be a 1 to 4 MW water-cooled reactor, using 3 per cent enriched uranium. This decreases the possibility of military utilisation.

However, there is another part of this parallel programme which is concentrated at the Aerospacial Technical Center (CTA), in Sao José dos Campos, and at the Energy and Nuclear Research Institute (IPEN), in Sao Paulo. The IPEN project was initially linked with the State of Sao Paulo, working in agreement with the Federal government, but the latter took over total control and withdrew it from State supervision before the inauguration of Governor Montoro from the opposition party. It is known now that there are security areas, with forbidden access, at IPEN and the presence of military engineers; there is talk about studies on nuclear submarines. Technically, the construction project of a submarine reactor is more difficult and expensive than that of a nuclear bomb.

At CTA, studies on Nuclear and Reactors Physics are being carried out; these are helped by a main frame computer and the construction project of a linear accelerator for intermediary energies. The expressed objectives were the acquisition of nuclear data for fast breeder reactor technology. This is also a more difficult problem than the construction of a fission bomb, even assuming that the raw material for this - very enriched uranium or plutonium - is available.

From known information and from what can be deduced, neither enriched uranium nor plutonium for the bomb exist today in Brazil. The technology to enrich uranium has not yet been mastered. Although development does exist, it is lagging behind Argentina in the light of the announcement, mentioned earlier, about the advances made in gas diffusion enrichment. Although plutonium is being generated in the Angra I reactor, its fuel has not yet been recharged, and therefore the spent elements containing plutonium have not been withdrawn. This recharging would normally occur after one year of operation, but it took a long time before the reactor started normal operation. Moreover, this material is under strict safeguards and international control. While forced to use enrichment services abroad, Brazil will have little margin to utilise the fuel for other purposes. As already stated, there is no reprocessing plant yet, although there are plans to construct it with German technology. However, it would be possible to operate a hot laboratory to reprocess small quantities of fuel and obtain some plutonium. This could be done, for example, at IPEN's prohibited area from where no information comes out.

It is of course possible to study the means to make the bomb, even before having enriched uranium and plutonium. These means are not restricted to nuclear technology and include problems of thermodynamics and optimisation. The operational problem is simple for a fission bomb, but for a fusion bomb, which would presumably follow the first one, the question is more complex and demands main frame computer calculations similar to CTA's.

In parallel with the nuclear studies which would aim at the bomb, CTA successfully developed the construction of rockets which may serve as launchers of nuclear warheads. The development of a Brazilian industry in conventional weapons is well known, having reached an important position in recent years, even in export. This industry includes light weapons, medium calibre heavy weapons, and light and medium combat vehicles, to more complex electronics control equipment, planes and rockets. This development cannot be separated from the concern about the nuclear bomb, since the latter makes sense militarily only if supported by adequate operational means.

It is interesting to observe that this industrial undertaking involved companies directly controlled by the State, such as IMBEL and EMBRAER, as well as national private companies associated with transnational groups which provide technology, for example the AMX airplane of Italian origin.

The Non-Proliferation Treaty

It would be a mistake to limit the discussion on nuclear weapons to the proliferation of technology sensitive to military utilisation, on the assumption that the political responsibility of the existing nuclear powers were a guarantee to avoid the existing nuclear war. In fact, in the past, these powers have been responsible for the worst devastation that the world suffered. It is important to place the problem in its true dimension; we have to reject military utilisation of nuclear technology in all countries, without exception, bearing in mind that the most serious threat to humanity is located in the arsenals of the great nations[2].

How can world peace be entrusted to these powers in the face of invasions like those of Granada and Afghanistan and the threats to Nicaragua?

However, it would be equally wrong not to consider the problem of new countries acquiring nuclear bombs, such as Israel, South Africa, Pakistan, as well as Argentina and Brazil. It is perfectly possible to follow India's example, which exploded a nuclear bomb but is incapable of resolving the problems of hunger and poverty of its population. It is

of fundamental importance to find the instruments of international politics to avoid nuclear adventures.

The Non-Proliferation Treaty puts restrictions on the
countries which do not have the bomb; this is the reason why
some of them did not sign it, as was the case of Brazil and
Argentina. In Latin America there is the Tlatelolco Treaty,
which forbids the production, ownership and placing of
nuclear weapons in the territories of the signatory countries. It was signed by all countries with the exception of
Cuba and Guyana. But the only two countries with the capacity to make the bomb within a relatively short period,
Argentina and Brazil, did not put the Treaty into effect
after signing it. The same applies to Chile. This situation
has arisen because of the insertion of certain clauses which
say that the Treaty will come into force only if signed by
all Latin American countries, as well as other countries with
interests in the region and, also, if all nuclear powers
commit themselves not to threaten the signatory countries.
Even so, nearly all signatories have already put the Treaty
into effect. In this context, a position which needs to be
supported is to enforce immediately the Tlatelolco Treaty in
Brazil and Argentina now that democracy has returned to these
countries. But even with the Alfonsin government, Argentina
has raised the question of the UK placing nuclear weapons in
the Malvinas, something considered unacceptable by the
Argentinians.

In 1984, during the annual meeting of the Brazilian Society
for the Progress of Science, there was a gathering of all
Latin American physics societies, under the auspices of the
Brazilian Society of Physics. A joint statement was approved
against the production of nuclear weapons, asking the newly
founded Latin American Federation of Physics Societies, to
institute a commission to study the matter. A proposal to
convene a meeting of Latin American countries to deal with
the question of nuclear weapons was also approved. Prior to
that, at the time when the announcement was made that
Argentina had mastered the technology of gas diffusion
enrichment, Brazilian and Argentinian physicists had already
made a joint anti-armament declaration.

This question was again discussed at the Brazil - Argentina
cooperation seminar at the aforementioned meeting. Support
for the Non-Proliferation Treaty was demanded as well as some
type of commitment for the reduction of nuclear weapons[3].

But there is room for further advance. Brazilian diplomacy
has a good tradition which was preserved even in the dark
years of our internal politics. Now that this darkness is
nearing its end, it is the right moment to press the
government to assume a more positive stand in relation to

world nuclear disarmament, both with respect to Latin America in general and, bilaterally, towards a pact with Argentina against the bomb.

There is the concrete danger of an 'armament race' in Latin America involving Brazil and Argentina, the two countries most advanced in nuclear technology. However, this is not inevitable. The bomb does not exist as yet, nor are there the conditions for making it in a short period of time. This offers plenty of scope for reaching political understanding.

References

1. cf. 'O Acordo Nuclear no Contexto do Modelo e da Crisa', Energia e Crisa, (Petropolis: Vozes 1984).
2. L.P. Rosa, Science and Technology in the Transformation of the World, (Tokyo: United Nations University, 1982) p.328.
3. J. Goldemberg, 'Brazil', in J. Goldblat (ed.), Non-proliferation : The Why and the Wherefore (Stockholm: SIPRI, 1984).

4 New Technological Developments (Vertical Proliferation)

Jean-Pierre Stroot

Vertical Proliferation

Vertical proliferation designates the continuous process of introducing new scientific and technical discoveries into the field of armament. It is associated with all new systems that are developed in order to replace obsolete armaments which are meant to improve national arsenals and bring them to a level of efficiency and reliability that is at least equivalent to, or better than that of potential adversaries. It is a nearly impossible game to determine what this equilibrium really means. Few political leaders are ready to make a fair evaluation of the minimum needs for defence (what might be called minimum deterrence) and to stick to their conclusions irrespective of outside deployments. Such a posture involves the political risk, which nobody is willing to take, of being called naive about national security problems by not providing all possible means to the military. It is contrary to the primitive tradition of power symbolism which requires a group to show at least an equivalent power to the opponent, whether of not this power may be of any use. Also first-strike capability remains the basic military doctrine in case of perceived menace (not necessarily because of an aggressive posture), and armies cannot really be satisfied with purely defensive means. In such conditions, equilibrium can never be ideally achieved because it cannot be defined objectively. Vertical proliferation is at the root of what is more commonly called the arms race.

Most features of vertical proliferation first occur in the laboratories, at the stages of conception, research and development, the final steps being production and deployment. The latter are the most visible ones and are often the only ones which are perceived by the public. It is then too late. Depending on the complexity, ten to twenty years have already elapsed and correspondingly large sums of money have been spent. Furthermore, the new system is already part of the

47

military doctrine and it proves extremely difficult to cancel
such a mature project.

This means that the technical developments we have to worry
about are not only those we are observing today, but even
more so the developments that will produce weapons to be
deployed in twenty years time and after. Or do we have to
worry?

The main basic scientific and technological breakthroughs
which are of importance for our topic have been with us for
40 years or more, in regard to the nuclear weapon itself; 30
years and more, in the matter of transportation, of microelectronics and guidance; and 25 years since the discovery of
lasers and opto-electronics. There will undoubtedly be new
discoveries that might revolutionise the whole field of
armaments, most probably in biotechnology, but all
ingredients for an accidental or purposeful destruction of
civilisation or even of the world ecosystem are available
now. What more is needed when the arsenals of the great
powers are awash with nuclear warheads that have an explosive
power ranging from one kiloton to several megatons (there is
no real upper limit except that there is no practical
usefulness for bigger weapons); when several other countries
have already by far passed the destructive power needed for
deterrence; and that quite a number may reach this stage in
the near future?

This does not mean that further developments will be less
frightening than existing systems, but I shall argue that
their effect will only increase destabilisation with all the
inherent risks of a politically and socially unstable world.
I will also argue that destabilising actions are based
entirely on illusions and misperceptions of the technical
reality.

Technical Trends

Three main features characterise the destabilising effects
of technical innovation: decrease or elimination of the
possibility of verification procedures; increase in
first-strike capability; and 'battlefield' nuclear weapons.
The first hinders conclusion of new agreements and
jeopardises existing ones, the second creates a permanent
temptation in times of crisis, and the third makes it easier
to start nuclear exchanges even in small or localised
conflicts. An example of the latter is provided by the recent
Declaration of the French Minister of Defence on the possible
use of prestrategic weapons, that is Hades missiles and
neutron bombs, to retaliate after an attack with chemical
weapons.

Nuclear Weapons

The field of nuclear armaments may be divided into three
sub-areas:
- explosives
- delivery vehicles
- command, control, communication and intelligence (C^3I).
Only the first sub-area - nuclear warheads - is specific.
The others have common features with modern classical arms.
Missiles with classical explosives have an accrued importance. Smart weapons (anti-aircraft, anti-tank, and so on)
essentially use the same basic techniques to track their
target as do nuclear missiles.

Apparently nuclear warheads are still being actively
developed in two directions: further miniaturisation for
easier delivery, and lowering of the explosive yield to be
able to bring the nuclear weapons closer to the battlefield.
There is also a diversification in the ratio of blast to
radiation according to the specific application. Not much
fuss is made any more about neutron bombs because the
expected psychological reactions to the idea of decreased
collateral damage together with increased anti-personnel
efficiency did not last long enough to have a durable impact.
It now seems, however, that the polemics were a smoke-screen
that diverted discussion from more important issues.
Enhanced radiation warheads, that is neutron bombs, are now
being introduced into arsenals as a matter of routine.

Improvements are also made in reliability and safety. As
nuclear warheads (mainly fusion ones which incorporate
shortlived tritium) have to be regularly maintained and
refurbished, there comes a time when it is cheaper to change
them completely with more modern components. This is a prime
example of automatic modernisation which plays such an
important role in disarmament negotiations.

More impressive are the developments towards more precise
and intelligent delivery systems, a field where the border-
line between nuclear and classical weapons is getting more
and more blurred. CEP (circular error probable, that is the
radius of the circle around the target with a 50 per cent hit
probability) are now in the tens of metres range for ballistic missiles equipped with terminal guidance systems.
Pershing II is the best known example. The precision of
submarine-launched ballistic missiles (SLBM) is also dramatically increasing so that in the near future SLBMs, which may
be located much nearer to targets, will be as efficient a
decapacitating force as ICBMs are now. The introduction of
manoeuverable autonomous re-entry vehicles is proceeding
along the same lines. Time here is an irresistible driving

force. Year after year new production of current missile
models benefits from improved electronics and fabrication
techniques which do not entail major modifications. These
improvements are natural developments which apply through all
technical fields, civilian or military, without advanced R&D.
So although no new arms systems are being deployed, existing
ones are getting more and more efficient.

Cruise missiles certainly are a destablising current
development. There is no way to distinguish between nuclear
and non-nuclear cruise missiles; moreover they are small
enough to be concealed easily from satellite observation and
thus escape the most reliable verification procedure. Many
discussions have taken place in Pugwash meetings on this
subject but the recommendations have been ignored up to now.
One more opportunity to avoid a dangerous deployment is being
missed. It is probably another illustration of the very
disturbing observation that once a system has reached the
production level, no way to stop its deployment has been
found so far.

There is also considerable activity in C^3I which may
become destabilising and work against at least the spirit of
the ABM Treaty. The Krasnoyarsk radar is a much cited
example.

'Star Wars'

Star Wars, the popular name for SDI (Strategic Defense Initiative), as it is presented today, is essentially a
non-nuclear defensive programme. As such it should not be
discussed in this context, except that it portends important
consequences for nuclear vertical proliferation and also
because its technical developments could result in the
generation of new offensive weapons which have not yet been
thought of.

SDI, as envisaged by Reagan, aims at a 100 per cent
fool-proof defence system. Should one party believe it were
mastering the solution to this challenge, it would be
strongly tempted to use its offensive nuclear weapons, being
sure of impunity. Reaction to this kind of programme can only
be an endless race to defeat its perceived efficiency by a
correspondingly enhanced offensive capability.

Before discussing the sheer impossibility of reaching the
intended goal, it should be mentioned that most components of
SDI do, or will have, recourse to many basic techniques which
would in any case be investigated independently in the field
of lasers, particle beams, computers, and so on, although
probably at a slower pace if only civilian applications were
under consideration.

Feasibility of New Projects and Decision Mechanisms

As long as it does not involve resorting to magic, every crazy idea that arises in the mind of conceivers of weaponry seems to be feasible today. It simply requires that the problem be correctly stated. Its realisation may take time and enormous amounts of money, but never seems a priori impossible. It may in the end prove unrealistic and of no practical use. The fundamental book of Herbert York, Race to Oblivion, dealt with the matter in a vivid and illustrative manner more than ten years ago.

In presentation everything looks so simple that even ignorant non-specialists do not fear to come out with their own pet schemes. The most typical and spectacular case is the Reagan speech of March 1983 on 'Star Wars'. This is by no means an isolated case, as witnessed by most high level political statements on the technical aspects of nuclear armament itself and on the doctrines for its use. It also shows that the attitude of power towards science, however rationalised, has little to do with rational thinking. Science is considered to be a magic power which cannot fail when properly invoked by the right people, that is the people who have the right on their side. Scientists are paid professionals, who are called upon to provide these formidable means which will forever eliminate the evil, that is the enemy, and their lesser magic. The trouble is that this approach does not work. Dominant technology does bring victory, and the question of good or evil is left to the victorious side to decide. This was the case in World War II and we were lucky that Nazi science and technology were weaker. But instances of the triumph of the most brutal forces are numerous, notably in modern colonial wars. Fortunately though 'neither good nor evil' have been definitely suppressed.

Old magic procedures are infallible. When their success is not complete the fault rests with the faithful not with the procedures. Whether this belief has or has not helped mankind to survive is not our subject. The important fact is that it will no longer help in a nuclear world. This is probably the central problem today. Technology will neither counteract nor suppress nuclear weapons. An SDI version might work in the end, but every such scheme will be at least partly defeated by a corresponding counter-measure, as well as by its own less than 100 per cent efficiency, and by the failures to which all systems are susceptible and which would be aggravated in the turmoil of a conflict. Given the available nuclear arsenals, even a small fraction of successful nuclear strikes would be a major catastrophe.

No strong, long-term argument may be presented against the

feasibility of technical proposals. We may be sure that somewhere somebody is still thinking of a nuclear-fuelled airplane that would have an 'indefinite' flight autonomy as a command centre in case of nuclear war. It is probably not worthwhile to try to defeat all the crazy ideas that flourish in some minds. SDI is most probably amongst them. However, it is fundamental to fight the idea that there is a magic called science that can maintain war as an effective means to fulfil political goals in a nuclear age.

This is not a pessimistic view of the situation. It simply states 'here we are'. Different attitudes are possible. One is empirical and has certain merits. It tries to move things from inside the technical field itself. It rests on the correct idea that techniques may be used or diverted for any purpose, good or evil, and that more benign techniques may be substituted for the most threatening ones. On the other hand, trying to replace dangerous systems by more intelligent and less reactive ones does not solve any long-term problem. The solution rests with the people and with their leaders. It is political, not technical, even if technical fixes may help at some stage for a limited period of time.

The question then is how vertical proliferation is driven, by whom it is driven, and what achievements can reasonably be expected in terms of technically successful systems.

Driving Vertical Proliferation

The impetus towards vertical proliferation rests on the perceived needs for defence against real or supposed threats, but, as mentioned before, it is not a rational process. In the case of nuclear armament, intentions are even less connected with the reality of a possible effective use than are classical armaments. Enormous amounts of equipment, un-imaginably large, are produced and prepared with the stated aim that they are never to be used. Nevertheless, all kinds of schemes for use are studied, as a basis for new requests to the laboratories or as a demonstration for the need to procure the latest laboratory developments. This kind of schizophrenia constitutes a major menace which in the end can be conquered by political will only. We need to understand the kind of mechanism that creates such a situation, how to dismantle it, how to explain it to the public and make proposals that would be perceived and understood by the political powers.

The energy release of nuclear explosions is many orders of magnitude larger per unit mass than that of all previous chemical explosives. This discovery is entirely due to fundamental science. It constitutes a sharp break with all previous knowledge. There is no wartime experience on the use of nuclear weapons and no experience can be gained in any limited conflict (Hiroshima and Nagasaki have been demonstrations with rudimentary small weapons). These two elementary and well known points have to be repeated and constantly kept in mind when one is dealing with problems associated with nuclear armament.

Who is Driving?

The whole history of this field which spans less than fifty years is an illustration of the ever more ambiguous relations between scientists in their laboratories, technicians at their drawing boards and test benches, industrialists on their production line, finance people backing industrialists with considerable amounts of money and political people exercising their powers under pressure from all the aforementioned groups.

The military occupy a position apart. They are in charge of the technical questions raised by a possible war, how to manage strategic and tactical problems. They are supposed to establish the doctrine for action both in the case of defence and attack. They exercise their trade within their own traditions, which are completely out of phase with the potential use of nuclear weapons. They normally were under strict control of the civilian decision centre of which they are the secular arm. But the formidable invasion of modern technology in the field of armaments, accompanied by rapid obsolescence and constant renewal of weapons systems has brought them together in close interaction with the same pressure groups, the laboratories, the factories and financial groups. The military is the principal funding source even for basic research in many countries.

There is one element missing in the story, however, and that is the people at large who have very little, if any, access to proper information in the field of armament.

Circulation of information is an important subject itself; it could reveal totally unexpected aspects of the sociology of power. Although it is outside the scope of this paper, it should be kept in mind that in matters of armament secrecy, for reasons of security and patriotism, is the rule. It will probably long remain one of the main obstacles to rational disarmament.

The Laboratories

Applied science laboratories are normally dependent on funds from agencies linked with industrial development when they are not integral parts of industries themselves. They naturally contribute to all activities of the factories, civilian or military.

Technological improvement is a continuous process. Old systems can be maintained for a limited period of time only, because spare parts may no longer be produced or are modified according to the latest procedures. Modernisation is automatic. Objects cannot be made today as they were yesterday. The reasons for this are many, they have to do with reliability, automation, new materials, survivability, subcomponent availability, price, and so on. Thus there arise endless arguments about whether a system should be new, upgraded or simply maintained. The fact is that maintenance alone either becomes unfeasible or does not make good sense. As a result of minor changes something may well appear to be new in the sense that the system now possesses entirely novel features or capabilities.

Specific R&D projects are clearly more likely to bring drastic changes with a destabilising effect. They are the object of strong competition among the laboratories which search out where money is abundant. Today the situation is such that a very large proportion of technical R&D is for military purposes.

Basic science laboratories are funded to a large extent, if not exclusively, by official agencies. Traditionally they had been very independent but with proliferation in the 1950s and through the 1960s they have become more vulnerable to money restrictions and have had to turn to military sources. In many countries more than 50 per cent of funds are supplied by the military. Some laboratories care about freedom, many are not free to care even if so inclined. Academic freedom is everywhere a rare condition indeed. Survival for many laboratories and employment for their researchers is thus heavily dependent on the interest and support of the military.

One may say that there is no common attitude, either in the scientific or in the technical community, towards the problem of proliferation. Technical developments are usually so divided into small components that no ethical question arises. The beauty of their own innovative work is also important in diverting people from moral issues. Here again the aforementioned book by Herbert York is illuminating. Challenge is an efficient driving force and it is always possible in any society to find people who are ready to perform any task, and scientists are no exception. It is no wonder that SDI is the object of so much interest by people who are competent enough to know that they cannot fulfil its promises.

It is by no means the role of the concerned Pugwash scientists to blame any particular group. What we should do is to see that the development of dangerous projects for the sake of corporate interests does not take place and that society provides other opportunities for scientific and technical talents.

Industries and Economic Powers

The enormous amount of money involved in building up the components of the arms race is a powerful incentive for industries and economic powers at large. Interaction between laboratories and the military provides a kind of positive feedback; new procedures developed for a given system may lead to more sophisitcated systems which then render obsolete the former and give rise to new procedures, which open new ways and so on. This mechanism starts an apparently endless process of so-called improvements that must be shown to be indispensable for the process of keeping going. This is also the rule of the game in industries directed towards offensive commercial objectives and having only marginal relevance for the nature of their product. It is up to the political authorities to decide at what point to stop.

There could be a profound and long-term destabilising effect on the economic level from a spiralling arms race. This might result in increasing the world economic crisis and instability both in developed and underdeveloped countries. The danger would be when a level is reached at which uncontrolled social movements might result in armed conflicts.

What Can Be Achieved Technically?

The basic question we have finally to face is: Is it possible for either side to obtain a decisive and workable military supremacy by technical means in the process of vertical proliferation?

The answer seems to be definitely NO. Whatever success may be obtained in any technical breakthrough, first of all they will never be 100 per cent efficient (count the peace-time missile failures today!);   second, there will always be countermeasures which require less efficiency to defeat the best system (flooding missile defence by increased numbers of missiles is the most simple-minded, if not the cheapest); third, any technical advantage erodes extremely fast.

This is well known and until now nobody has ever found a way of using nuclear weapons that would be advantageous to the initiator.   This does not however prevent the military from devising tactics 'in case', but in what case?

But the dream seems to live on in some minds.

If nevertheless ...?   The most disturbing possibility would be that one side would at some stage believe that it has gained complete superiority.   Apart from accidents, this is the greatest risk one has to face.

What Can Be Done

It has to be accepted that laboratories have a large respons-iblity in promoting most new ideas and in providing all the necessary building blocks for an unlimited vertical weapon proliferation.   The economic pressure of the industrial communities is another factor.   It is probably true that the great majority of both these communities would show the same enthusiasm towards civilian-orientated tasks.

But the responsibility for the decision on what to make or to renounce rests finally with governments.

There lies the real challenge to concerned scientists: to let societies at large, and their political leaders, under-stand that in the nuclear age there are no technical means, neither offensive, nor defensive, that can make a large-scale war possible without utter catastrophe for all sides, the initiator and the others.

Such a challenge is not a simple one because dreamers tend to listen to those who go along with their phantasmic ideas. Nevertheless, when the public is given access to this information and to the notion of a self-defeating techno-logical race, decision-makers will probably redirect R&D efforts toward civilian purposes.   It will then be time to start progressive nuclear disarmament.

Perhaps a systematic analysis and presentation of the technical limitations of existing and projected systems, of countermeasures and verification methods, their meaning and their development, need to be undertaken.

5 'Workshop on Nuclear Forces, May 1985'

Pugwash Executive Committee

The 12th Pugwash Workshop on Nuclear Forces was held in Geneva, Switzerland on 25 and 26 May 1985. Participants in the Workshop comprised 34 scientists and public and military figures from 18 countries. This meeting continued a series that began in January 1980 with an initial focus on European and intermediate-range nuclear forces; the current focus is on nuclear arms control more generally, including defence, the prospect of the weaponisation of space, and the relation of nuclear to conventional forces.

Three interrelated themes were especially prominent in the May 25-26 discussions: first, that the pursuit of nuclear-war-fighting capabilities by both sides has been steadily undermining the security of everyone; second, that the continuation of these trends and their extension into space weaponry now threaten the entire array of treaties that have provided the main restraints on the nuclear arms race to date; and, third, that this unprecedented level of threat also provides an unprecedented opportunity to develop a more durable and comprehensive approach to reducing the nuclear danger.

The participants in the Workshop took part as individuals, not as representatives of their governments or other agencies. The present statement was prepared following the meeting by the Executive Committee of the Pugwash Council, which has sole responsibility for its contents. It should not be interpreted as a consensus of the Workshop participants, among whom a wide range of views was represented.

The nuclear arsenals of the United States and the Soviet Union number tens of thousands of nuclear weapons each. These enormous quantities far exceed the requirements of a pure deterrent strategy, in which the only role for nuclear weapons would be to deter others who possess them from using theirs. For that purpose, a few hundred invulnerable weapons on each side would be more than enough. The much larger numbers both sides possess have resulted mainly from long

continuation of an action-reaction competition in which,
following traditional military logic that actually is invalid
in the era of nuclear deterrence, each has sought the capability to destroy the nuclear forces of the other. In this
situation, every 'counterforce' nuclear weapon added to
either arsenal reduces the other side's confidence in its
retaliatory capacity and thus motivates further deployments
in reaction; if, moreover, an added counterforce weapon is
itself vulnerable to attack, its addition to the adversary's
target list adds to the incentive for a build-up in response.
In aiming nuclear weapons at other nuclear weapons, then, the
two sides have found a prescription for growth of nuclear
forces without limit.

The resulting upward spiral in nuclear armaments has not
merely wasted vast sums of money in the accumulation of
enough destructive power to threaten the existence of civilisation itself, it also has generated a level of fear and
mistrust that has seriously aggravated the confrontational
dimension of the US-Soviet relationship that gave rise to
this arms race in the first place - the worst sort of vicious
circle. And it has further increased the probability of
nuclear war by multiplying the pathways for escalation from
conventional conflict and by increasing the temptation to
attack pre-emptively in a crisis.

Today each side still retains, by a substantial margin, the
assured capacity to retaliate overwhelmingly against the most
devastating pre-emptive attack its adversary could mount.
But the already staggering cost of maintaining this capacity
is growing rapidly as counterforce capabilities are
'improved', and each side now professes to be persuaded that
the other is actively pursuing the capability to execute a
disarming first strike. Each new weapon with counterforce
potential reinforces these impressions: concern is expressed
in the Soviet Union about the MX, Pershing II, and Trident 2
(0-5) on the US side; concern is expressed in the USA about
the Soviet SS-18, SS-19, and SS-20; and the worry on both
sides about survivability of retaliatory forces continues to
grow.

The march of folly almost surely would have been even
faster, however, but for the fragile web of restraints
imposed by a handful of crucial arms-control agreements: the
Anti-Ballistic Missile (ABM) Treaty of 1972, which averted a
runaway offence-defence arms race by tightly constraining
defence against ballistic missiles; the SALT II agreements
of 1979, never ratified but so far observed by both sides,
which put numerical ceilings on the multiple-warhead ballistic missiles that are the most formidable of counterforce
weapons; the Partial Test Ban of 1963, which restricted

investigation of certain weapons effects ('fratricide'; electromagnetic pulse) that might play a role in first-strike capability; and the Non-Proliferation Treaty (NPT) of 1968, which has helped restrain other countries from mimicking the major nuclear powers in staking their security on these weapons.

Now, in 1985, a convergence of dangerous developments threatens the continued viability of all these agreements - threatens, in other words, to unravel the arms-control web completely, removing the main restraints against drastic expansion of the nuclear arms race both 'vertically' (bigger, more dangerous arsenals) and 'horizontally' (nuclear arsenals in the hands of more nations). Specifically:

- The ABM Treaty is threatened by the prospect of clear violations of its prohibitions against either side's pursuing 'ABM systems or components which are sea-based, air-based, space-based or mobile land-based' (Article V).
- Abandonment of the ABM Treaty to pursue strategic defence would lead inevitably to the demise of the SALT II regime, as each side insisted on expanding its offensive forces to assure penetration of its adversary's defences. Observation of the SALT II limits could collapse even sooner if scheduled sea trials of an additional US Trident submarine in late 1985 go ahead without some dismantling of other US weapons to preserve the ceiling on MIRVed launchers.
- The loss of both the ABM Treaty and the SALT II ceilings would create powerful pressures for abrogation of the Partial Test Ban Treaty to pursue defensive and anti-defensive use of nuclear explosions in space and in the atmosphere. (The Outer Space Treaty and the Threshold Test Ban probably would be lost as well.)
- All these drastic manifestations of the superpowers' continuing failure to honour their obligations under Article VI of the NPT might well lead to the disintegration of that Treaty as well.

The preservation of the ABM Treaty is clearly a prerequisite for avoiding this disastrous unravelling of arms-control restraints. Dissatisfaction with deterrence by threat of mutual annihilation is understandable, and so therefore is the desire to seek a defence against the threats posed by offensive nuclear weapons; but simply wishing for an escape from mutual vulnerability cannot provide one. No realistic prospect for the defence of populations against nuclear weapons is in sight, notwithstanding claims being made for the Strategic Defense Initiative ('Star Wars') in some quarters in the United States. Partial defence of hardened military targets (such as missile silos and command bunkers) against nuclear attack is possible, as it has been for decades, and some increase in this capability is the most likely output of the research programmes in missile defence that are underway on both sides.

Without firm restraints on offensive forces, however, even the limited (and largely unpublicised) goal of partial defence of retaliatory nuclear forces is problematical: its pursuit will simply provoke compensating offensive build-ups, and the deployment of defensive systems that are (inevitably) leaky and themselves vulnerable to direct attack would actually **decrease** crisis stability by increasing the relative advantage of the side that strikes first.   Offence and defence thus are not only tightly linked, in the sense that build-ups of either tend to provoke build-ups of the other;   they are **indistinguishable** in the important sense that deployment of 'defensive' systems in combination with powerful offensive forces can increase first-strike capabilities and incentives.   These relations were recognised fifteen years ago and became the basis for the ABM Treaty; nothing has happened in the meantime to change them.

The unprecedented danger posed by the current combination of threats to the whole array of arms-control constraints is also an unprecedented opportunity, because the danger has made clearer than ever before why a comprehensive approach to the problem is essential.   In particular, it is now clear not only that limits on offensive forces cannot be maintained without limiting 'defences' as well - and **vice versa** - but also that any practical solution to the arms race must address and eventually eliminate the mutual fear of pre-emptive attack that has been engendered by long pursuit of counter-force capabilities on both sides.

Given these fundamental propositions, the basic ingredients of a solution become clear:

- The ABM Treaty must be preserved and, if possible, strengthened by agreed-upon clarification of some of the ambiguities inherent in the language of the Treaty (for example, 'develop', 'test', and 'component').   Clarification of restraints on testing may provide the key to maintaining verifiable limitations on research and development short of the point where destabilisation of the control regime becomes inevitable.
- The ABM Treaty needs to be complemented by independent moratoria on testing of anti-satellite weapons (ASAT), followed eventually by a permanent negotiated ban.   These measures are essential because the linkages between ASAT technology and ballistic missile defence are such that

neither can be controlled unless both are controlled.
- The SALT II ceilings must be observed and maintained, as a precursor to deep cuts in nuclear forces wherein emphasis is given to reducing the ratios of each side's counterforce weapons to the vulnerable weapons on the other side.
- Experience suggests that pursuit of negotiated reductions should take place in a comprehensive context wherein nuclear weapons of all types and ranges are included in a single negotiating framework.   Ambiguous and often artificial distinctions among categories of weapons only serve to divert the attention of the negotiators into fruitless disputes about the boundaries of the categories, to reduce much-needed flexibility for trade-offs among different classes of weapons, and to divert the nuclear arms race into uncontrolled channels.
- Cruise missiles are a category of nuclear weapons insufficiently constrained in prior agreements.   Within the comprehensive framework mentioned above, limits on cruise missiles should be sought with special emphasis on the sea-based type – the deployment of which on both sides threatens to open up a major new area of arms-race competition and to complicate considerably the verification (and hence also the achievement) of future arms-control agreements.
- Negotiations towards a comprehensive ban on the testing of nuclear explosives (CTB) should be resumed and pushed to an early successful conclusion.   This step is important as a complement to the arms-control agreements already in place, as a sign that the nuclear powers are willing to abandon the pursuit of greater 'usability' of nuclear weapons through modifications in their characteristics, and as a reinforcement of the NPT by signalling the commitment of those powers to honour their obligations under Article VI of that Treaty.

In addition, moving away from the emphasis on nuclear-war-fighting that has shaped the characteristics of the nuclear arsenals on both sides would seem to require eventual abandonment of the policy of 'extended deterrence' – attempting to deter conventional attacks by threatening to respond with nuclear weapons if necessary – that has long been an explicit part of NATO strategy. NATO has been reluctant to match the Soviet Union's pledge of 'no first use' of nuclear weapons for fear that such a posture would reduce the barriers to conventional conflict;   but the risks of the present policy of 'first use if necessary' seem intolerable in the long run. NATO should re-examine its position and make any changes in its posture needed to permit reliance on nonprovocative conventional deterrence of conventional threats. It should then be possible to match declarations of no-first-use (of nuclear weapons and of force in general) on both sides with observable changes in force structures that provide confidence in the declarations, and generate concrete benefits in the form of reduced chances of accidental escalation.

We stress, finally, that concern over the probability of war and the prospects for peace cannot be confined to the nuclear arms race between the United States and the Soviet Union.   US-Soviet discussions on arms control, crisis avoidance, and tension reduction should continue and expand, and attention be given to the role of other countries in international security matters,   including especially crisis areas in the Third World.   Establishing a framework for a sustainable peace will require accommodation and cooperation encompassing North and South as well as East and West.

The opportunity to deal comprehensively with all these problems in the months and years immediately ahead is as compelling as the danger of failing to do so.   Piecemeal measures will not be effective, and the 'window of opportunity' for comprehensive measures will not be open for long. Collapse of the ABM Treaty and mutual break-out from the SALT II limits could very quickly become essentially irreversible. It is time for publics to demand and decision-makers to deliver a comprehensive strategy to reduce the nuclear danger.

6 'Strategic Defences: Technological Aspects; Political and Military Implications'

Pugwash Executive Committee

The Pugwash Conferences on Science and World Affairs, which for 28 years have been bringing together prominent scientists and public figures from around the world for private discussion on reducing the peril of nuclear war, convened the 47th Pugwash Symposium in London from 5 to 8 December 1985. The 50 participants came from the United Kingdom, the United States, the Soviet Union and 11 other countries.

Under its general theme of 'Strategic Defences', the Symposium reviewed the technological prospects and limitations of defences against ballistic missiles, the positions of the US and Soviet governments regarding such defences, and the reactions of European governments to recent developments on this issue. The discussions gave particular attention to the potential impacts of strategic defence programmes on the Anti-Ballistic Missile (ABM) Treaty as well as on other existing and prospective arms-control agreements; to the effects of such programmes on the nuclear arms race, on the weaponisation of space, and on the chance of nuclear war, and to the nature and implications of participation by Western European countries in the Strategic Defence Initiative (SDI) being undertaken by the United States.

The views of a number of the participants on these topics were expressed at a public meeting sponsored by the Institute of Physics and the British Pugwash Group on 6 December, at the Royal Society. As has been the case with Pugwash meetings since the organisation's inception in the 1950s at the instigation of Bertrand Russell and Albert Einstein, the Symposium itself was closed to press and public to facilitate uninhibited discussion of politically sensitive issues.

Also according to Pugwash custom, the participants in the Symposium took part as individuals, not as representatives of their governments or other agencies. The present statement was prepared following the meeting by the Executive Committee of the Pugwash Council, which has sole responsibility for its contents. It is not intended to represent a consensus of the

Symposium participants, among whom a wide range of views was represented.

The Problem and the Solution in Summary

The world stands at the threshold of a massive expansion of the nuclear arms race, including the extension of the deadly competition into space. This new dimension of our nuclear peril arises from the prospect that pursuit of space-based defences against strategic ballistic missiles will breach the ABM Treaty, precipitating an unrestrained competition in offensive and defensive weapons on Earth and in space, unravelling in the process the entire web of existing arms control agreements, increasing the chance of nuclear war, and scandalously wasting the scientific, technological, and economic resources of most of the industrial world.

This debacle can still be averted, but there is little time left in which to do so. The two most essential steps for the moment are maintaining strict adherence to the ABM Treaty (which permits continuing research on ballistic-missile defence but not development or testing of space-based and other mobile ABM systems and components) and preserving the SALT II ceilings on strategic nuclear forces as a precursor to deep reductions of the sort put forward by the leaders of the United States and the Soviet Union just prior to their recent summit. Other steps that should be implemented as quickly as possible include a ban on further testing and deployment of anti-satellite weapons and a comprehensive ban on testing of nuclear explosives.

Strategic Defence, Weapons in Space, and the ABM Treaty

The ABM Treaty of 1972 between the United States and the Soviet Union codified the recognition that failing to restrain defences against nuclear-armed ballistic missiles would inevitably produce a runaway offence-defence arms race without producing protection for either side. This conclusion followed from the vulnerability of defensive weapons to direct attack by the side striking first, from the corresponding concern that deployment of defences would increase pre-emptive pressures in time of crisis, and from the circumstance that any measure taken by the defence could be overcome by the offence at lower cost; and it meant that mutual vulnerability of populations to nuclear attack would continue to be the basis for deterrence. The ABM Treaty did not **create** this vulnerability; the characteristics of nuclear weapons did. The Treaty simply brought the declared intentions of both sides into consonance with technological reality by precluding pursuit of defences likely to be as dangerous and expensive as they were illusory.

Now, in the 1980s, a new debate has arisen about the feasibility and advisability of defences against strategic ballistic missiles. Have the arguments against it changed since 1972? Although the technologies relevant to both offence and defence have changed substantially in these 13 years, we see no basis for the hope that an escape from mutual vulnerability is now within reach.

The US Strategic Defence Initiative (SDI), which is the main focal point of the debate, although it is not the only relevant issue, was said to be aimed mainly at finding out whether the essentially leakproof defence of entire populations needed to render nuclear weapons 'impotent and obsolete' is attainable, making possible an escape from deterrence in the form of the threat of mutual destruction and its replacement by 'mutual assured survival'. Nearly all technical authorities (including those working on the SDI) already have agreed, however, that the goal of protecting populations is so unlikely of attainment that it should not serve as a basis for public hopes or government policy.

Those analysts who are at all optimistic about the prospect of defence talk not of defending people but of defending retaliatory nuclear missiles and other 'hardened' military targets, which would represent not an escape from deterrence in the form of mutual assured destruction but a reinforcement of it. This of course is a much less appealing goal politically than the defence of people, so it is not so often stated plainly in public.

Nearly all serious analysts concede, moreover, that even the limited goal of partial defence of retaliatory forces will be achievable in satisfactory measure only if the possible responses of the offence to such defensive deployments are somehow constrained. In other words, not only is no escape from the threat of mutual destruction offered by this version of the SDI even if it 'succeeds'; it also requires cooperative arms control in order to have a chance of succeeding.

If such cooperation is a possibility, however, it would be far better to address the dangers of the nuclear confrontation through arms control alone, without the enormous complications, costs, and risks of pursuing defensive weapons. Indeed, that pursuit is almost certain to make impossible the very arms control it requires for success, given the strong incentives (which have not changed since 1972) for each side to respond to its adversary's defences by building up its own offensive forces. The diverse means for basing components of a defensive system in space, many of which are new since

1972, have only made things worse: the great vulnerability
of space-based defensive components to direct attack (a
vulnerability much greater than that of the boosters and
warheads the defence proposes to shoot down) enhances the
incentives for pre-emption while promoting the proliferation
of weapons in space; and the premium on fast response
created by all this requires that everything be fully auto-
mated, increasing the chance that war could be started by an
electronic mistake in a time of crisis.

There is therefore no reason to seek release from the
restraints of the ABM Treaty. Yet the Treaty is clearly
endangered by the possibility of abrogation (or,
equivalently, radical reinterpretation) in order to pursue
prohibited programmes in strategic defence openly, as well as
being threatened by piecemeal erosion of its restraints
through increasingly troublesome activity in ambiguous or
multi-purpose technologies such as early-warning/space-
tracking radars, anti-satellite weapons (ASAT), surface-to-
air missiles, and anti-tactical-ballistic-missiles (ATBM).
(SAM and ATBM are not prohibited by the ABM Treaty, although
testing them in an anti-long-range-ballistic missile mode is
prohibited).

The loss of the ABM Treaty would be a disaster. It would
lead almost inevitably to the unravelling of the entire
fragile web of arms-control agreements of which the ABM
Treaty is the centrepiece, and which has provided at least a
modicum of restraint on the accumulation of nuclear weaponry
to date. First to go would be the SALT II agreement with its
numerical ceilings on strategic nuclear forces (never ratified but still being observed by both sides), opening the way
to tremendous increases in the number of strategic nuclear
warheads deployed. And the loss of the ABM Treaty and the
SALT II ceilings together would create powerful pressures for
abrogation of the Partial Test Ban Treaty of 1963 and the
Outer Space Treaty of 1967 in order to pursue defensive and
anti-defensive uses of nuclear explosions in the atmosphere
and in space. This acceleration of the nuclear arms race
between the United States and the Soviet Union, moreover,
could hardly fail to add to the pressures on the Non-Proliferation Treaty.

Besides imperiling the whole array of existing arms-control
agreements, of course, loss of the ABM Treaty would damage
severely the prospects for achieving the additional agreements in this field that are so badly needed. With even the
Partial Test Ban Treaty at risk, for example, a Comprehensive
Test Ban would be out of the question. Similarly, there
would be little hope of an agreement constraining anti-satellite weapons, because these would be seen as useful for

attacking the temptingly vulnerable space-based components of missile defences. As a result, an enormously expensive as well as dangerous arms race in space would become impossible to avoid. And the prospects for deep cuts in offensive forces would disappear for the same reason that the SALT II limits would not survive: each side would be building up its offences to be certain of being able to overwhelm the other side's defences.

Ingredients of a Solution

The interconnected nature of these threats to the entire arms-control regime underlines the need for a comprehensive solution. It is clear that limits on offensive nuclear forces cannot be maintained without continuing to limit defences as well, that pressure to develop defences will not cease until the buildups of offensive nuclear forces that have been taking place on both sides are halted and reversed, and that preventing an arms race in space is a prerequisite for maintaining limits on offensive and defensive forces on Earth.

It is just as plain that the cornerstone of the needed comprehensive solution must be strict adherence to the ABM Treaty by both parties to it, together with a recommitment by both sides to use the existing mechanism of the Standing Consultative Commission to clarify ambiguities and to work out mutually acceptable solutions to disputes about compliance.

It must be emphasised, in this connection, that there is no plausible 'alternative' interpretation of the ABM Treaty on the question of ABM systems based on 'other physical principles' (that is, other than those being utilised in the ABM technology of 1972). The text as well as the intentions and understanding of the drafter, signers, and ratifiers of the Treaty on this point are clear: Article V's prohibition of development, testing, or deployment 'of ABM systems or components which are sea-based, air-based, space-based, or mobile land-based' applies no matter what physical principles such components and systems employ; the Treaty's Agreed Statement D dealing with 'other physical principles' is explicitly aimed at strengthening Article III's restrictions on what kinds of fixed, land-based systems may be deployed at the single ABM site permitted to each side, **not** at weakening Article V's comprehensive prohibitions on mobile systems of all kinds.

It should be noted also that adherence to the ABM Treaty does not preclude continuation of **research** on defence against ballistic missiles. (Indeed, for fixed, land-based systems, even development and testing are permitted at specified sites.) Both the United States and the Soviet Union had been doing such research for some years before the ABM Treaty was signed in 1972, and both have continued their research programmes since that time, within the constraints established by the Treaty. The new and dangerous parts of the SDI - as distinct from continuation of pre-existing research programmes - are (a) the expression of a Presidential commitment to move as rapidly as possible towards deployment of a territorial defence if this seems practical, and (b) in the name of finding out whether it is practical, a programmed transition from research to development and testing that would violate the ABM Treaty within the space of a few years. It is these threatening elements of the SDI - not the continuation of research - that would be given up in consideration of strict adherence to the ABM Treaty.

Beyond maintaining the ABM Treaty itself, additional measures are needed to deal with the problem of anti-satellite weapons. Just as ASAT activities will be uncontrollable if space-based defences against ballistic missiles are pursued, so also does controlling ballistic-missile defence require limits on ASAT; without such restrictions, it would be all too easy to carry out prohibited kinds of ABM development under the guise of testing ASAT systems.

The best approach to this problem would be a comprehensive ban on testing and deployment of ASAT systems. Such a ban would be easier to verify than more complicated restrictions permitting limited numbers of systems or limited capabilities, as well as closing off a wider range of undesirable developments. The dedicated ASAT capabilities developed on both sides up until now are modest, and could well be dismantled. In any case, neither they nor the **de facto** ASAT capability associated with the option of using ballistic missiles or ABM interceptor missiles in an ASAT mode should be allowed to stand in the way of prohibiting the much more dangerous and open-ended ASAT developments likely to occur in the absence of a comprehensive ban.

Additional ingredients of the needed approach to the present predicament should include a comprehensive ban on the testing of nuclear explosives (CTB) and continued observance of the SALT II ceilings as a precursor to deep cuts in nuclear forces. Among many other benefits of a CTB would be prevention of the development of the bomb-driven X-ray lasers so beloved of the more ardent proponents of the weaponisation of space. Deep cuts in strategic nuclear forces, emphasising reduction in the ratios of each side's very accurate weapons to the vulnerable weapons on the other side, would reduce the first-strike fears that help promote interest in strategic defences.

The European Dimension

The Strategic Defence Initiative of the United States has aroused a variety of concerns among that country's European allies and in Canada. These include: dismay at the emphasis in the announcement of the SDI (and in official statements since) on the defects of deterrence without having any alternative in hand, and at the possible reduction in the US interest in arms control signalled by the announcement; concern that the nuclear deterrent forces of the United Kingdom and France could be undermined by Soviet defensive efforts paralleling those of the US (evidenced already by France's announcement of new modifications in her strategic warheads to increase their capacity to penetrate defences); apprehension about 'decoupling' in the unlikely event that the United States develops an effective defensive umbrella and it does not extend to cover Europe (an apprehension reinforced, perhaps, by the ABM Treaty's proscriptions against the transfer of ABM systems or components from the signatories to other countries);   and fear of being left out of the benefits of 'spin-off' into the civilian and non-nuclear military sectors from SDI research and development.   There has also been resentment at the lack of consulation in the initial formulation and announcement of so far-reaching an initiative affecting the security interests of the NATO alliance.

Belated US promises of consultation prior to a decision to deploy anti-missile defences have scarcely allayed these concerns, nor has the US invitation to its allies to join in the research and development effort.   (Indeed, Canada, France, and the Netherlands already have refused the US invitation, and only the United Kingdom has accepted).   The President's apparent reluctance to give up the threatening parts of the SDI even if doing so is the **sine qua non** for avoiding the complete collapse of arms control must make the allies wonder how much weight their views will carry in future consultations on the topic;   and they have reason to be far from certain about the benefits of collaboration in SDI research and development.   Indeed, the diversion of scientific and technical resources from much more directly productive tasks could be a debilitating burden for US allies who become heavily involved in the project, as it already is becoming in the United States itself.   A joint technological venture of far greater promise would be a cooperative East-West programme for the peaceful utilisation of space, which would increase mutual confidence and trust and could lead to great benefits for all humankind.

As for the possibility of direct benefits from ABM technologies for European defence, much weight seems to be given to the prospects of developing anti-tactical-ballistic-missile options that would not be constrained by continuing US adherence to the ABM Treaty (which the allies of the United States all seem wisely to hope she will do). We think these ATBM prospects are dismal, however. While the technical difficulty of the ATBM mission is smaller than that of intercepting longer-range missiles in some respects, it is greater in others (due, for example, to the shorter flight time). ATBM systems will be likely to be vulnerable to decoys, other forms of spoofing, and direct attack, and they will encourage offensive build-ups in response in the same way that defences at the strategic level do. The more impressive the capabilities of the ATBM systems developed on both sides, moreover, the more they may contribute to eroding the ABM Treaty through the ATBM 'loophole' - with all the above-described dangers that such erosion would entail.

PART TWO
Non-Violent Management of Crises

7 Solving Conflicts Without the Use of Force

Toshiyuki Toyoda

Introduction

There have been, and will be, many conflicts in the world because of the many economic, ethnic, and cultural differences among nations, as well as the unequal degree of industrial development, which are unlikely to disappear in the foreseeable future. On the other hand, due to the remarkable progress of technological means of communication, transportation, as well as destruction, a single local conflict can quickly grow into a global one. At the same time as complex economic systems have covered the entire world, the gigantic nuclear strategies of the two superpowers have been encompassing the whole globe, extending to outer space. There is no doubt that any local conflict can easily ignite a catastrophic war.

There is now an urgent need to find some effective means to solve conflicts without the use of force. Since the First Pugwash Conference in 1957, several international institutions for peace study have been set up, devoted to research on this issue. Peace researchers have elaborated the categorisation of many post-war conflicts and analysed them from various points of view. Some of them have studied extensively the issue of non-violence, drawing lessons from history such as Mahatma Gandhi's principle of civil disobedience.

This paper is not an attempt to review or summarise their contributions, much less to extend them. Instead, I shall confine myself to an analysis of the interrelation between the current local conflicts, which are taking place in the so-called Third World, and the global nuclear strategies. In presenting my argument I shall maintain the standpoint of a Pugwash scientist, that is, representing solely my own conscience.

Peace Building versus Peace Keeping

As is well known, the leaders of the two superpowers have

repeatedly stated that thanks to mutual nuclear deterrence there has been no war between the United States and the Soviet Union, nor between the NATO and the WTO blocs since World War II. According to them, the doctrine of nuclear deterrence has been working effectively in maintaining the **status quo.**

Usually, conflict resolution without use of force has connoted a **peaceful** settlement of disputes, where the word 'peaceful' is used to mean 'no alteration in the **status quo'.** Such an interpretation of peace is more explicitly represented by the term 'peace keeping', which has often been used to justify the maintenance of intolerable domestic or international socio-political structures, and sometimes to repress the people's voice demanding change. One ridiculous use of the word is seen in naming 'PEACE KEEPER' the latest model of the US ICBM, which will be deployed by the end of 1986. This choice of name probably reflects the expectation that the advanced single-warhead missile will serve to maintain the **status quo.**

It may be of some interest that peace researchers have recently proposed a new term 'peace building', to replace 'peace keeping', so as to focus arguments for peace towards the realisation of a livable world. What is a livable world? In my understanding it will be a world based on a common value system for all nations and peoples in the world. This value system would consist of the principles of social justice and welfare as were stated in the Charter of the United Nations, when it was set up after World War II.

Social justice, as far as I understand, implies a social condition to guarantee human rights, and welfare signifies a satisfaction of basic human needs. A livable world is a new order which fulfils the conditions to implement these values. Our primary objective of solving conflicts without the use of force must be orientated toward this goal.

To achieve the aim by means of **peaceful change** one needs free access to information. Concealment or monopolisation of information is a serious obstacle on the way to peaceful change. Absence of objective information and artificial manipulation of information always make conflicts more fierce and violent. In this connection, the earliest establishment of the New International Information and Communication Order adopted by UNESCO in 1980 should be encouraged, if its genuine purpose can be pursued. Needless to say, chauvinism and militarism are intrinsically fond of secrecy.

If one accepts the notion of 'peace building' instead of 'peace keeping', one must undertake conflict resolution in a spirit of active non-violence, relying on the power of public opinion based on humanitarian and rational precepts. In the past, such a way of thinking might have been regarded with some contempt as Utopian. The advent of nuclear weapons, however, has drastically changed the situation. Whether one likes it or not, war can no longer serve as a political means even in the pragmatic sense. The majority of people in the world have begun to contemplate the fate of the earth.

The recent scientific assessment of the 'nuclear winter', now examined by the SCOPE/ENUWAR group[1], has given a considerable shock to many people, including the decision-makers of the superpowers. This is a good example of how world public opinion can exert a significant influence on global political society, if it is properly awakened. The roles of existing international organisations such as the United Nations and its infrastructures, UNESCO, NGO, UNU, and others, are highly appreciated and should be further acti-vated. The recent tendency in some countries to belittle the importance of these organisations is historically regressive.

Third World Conflicts and the Superpowers

These days it is seldom necessary to use force in solving or settling domestic conflicts. In most countries peaceful means of dispute resolution have been institutionalised to a considerable extent. Regrettably, however, with respect to international conflicts there still remains a tendency to resort to violence, explicitly or implicitly. The excuse usually given is that the present state-system is practically in a state of anarchy. Such a view seems to prevail, particularly among nuclear strategists, but it is misleading and contradictory because they themselves have been looking for effective arms control agreements. In the nuclear age all of us ought to believe that peaceful transition from a state of anarchy towards a just order is possible.

Obviously, each conflict has its specific historic back-ground. The present-day industrialised countries are more or less to blame for many local conflicts occurring in the developing countries, attributable to past colonialism, artificial borders drawn by the self-interested powers, exploitation of resources, and so on. They are apt to obscure these historical reasons in an effort to hold on to their vested interests. Indeed, neglecting history is dangerous. This is especially relevant when we search for means to solve conflicts in the developing countries.

On the other hand, major powers and, in particular, the two superpowers are now very much concerned with the conflicts in the developing countries from both the military and economic points of view. In spite of the enormous quantities of modern weaponry at their disposal the two superpowers feel, and are concerned about, a decrease of their own security. As their nuclear strategy has been extended so widely, even to outer space, they have become extremely nervous about any kind of disturbance which may abruptly destroy the delicate balance of terror. Thus, even when they consider a small local conflict far outside their territories, their primary concern focuses on its military effects.

In these circumstances, it may be impractical to discuss conflict in a framework isolated from the issue of nuclear strategy. In fact, the superpowers intervened in post-war conflicts in most cases mainly from the standpoint of their military security, and not from the contemplation of human rights and welfare of the people involved in the conflict. Naturally, their interventions have always been accompanied by military actions, explicitly or implicitly, despite various other pretexts.

Unfortunately, given the milieu of world-wide militarism, people in the conflict-ridden developing countries are easily tempted to acquire modern weapons when they abandon the will to solve conflicts by peaceful means. The temptation is intensified by the arms dealers who are greedily looking for new clients. Munition industries are intrinsically committed to continuous innovation in the manufacture of new weapons resulting from progress in military R&D. It is a great tragedy that many conflicts that take place in the Third World have been exploited by munition industries in order to test their instruments of human annihilation.

Reaffirming the two main themes of the Pugwash Conferences, disarmament and development, we should criticise more severely the arms transfer from the industrially advanced countries to the Third World. Acceptance of the arms trade undermines the basic principles of world disarmament, and also makes conflict resolution by peaceful means very difficult. It is of some interest that although the nuclear-weapon states have never exported nuclear warheads, they vigorously sell the sophisticated missiles and other modern weapons, which have been developed in connection with nuclear weapon systems.

The concept of development is essentially opposite to that of **status quo**. While we can hardly accept any violent revolution or liberation war in the nuclear age, we must insist upon peaceful change, however difficult it may be. In my view, ideological controversy makes little sense these days, because all of us are on the brink of nuclear catastrophe. Consequently, what we have to do is to find or create means to implement the principles of peaceful change as soon as possible. This will never be achieved by technological development alone. On the contrary, only political wisdom emerging from a profound recognition of human rights and welfare, strongly supported by public opinion, can provide reliable means for peaceful change.

Prescription for Peaceful Resolution of Conflicts

Conflict is essentially a social phenomenon, reflecting different traditions, customs and conditions, which are deeply rooted in a given local geographic situation. Usually, each conflict is treated on a case by case basis. In practice, it has been taken for granted that there is no general prescription applicable to various kinds of conflicts. However, in my opinion, it is of the utmost importance to work out such a prescription as a means of non-violent direct action for conflict resolution. To this end, it is strongly recommended that some global institution be set up to study these problems. The United Nations University may be one of the most suitable international organisations to undertake the task, since it was established to carry out research work as defined under the United Nations Charter: peaceful settlement of international conflicts and disputes. In this connection, it should be mentioned that the United Nations University has been doing a good job, but there is the need for world public opinion to support and encourage its activities.

Looking back on the past activity of the Pugwash Conferences in this field, I found the following important passages in the report of Committee Three attached to the Statement from the First Pugwash Conference in 1957, which states[2]:

> In the past, nations have often resorted to force in the quest for natural resources and fruits of labour. These methods must now be replaced by common effort to create wealth for all.
>
> Tradition tends to place the emphasis in the education of youth on separate ideals of single nations, including the glorification of wars. The atomic age urgently requires a modification of these traditions. Without abandoning loyalty to national heritage or fundamental principles of the different societies, education must emphasize the fundamental and permanent community of the interests of mankind, in peace and co-operation, irrespective of national boundaries and differences in economic or political system.

The tone is rather low-key, and comments on the history of education in individual countries are omitted. On a deeper level, however, the message implies that the unconditional glorification of a nation's history is perilous, leading to feelings of discrimination or national superiority. As shown in debates on nuclear issues, these feelings or attitudes still remain among the people in the countries of the major powers. Discrimination is always accompanied by fear, and a superiority complex gives rise to aspirations for military superiority.

Thus, what is first called for is a sincere self-reflection on the part of major powers regarding their behaviour before and after World War II. Without this, the major powers can hardly be qualified as moderators or advisers with respect to conflicts occurring in the Third World. Specifically, the substance of their vested interests should be thoroughly examined from various aspects in the light of the nuclear age. The emerging new colonialism, as well as the residues of past colonialism, must be wiped out immediately.

In parallel with these efforts, the people of the developing countries should strive to establish their autonomy in solidarity with other nations. This task looks extremely difficult in the heavily biased economic system of the present world. However, one should not overlook the recent moves for de-alignment in various parts of the world. The process of de-alignment is, of course, one of the first steps towards national autonomy. Furthermore, this contri- butes to the ending of the hegemony of the nuclear powers, because the present-day network of nuclear strategy is sustained through military alliances.

It is true that there is still a keen desire for military power among the political leaders in the developing coun- tries. Moreover, the acquisition of sophisticated modern weapons is so easy that any conflict resolution involving the use of force may easily escalate to fighting with these weapons. It should also be kept in mind that nowadays terrorists are using highly sophisticated missiles. In these circumstances, the peace-oriented autonomy of small countries cannot be achieved as long as the arms trade and the dispatch of military advisers to these countries continues.

No one can deny the fact that most current conflicts are taking place in the ominous shadow of the world-wide nuclear strategies of the two superpowers. Their gravest responsi- bility is to initiate nuclear disarmament and to refrain from any kind of military intervention, including the supply of arms and military advisers. They are also obliged to fulfil their pledge in Article VI of the Non-Proliferation Treaty. These are minimum conditions for providing the means to solve conflicts without the use of force.

In this respect, mention should be made of the Inter- national Court of Justice, renewed after World War II. Although its activity has not often been effective in resolving international conflicts, its function ought to be strengthened, and international law should be elaborated in order to better accommodate the needs of the nuclear age. Concerning international law, we should consider seriously the following proposition: 'The use or manufacture of nuclear weaponry is illegal under international law and constitutes a crime against humanity and an international tort'[3].

If the above conditions were realised, the political climate in the conflict area would be greatly improved and many conflicts will cease or be resolved peacefully by the wisdom of the local participants.   If they do not succeed, despite all these efforts, then some neutral international organisation should undertake mediation efforts. The United Nations' responsibility for this task should be considerably strengthened and acknowledged by world public opinion. Beside the United Nations, some non-governmental organisation consisting of independent expert personnel from all over the world should be established for this purpose. Pugwash would be one of the most appropriate bodies to take the initiative.

The Pugwash Conferences started as a gathering of conscientious scientists who realised their social responsibility in the nuclear age. In the beginning most of the participants were natural scientists, especially nuclear physicists. Despite their efforts through successive conferences and other media, it is a sad fact that the main actors in the escalating nuclear arms race are undoubtedly those who have received substantial training in the natural sciences and technology. Furthermore, the recent 'science fiction pipe dream', SDI, has been inspired and advocated by physicists. These facts should be seriously considered; the naivety of natural scientists in respect to socio-political affairs does not grant them immunity from their social responsibility.

References

1. SCOPE 28, Environmental Consequences of Nuclear War Volume I: Physical and Atmospheric Effects; Volume II: Ecological, Agricultural and Human Effects, Scientific Committee on Problems of the Environment (1985).
2. J. Rotblat, Proceedings of the First Pugwash Conference on Science and World Affairs. Pugwash Council 1982.
3. C. Weeramantry, Nuclear Weaponry and Scientific Responsibility, presented at UNU & SCOPE/ENUWAR Tokyo Seminar on Nuclear Danger, 4-9 February 1985.

8 Crises and Conflicts: Management And/Or Prevention

Istvan Kende

Crises and Conflicts

The conflict of interests, the discrepancy of aims of different social classes, strata, groups and so on, is due not to misunderstandings, it is not the consequence of lack of flexibility, it is not a fault or a phenomenon to be condemned; it is the inevitable and logical reality. It is a fact of history, resulting from the nature of societies in our age, from a situation that has gradually evolved.

If the different interests - at social or other levels - clash, if in a given situation the discrepancies become sharper, **crises** arise that may grow into a **conflict**.

By **crises** I mean a high level of aggravation of differences that **precedes** the real or potential outbreak of discrepancies, that is to say the condition **prior to** the potential conflict. By **conflict** I mean the more or less violent outbreak of discrepancies that may manifest itself as sporadic clashes, a low profile war, or a real war on a wider scale and at a higher level.

The interests and aspirations that are in sharp contradiction with each other are not automatically bound to clash. They can subsist collaterally, co-existing peacefully, each side acknowledging and respecting the entity of the other and its rights for existence and security.

Crises and conflicts come into being not **per se**, by the very existence of discrepancies of interests. The existence of these differences does not necessarily lead to a crisis or conflict. For a crisis to arise it is necessary that the differences become - or are perceived to have become - antagonistic. The real incompatibility of interests or aims is usually known and recognised by both parties. However, a **modus vivendi** can still be attained without complete conciliation of interests. If one of the parties wants to alter the given situation by force, if it wants to eliminate the contradictory interests and compel the other side to

accept its interests and/or aims, or if it threatens to do
this, a **crisis** situation is created which may grow into a
real **conflict**, as presumably the other party does not
accept the imposed change.

Such a situation may arise in relation to **interstate** as
well as the **intrastate** differences. Although the two are
basically different from each other in the way of their
settlement, they can both endanger international peace and
security.

Whether international peace and security are endangered
depends on the level and nature of the differences, on the
size of the forces concerned, and on the political, economic
and military significance of the antagonism. It is the task
of the UN Security Council to make an assessment of the
danger at the international level[1]: 'The Security Council
may investigate any dispute or any situation which might lead
to international friction or give rise to a dispute in order
to determine whether the continuance of the dispute or
situation is likely to endanger the maintenance of
international peace and security'.

Interstate Crisis

The primary task of the management of **interstate crises**
is the elimination or prevention of the use of force, that is
the prevention of the transformation of the crisis into a
conflict. Nevertheless, this aspiration need not necessarily
be achieved by a return to the pre-crisis situation. In some
cases that situation might be contradictory to development,
to the natural enforcement of historical processes, or it
might mean the preservation or maintenance of a previous
fait accompli that came into being by force. One such
case is the regaining of the territories occupied by Israel;
the purpose of crisis management should not be the securing
of peace in a manner that would perpetuate the current
situation, that is the occupation. In general, however,
crisis management has to adhere to the principle of
unalterableness; valid frontiers should remain unaltered.

In theory, even frontiers may be altered by mutual consent,
although such agreement is rather unlikely to be achieved in
our days.

The main task of crisis management is **conflict prevention**: the avoidance of the use of force. It should be the
basic principle of management that **international differences cannot be solved by military means**. A military
victory (or defeat) scarcely provides a lasting solution.

It is sometimes hard to dispute the justifiability of armed
repulsion of an armed aggression, or the need to take

military measures to force back the aggressor over one's frontiers. But such cases, like the example mentioned above, are exceptions which prove the rule: violence is engendered by violence.

Intrastate Crises

The situation, and the competence of the UN for instance, are different in the case of internal, **intrastate crises**, or **intrastate conflicts**. The majority of the more than 150 wars that have taken place since World War II were of the **intrastate** type.

Although being internal, most of these wars were not free from a certain degree of 'internationalisation', primarily because of the participation of troops alien to the territory in struggles taking place inside a country. This includes the troops of the former colonising power still present in the country by 'right' of colonisation. However, 'internationalisation' also appears in an indirect manner, if one or several of the industrially advanced countries are involved in the form of economic and military aid, advice, delivery of arms, spare parts and so on.

From the point of view of management, internal, intrastate conflicts have to be judged differently from interstate ones, which stretch across frontiers. In case of internal crises and conflicts the main objective of management should be to ensure that exterior forces refrain from intervention, so the fighting could be considered as a strictly internal one. This means that internationalisation of those conflicts must be avoided; even indirect exterior influence can be diminished by agreements like those discussed later.

The judgement and management of internal conflicts are one of the most important political issues of our days, because of the significant number of those conflicts in the past and the high probability of many new ones. To condemn the use of force is an important matter of principle. Nevertheless, it is necessary to make clear that in certain cases one cannot pre-condemn the party 'shooting first'. Examples are the openly violent, or even armed, revolt against regimes like those of Somoza, Batista, Trujillo. I mention these names just as examples in order to clarify what I mean to say, and not to discuss these concrete cases, which are nothing else but a response to existing violence that cannot be eliminated by other means. In other words, the side that initiated violence was in these cases the regime itself and its repressive force; the open violence against them was not more than a response, or, in military sense, a second strike.

To prove that the aforementioned conclusions or opinions

are not exclusive to a scholar who claims to be a marxist, it is possible to quote opinions, relating for example to South Africa or Latin America, from different scholars or politicians who do not adhere to any revolutionary ideology, from different churches, or from other groups belonging to political circles of highly peaceful aspirations. I can mention, for example, outstanding figures like Luthuli or Tutu, Nobel-prize winners from South Africa, or a number of statements from Latin-American church leaders who cannot in any way be considered to be devotees of marxism. In this connection I would like to present my view that the circumstances in South Africa are such that it is hardly possible to avoid the outbreak of more open violence against the regime in power; for this the African black population, the majority, should not be condemned!

In cases like this, a crisis and conflict management position automatically condemning the side that resorted to open violence is not acceptable. It would be equivalent to saying that the **status quo**, which means apartheid - should be perpetually maintained. It would represent crisis and conflict management only seemingly, but in reality it would contribute to maintaining racial oppression.

These examples show that crisis and conflict management is not at all simple; no single pattern can be applied in this field. This is not primarily an issue of method or procedure, it is mainly a **political** issue and task. As I have shown, in case of certain internal matters, to solve the conflict without the use of force is simply not feasible: the violence is inherent in the very situation brought into being by the forces in power themselves.

United Nations Activities

In case of disputes the continuance of which 'is likely to endanger the maintenace of international peace and security', the UN Charter prescribes several possibilities for settlement[2]: 'First of all a solution by negotiation, enquiry, mediation, conciliation, arbitration, judicial settlement, resort to regional agencies or arrangements, or other peaceful means of their own choice'. With regard to explicitly international disputes the UN Charter established that[3] 'all Members shall settle their international disputes by peaceful means in such a manner that international peace and security, justice, are not endangered'. As is known the Charter also regulates the role of the international Court in The Hague in cases of legal disputes. However, the significant task of management belongs to the activities of the Security Council, as the main body to preserve peace and security.

Without going into a detailed analysis of the UN activities in this field - there is an extensive literature on this subject - I think it is necessary to make a brief reference to the fact that among the activities conducted by the UN in this field, some were restricted to observing only (Palestine - United Nations Truce Supervision Organisation in the Middle East; Kashmir - United Nations Military Observer Group in India and Pakistan; Lebanon 1958 - United Nations Observation Group in Lebanon), while in others UN armed forces were used (Western-Irian or New Guinea - United Nations Emergency Force; Cyprus - United Nations Peace-Keeping Force in Cyprus).

In most cases the success of these activities was unfortunately rather moderate, not to mention the cases the impact of which explicitly contradicted the objectives of the United Nations, such as the intervention in Korea carried out under the auspices of the United Nations. Most authors tend to ignore the Korea case, when discussing the peace-keeping activities of the UN. Another example is the activity of UN troops in Congo (Zaire), where the task of solving the conflict was interpreted in such a manner that it resulted in passive assistance to one of the meanest political assassination of the last decades, the murder of Lumumba.

Thus, the peace-keeping missions of the UN cannot pride themselves on great achievements. This does not imply the need to reject the prescriptions of the UN Charter, nor that they are not appropriate. I still consider the possibilities offered by the UN to be a significant resource for peace-keeping and conflict management.

I may refer to the Declaration accepted by the UN General Assembly on 9 December 1981 about the problem of interventions[4], and especially to the so-called UN Manila Declaration[5]. They stipulate certain important principles condemning any intervention into the internal affairs of states and emphasise the role of negotiation in cases of conflicts. But I want to point out that the statement by Caspar Weinberger, enumerating 'six main criteria' when the US armed forces may intervene in foreign countries[6], seems to be in flagrant contradiction to the Manila Declaration which was unanimously accepted (adopted without vote). Another Pentagon document, also signed by Weinberger, claimed the same 'right' for the US armed forces, before the adoption of the Manila Declaration but after the acceptance of the 'Intervention Declaration'[4]. It stated[7]: 'the (US) strategy for Southwest Asia, including the Persian Gulf, directs American forces to be ready to force their way in, if necessary, and not to wait for an invitation from a

friendly government, which has been the publicly stated policy'.

Role of the Great Powers

Considering the already outlined reality of our age I regard **crisis/conflict prevention** to be the most important element on the road to the solution of crises and conflicts. It must be a sober-minded political activity, not based on the illusion that the contradictory interests can or should be dissolved. One has to start from realities, from the acknowledgement of the existence of contradictions, when endeavouring to prevent resort to the use of force as long as and where it is possible.

We know from current experience that international and internal crises and conflicts emerge primarily on the continents of the developing countries. However, the ways to their solution and elimination should not be sought only in that theatre. Global **interdependence** of different phenomena and events is an important factor in our age.

For this reason, agreements between certain powers not directly involved in the given controversy might have a positive and preventive impact in some cases of international crises or conflicts. An example for this is the joint statement of the USA and the USSR (October 1977) according to which they should take part jointly in the settling of the situation in the Middle East, and that UN observers and troops should be used for providing security under the guarantee of the two signing powers. Other examples were: the talks in Bern between the two 'superpowers' on the limitation of the militarisation of the Indian Ocean, still taking place in December 1977; the talks of a different nature, but with strongly conflict-preventive possibilities, that took place between the USA and the USSR in Mexico City at the beginning of 1978 on the mutual reduction of arms sales. Regrettably, the bilateral statement concerning the Middle East has been annulled by the known Camp David agreement in the autumn of 1978, and both of the other talks mentioned were interrupted by the United States also in the course of 1978. These agreements could have had a significant impact on crisis and conflict prevention. I am convinced that some of the dangerous conflicts could be solved, prevented or at least limited by agreements of the most influential powers of world politics.

Of course, there is no mechanism that would automatically guarantee the prevention of the emergence of conflicts. Attempts should still be made to solve the conflicts locally. Experience has shown that the success of the process of

mediation, or of a search for a compromise, is often more
promising by local effort than a solution involving the
direct participation of UN forces. In the current situation
it is rather difficult to imagine effective and successful
security measures being taken by consensus of the parties
concerned as well as of all the permanent members of the UN
Security Council. The example of applying sanctions has
proved the difficulty of attaining an effective result.

Management of the Main Danger

The fundamental problem threatening mankind, the main crisis
and conflict potential, is the sharpening of the contradictions **between the main forces** (USA and USSR, or NATO
and Warsaw Pact) which may lead to an **open conflict.**
This is **the chief danger** of our age. Despite the menace
from the numerous 'local' conflicts on our globe, in spite of
the fact that all of them contain the threat of escalation
into a broader, even world-wide conflict, the prime danger
continues to derive from the differences between the
interests and social orders of the main powers. Hence the
chief task for mankind is the securing of the kind of
management that would prevent the transformation of the
contradictions into an active crisis and then into an open
confrontation. In other words, the **only issue** is to bring
about a peaceful coexistence of powers belonging to different
social orders.

There may be no possibility for a real conflict-management
once an open conflict between the main forces has arisen.
There may be no way left to save the world. Therefore, talks
and agreements between the main powers offer the only way to
save the destiny of mankind. One has to start from realities
on the level of the main differences and the main danger;
from the **fact** that there **are** two basically contra-
dicting systems existing, living simultaneously.

For this reason I cannot accept the thesis that a solution
must be found 'beyond' the differences, 'above' the two
contradictory world systems. We can avert the most dangerous
conflict only by keeping our feet firmly on the ground, and
not at abstract levels; not by denying reality but by
acknowledging the existing differences and discrepancies.

The difference between the two systems or groups of states
can be kept on a peaceful path only if each of the parties
acknowledges the existence of the other and its right to
existence; if they realise that none of them is capable of
protecting its own interests to the disadvantage of the
other, that it cannot provide its own security to the detriment or against the security of the other party. If this were

recognised by both parties it would make it possible to attain an agreement that would **exclude the use of force in international relations.**

An important first step towards the elimination of violence from the settlement of international controversies would be the renouncement of the use of force, or at least of the **first strike** (not exclusively of a nuclear strike). With such an agreement, at least a certain level of confidence could be re-established between the two contradictory forces.

The rejection of even such a primary, no-first-use, obligation raises the question whether the powers that are incapable of formally and openly renouncing the use of force in the solution of their own differences, have any moral standing in the management of other conflicts of lesser importance. In spite of the fact that many proposals in this direction have been made from the Soviet side, unfortunately there has scarcely been any joint agreement yet. Proposals concerning limitation of the arms race on every level, including space, others concerning non-aggression agreements between the two main military blocs, proposals intended to diminish or perhaps eliminate the main and global areas of conflict, have met with the same fate.

References

1. United Nations Charter, Article 34.
2. United Nations Charter, Article 33, para. 1.
3. United Nations Charter, Article 2, para. 3.
4. United Nations General Assembly, Resolution 36/103.
5. United Nations General Assembly, Resolution 37/10.
6. Speech at the National Press Club, 20 November 1984.
7. New York Times, 30 May 1982.

9 Force Postures and European Security

Michael Clemmesen

Reduction of Offensive Capability

Conventional military forces can be structured for operational versatility, or they can be structured for a limited set of missions. They can be equally capable of offensive and defensive operations, or they can be specialised for the defensive.

In this paper I try to describe how we could reduce the offensive capability of the forces in, or earmarked for, Central Europe while enhancing their defensive characteristics. This could influence one central element of the European confrontation: the fear that the opposite side starts war by launching an offensive, possibly later supported with, or countered by, nuclear weapons.

In order to make progress in this direction we have to follow three tracks simultaneously:

Firstly, we should start reducing the number of those elements that carry the offensive capability of the military forces: tanks, other armoured combat vehicles, attack helicopters (not light anti-tank helicopters), tactical transport aircraft, light and medium amphibious assault shipping, and engineer equipment for crossing water-obstacles and minefields under fire. The conventional artillery should be reduced to the quantity necessary for the support of the defensive. The development should - of course - be a gradual one. Until the necessary degree of reciprocity is reached, the ability to carry out local counter-attacks as an integrated part of the defence must be maintained.

Secondly, we should emphasise the introduction of equipment that enhances the defensive. Within the next few years several types of such weapons will be available. Some are improved versions of relatively light direct-fire weapons capable of destroying armoured vehicles. Others - delivered by artillery or aircraft - will be able to destroy, damage or delay concentrations of armoured vehicles with submunitions

consisting of mines or 'intelligent' munitions with a
terminal-homing capability. Transport helicopters will be
available for the fast laying of minefields or movement of
troops to bolster the defence or contain a breakthrough.

Thirdly, agreements should be reached that ban new types of
munitions with a clear defence-suppressing capablility. Gas,
fuel-air-explosives, and the new anti-personnel cluster
muntions that explode on impact (not mines as they are
defence-enhancing) should be banned by arms control agreements.

By both sides following these three tracks we would gradually improve the conditions for defence in Europe to such an
extent that it would be evident that offensive operations
without the support of nuclear weapons to blast a hole for
the breakthrough are simply not feasible. Thereby a better
basis for stability and the building of trust would have been
developed. Only the 'third track' will demand on-site
inspections. That the other two tracks are followed can
probably be monitored from a distance.

Battlefield Nuclear Weapons

The recommended steps in the conventional field influence the
demand for the use of battlefield nuclear weapons. One of the
missions of these weapons is to prevent or destroy concentrations for breakthrough, and as the potential for attack is
reduced the need for weapons to prevent or counter an attack
is reduced as well.

On the other hand, there is a risk that other battlefield
nuclear missions gain in relevance. If the recommended steps
have been taken on both sides, a breakthrough offensive is
still possible, if nuclear weapons are used massively to
clear a lane through the defences. But such a massive use
would involve a considerable risk of escalation, and because
of that it is not very likely. And it is possible to make
such use less destructive to the defence, and thus less
tempting to the attacker. This can be done by dispersing,
hiding and decentralising the command-and-logistic
structures, and by making the fighting element less
vulnerable prior to employment.

Thus the steps in the conventional field, supplemented with
a reduction of vulnerability, would diminish both the demand
for and temptation to make first use of battlefield nuclear
weapons. This could make it possible to start limitations in
the number of these weapons and in those longer-range nuclear
weapons that are more or less directly linked to the deterrence of a conventional attack in Central Europe. Longer-
range nuclear forces - including some Euro-strategic ones -

that are primarily meant for deterrence of a nuclear attack on one of the nuclear powers, are not directly linked to the confrontation in Central Europe. But even in this field the spin-off effect of a lessening of the military tension in Europe could be considerable.

Unilateral Steps

Some of the steps mentioned here could be taken unilaterally without any security risks, for instance the reduction of vulnerability. Others are only possible if followed by a certain degree of reciprocity. The degree depends on the current situation. The unilateral implementation of a wholly defensive force-structure is not a good idea, as the attacking party could counterbalance the advantages of the defence by a massive and systematic use of artillery and close air support; by having the initiative; and by being able to take his time doing the job. The attacking party could act deliberately since his home territory would be safe, except in the unlikely event of the defending party risking escalation to the strategic nuclear level directly from the relatively low-intensity warfare. It would be especially tempting for the side with offensive capability to carry out operations with politically or geographically limited objectives. This is so because the defender would have re- nounced beforehand the possibility of making a similar move, or of recapturing the lost territory through counter-attack. Looking at the actual situation in Europe it should be added that NATO forces have a less all-round force structure than the forces of most Warsaw Pact countries.
To change the forces on one side only would hardly be an attractive solution. On the other hand, it would be absurd, if progress is intended, to ask for an accurate balance of capabilities. Such a balance does not exist to-day, it would be nearly impossible to define it, and it would thus be useless to ask for it at each step in a mutual restructuring process. The aim should be to reduce any real fear of the offensive capabilities of the opponent through establishing 'confidence-building'-characterisitics in the force postures. Since the suggested steps are verifiable, they could hardly fail to enhance real detente by creating visible reasons for trust. In this way we would undermine the position of fear in the motivation behind force modernisation. The MBFR talks have clearly demonstrated the futility of the traditional approach to a more acceptable situation in the conventional field. Even if warheads could be defined, and thereafter counted and reduced in number within this - rather arbi- trarily limited - area covered by the talks, no balance of

capabilities would have been reached, and a reduction in number could have created an even more unstable situation than the present, since the defender would find it even more difficult to establish a continued defensive system with enough strength to intercept and contain a surprise attack.

To have all-round structured forces is not enough to give an offensive capability. They must be either standing or with a very well developed system for refresher training. Their cadres must be specialised in offensive operations. They must have the infrastructure necessary to support and sustain the offensive. Forward stocking of special equipment and ammunition must have taken place.

If one's forces are to succeed in offensive operations, the formations planned to lead the attack must be very close to wartime strength in time of peace, or they must be called-up with short intervals for long refresher training periods, like the Israeli reserve army. Otherwise, the level of training will be insufficient until three to four weeks after mobilisation. If the formations best equipped for offensive operations are kept at cadre strength, and especially if they are also kept based far away from the border, they are more likely to be used in the final part of the defensive strategy, the counter-offensive, than in a surprise offensive in Central Europe.

In peacetime one has only limited time and resources for the training of military formations. Therefore, one has to use exercises to train the staffs of those formations in carrying out their planned war-time duties. Full operational versatility simply cannot be reached anywhere but in small elite units. If one intends to fight a war offensively, one must practise offensive operations in large-scale exercises. If, however, one only plans to defend one's territory, this will be mirrored by what one practises in time of peace.

If one's strategy is an offensive one, this will influence the way both the logistic and airfield infrastructure are arranged and operated. Expanding the number of airfields for the operations of fighter bombers and heavy attack helicopters within 100 km from the border between East and West Germany is fully justified, as is exercising forward concentration of aircraft to those airfields - if the plan is to fight offensively. If the plan is to fight on one's own territory, the airfields are placed at a more safe distance from the border. In the same way, the forward concentration of the logistic structure is only appropriate if one intends to move forward in case of war.

Heavy engineering equipment for river-crossing will only be stocked in the forwarding area if it is meant for rivers ahead, otherwise it is kept distributed near the river-lines to the rear. In the same way heavy stocking of artillery ammunition in the forward area is irrelevant if one plans to fight defensively.

Thus even before the move away from all-round capable forces in Europe gets underway, steps could be taken to reduce the capabilities for surprise attack. Putting a stop to forward exercising, pulling back river-crossing equipment and artillery ammunition, changing the exercise-pattern toward emphasising the defensive, and downgrading armoured formations to mobilisation status while upgrading more infantry-heavy formations to standing status, could take place or start unilaterally without any significant loss in security.

At the same time as such unilateral steps are taken to show the intent to establish the basis for a military detente in Europe, informal talks should start between East and West. The object of these contacts should be to reach a common understanding about what type of force structure could ensure the defence, while having only very limited offensive capabilities. Following these initial talks, the forum should primarily be used for communication of the specific concerns about the conventional force posture of the other side, giving priority to capabilities most harmful to the defence. If or when both sides take steps to remove those concerns, and thereby demonstrate their intent to reach a mutually more acceptable situation, the development would have started, and more formal talks about the final force posture of the two sides could be initiated.

10 The Implications of the Increasing Accuracy of Non-Nuclear Weapons

Robert Neild

Introduction

Some people say that, with the advent of precision-guided munitions, the defence is coming into the ascendant again in non-nuclear war. Others say that the use of manned platforms to carry weapons cannot last much longer[1]; tanks, aircraft and warships will all become obsolete because they will be so vulnerable to future generations of precision-guided munitions.

These statements may prove to be right. But it is hard to be sure. They are often ad hoc propositions referring to particular vehicles (usually tanks), and particular weapons designed to destroy those vehicles (anti-tank weapons). They are vulnerable to ad hoc counter propositions and, consequently, to untidy, inconclusive argument. For example, the experience of the 1973 Middle East war is often cited as if that war, more than ten years ago, provided a definitive demonstration of the new technologies and the possible strategies for their exploitation.

The purpose of this paper is to describe a general principle that illuminates the relationship between accuracy and defence. It is a proposition I came across in the course of work I am doing with Anders Boserup on the theory of strategy. The principle also shows why, when accuracy is high, it may pay the defender to disperse his forces rather than concentrate them.

The subject whether increasing accuracy favours dispersion or concentration, defence or offence, merits some consideration. We have recently been reminded of the failure, before the 1914-18 war, to recognise that advances in firepower, notably the development of the machine gun, had brought the defence into the ascendant. The conventional wisdom in 1914 was that the attack would be supreme[2]. In retrospect, that seems astonishing. It is tempting to reflect that, had the supremacy of the defence been foreseen, perhaps war would

93

have been avoided. Perhaps the massacre in the trenches, caused by the supremacy of the defence, would have been avoided. Who can say?

Technology is changing again. Whether it redounds, or can be made to redound, to the advantage of the defender or attacker is a question we should try to get right. The only way to find out is by theoretical analysis of the implications of changing technology and by examining evidence yielded by simulations, field exercises and war. What is offered here is a tentative attempt at theoretical analysis.

Lanchester's Law

It is convenient to start by considering a simple model of the exchange of fire between two forces using weapons that are not highly accurate. The model applies equally well to any exchange of fire where there is repeated shooting by one force against another in conditions that are symmetrical as regards cover, the absence of surprise, and other variables. For example, it can be applied to an artillery duel, a naval engagement, or an infantry engagement. What matters is that there is an open 'shoot-out' in symmetrical conditions.

We shall call our numerical example an infantry engagement.

Suppose two forces of soldiers, Blue and Red, start shooting at each other in symmetrical conditions (that is with the same rifles and standard of aiming) so that the hit probability is the same on each side. The only thing that is assymetrical is the number of men.

Suppose there are twice as many Blues as Reds. At the first round of fire (supposing they start firing simultaneously) the Reds can aim at only half the Blues. But on the other side two Blues can aim at each Red. The result is that the Reds, who were fewer to start with, lose nearly twice as many men as the Blues. Consequently, at the second round of shooting, the ratio of Blues to Reds will be even more favourable to the Blues than at the first round. There will be only enough Reds to aim at less than half the Blues; and there will be more than two Blues to aim at each Red. The difference in casualty rates will, therefore, be greater than at the first round, and the ratio of Blues to Reds will show a further and bigger change in favour of the Blues. In this way the differential advantage to the Blues will accelerate dramatically as shooting continues.

To construct the mathematical example shown in Table 1, I make these assumptions:

a) 2000 Blues fight 1000 Reds. (Large numbers are used so as to avoid fractions of a man).

b) The kill probability per shot (k) is 0.2 on both sides and is assumed, in this simple example, to be the same as the hit probability, that is all hits are fatal.

c) In each round all the Blues and Reds shoot simultaneously and the bullets cross mid-air. (In order to isolate and examine the consequences of numerical superiority and nothing else, we rule out the possibility that one side or the other may gain by shooting first; and we rule out the possibility that the numerically superior side may stagger their fire within each round).

d) Each man on each side in each round is given a target, selected on the basis that fire is allocated evenly to targets so as to maximise total kills. (If it is assumed that each man chooses his own target and target selection is random, the rate of kills will be less than in this example).

The figures can be explained as follows:

a) In Round 1, 1000 Reds aim at 1000 Blues and kill 1000 x 0.2 = 200 Blues. The number of Blues surviving at the beginning of Round 2 is 2000 - 200 = 1800.

b) In Round 1 on the other side, 2000 Blues aim at 1000 Reds, spreading their fire evenly so that they aim two shots at each Red. Consider their shots as two waves, even though they are, by assumption, simultaneous. The first wave of 1000 shots will hit and kill 1000 x 0.2 = 200 Reds. The second wave will hit 1000 x 0.2 = 200 Reds. But because 200 of 1000 Reds will have been killed by the first wave, the number killed by the second wave will be only 800 x 0.2 = 160. So the Red losses in Round 1 are 200 + 160 = 360. The number of Reds surviving at the beginning of Round 2 is 1000 - 360 = 640. The ratio of Blues to Reds at the beginning of the second round is 1800 to 640 or 2.8 to 1.

c) In Rounds 2, 3, 4 and 5 the process continues with the ratio of Blues to Reds taking off dramatically. Every shift in that ratio means fewer Blues will be shot at and that more shots will be fired at each surviving Red. These are two sides of the same coin - the coin which generates the accelerating change in the ratio.

Table 1. Simultaneous fire between Blues and Reds
k = 0.2

Round	Blues		Reds		Ratio of Blues to Reds
	Number at beginning of round	Losses during round	Number at beginning of round	Losses during round	Ratio at beginning of round
1	2000	200	1000	360	2:1
2	1800	128	640	297	2.8:1
3	1672	69	343	227	4.9:1
4	1603	23	116	111	13.8:1
5	1580		5		316.0:1

Whether this law is applied to an artillery duel, a tank battle or other forms of exchange, the same conclusion follows, namely that it pays to concentrate your forces for the sake of numerical superiority.

This is a principle that was discovered 70 years ago by Lanchester, an English engineer and inventor[3]. He called it 'The Principle of Concentration'.

It is impossible not to admire the beauty of Lanchester's Principle of Concentration. It provided a brilliant rationale for concentrating your forces - and dividing those of the enemy if possible - so as to achieve superiority of fire-power, something which military men knew from experience to be of the greatest importance.

But the law depends on two implicit assumptions. The first, and more obvious, is that the advantages of being on the defensive, with dug-in positions, knowledge of the ground and so on, are assumed away, as are the advantages the attacker may enjoy if he achieves surprise.

The second implicit assumption, whose significance is less immediately obvious but which is of interest today, is that the hit probability of the weapons is fairly low, so that repetitive shooting is needed for an assured hit.

Suppose the hit probability was one, meaning that every shot was sure to destroy its target. There would be no point in numerical superiority in an exchange of fire - as distinct from superiority in total forces available to a nation or commander. The Blues, with their first shots, would hit one thousand Reds. There would be no point in having more Blues to kill each Red more than once. One thousand Reds would simultaneously kill one thousand Blues with their first shots, if the bullets of the two sides cross in mid-air. Of course that would not happen. The fact that it would not happen is a key point; it brings us to a conclusion: **as kill probabilities rise, the value of shooting first in an engagement increases.**

But higher kill probabilities have a second effect. They mean that the rate of change in the ratio of forces in favour of the superior increases. The latter point is illustrated in the numerical example in Table 2. The assumptions are the same as in Table 1, but kill probabilities of 0.5 and 1.0 are introduced.

Table 2. Simultaneous fire between Blues and Reds
$k = 0.2, 0.5$ and 1.0

Round	Blues		Red		Ratio of Blues to Reds
	Number at beginning of round	Losses during round	Number at beginning of round	Losses during round	Ratio at beinning of round
			$k = 0.2$		
1	2000	200	1000	360	2:1
2	1800	128	640	297	2.8:1
3	1672		343		4.9:1
			$k = 0.5$		
1	2000	500	1000	750	2:1
2	1500	125	250	246	6:1
3	1375		4		344:1
			$k = 1.0$		
1	2000		1000	1000	2:1
2	1000		0		

If we consider the combined result of these two effects of higher accuracy - the rising premium on shooting first and the more rapid gain to the superior force when fire is simultaneous - we can arrive at the following conclusions:

a) If the two sides are unequal and the inferior side shoots first at the first round, it will thereby reduce its rate of relative decline - or achieve superiority. Whether it achieves superiority depends on whether the kill probability per shot is high enough in relation to the numerical superiority of the enemy. (The condition that must be satisfied if the inferior side by shooting first is to achieve equality or superiority is $1 + k > r$ where k is the kill probability and r the ratio of the superior to inferior force). What happens beyond the first round depends on the sequence of fire. With high accuracy, the outcome of an engagement is sensitive to the sequence of fire at all stages. For example, if it is assumed that there is alternating fire, rather than simultaneous fire (which is an approximation to random fire), **after** the first round, the rate of change in relative strength is affected. If the inferior side (Red) has shot first at the first round, gaining unilaterally, it will lose uni-laterally at the second round when, with alternating fire, the superior side (Blue) shoots alone. The evaluation of the ratio of forces will be less favourable to the inferior side than if the fire after the first round is simultaneous.

b) Similarly, if the superior side (Blue) shoots first, the gain that it derives (in terms of the evolution of the ratio of forces) will be less if in subsequent rounds there is alternating fire than if there is simultaneous fire. These points are illustrated in Table 3.

c) If the two sides start with **equal** numbers and one side shoots first, the evolution of the ratio of forces will not be significantly affected if accuracies are low. But if accuracies are high, the balance of forces will be tipped decisively in favour of the side that shoots first, that is, the outcome will be decided by who shoots first, a point illustrated in Table 4.

d) The fact that the rate of change in the ratio of numbers in favour of the superior force increases with accuracy implies that there is less advantage in achieving large superiority in numbers than there is with low accuracy. With high accuracy, moderate superiority in numbers will do, the more so if by deploying smaller numbers you increase the chances of concealing your force success-fully and shooting first. On the other hand, to be out-numbered in an open exchange or surprised when accuracies are high is more costly than it is when accuracies are low.

Table 3. Ratio of Forces after Successive Rounds of Fire with Three Different Sequences of Firing

Initial Ratio of Blues to Reds   2:1
Kill Probability of Both Sides   0.5

Simultaneous Fire	Reds Shoot First followed by		Blues Shoot First followed by	
	(a) Alternating fire	(b) Simultaneous fire	(a) Alternating fire	(b) Simultaneous fire
2:1	2:1	2:1	2:1	2:1
6:1	1.5:1	1.5:1	8:1	8:1
344:1	4.0:1		7.5:1	
	3.5:1	2.7:1	1280:1	1920:1
	37.5:1		12795:1	
	37.0:1	26.2:1	:1	:1

Table 4. Ratio of Blues to Reds after Successive Rounds of Fire with Different Sequences of Firing

Initial Ratio of Blues to Reds   1:1
Kill Probability of Both Sides   0.01 or 0.5

	k = 0.01			k = 0.5	
Simultaneous Fire	Blues shoot first followed by		Simultaneous Fire	Blues shoot first followed by	
	Alternating fire	Simultaneous fire		Alternating fire	Simultaneous fire
1:1	1:1	1:1	1:1	1:1	1:1
1:1	1.01:1	1.01:1	1:1	2:1	2:1
1:1	1.0001:1		1:1	1.5:1	
	1.0102:1	1.0102:1		4:1	6:1
	1.0002:1			3.5:1	
	1.0103:1	1.0103:1		37.3:1	344:1

These are the sort of trade-offs that need to be analysed in an assessment of alternative strategies in a world of high accuracy. Clearly, it is no longer safe, as it is in a world of low accuracy, for the analyst, let alone the soldier, to assume that it does not matter who shoots first or what the sequence of firing is.

The Principle of Dispersion

We shall for the moment assume that there is a kill probability of one for weapons with single heads aimed at single targets (that is, aimed at one man or one weapon).

We shall temporarily leave aside weapons which characteristically will kill more than one man or weapon, a category that includes projectiles with multiple aimed sub-munitions, as well as weapons that cause destruction over an area, whether by blast, splinter, fire, chemical contamination or nuclear reaction. We shall turn to multiple target weapons later. For a single-target weapon the maximum value of k, the kill probability, specified in terms of numbers of men or weapons killed, is one. For the multiple target weapon there is no general upper limit to the kill probability.

The assumption that the kill probability for single-target weapons is one has these implications for an engagement:

a) who sees first, by eye or sensor, kills;

b) therefore, concealment from the eye or sensor, pays;

c) if dispersion helps concealment, as it will in most geographical setting, dispersion pays.

Thus, we are led in a few steps to the opposite conclusion from Lanchester. In his low accuracy world, concentration pays. In our perfect accuracy world, dispersion pays.

In mathematical terms, we could write that the chance of being killed were a function of two probabilities, the probability of being detected (P_d), and the probability of being killed once you had been detected (P_k). Thus, the probability of being killed = $P_d \cdot P_k$, and the chance of survival = $1 - P_d \cdot P_k$.

Lanchester implicitly assumes that there is no problem of detection: $P_d = 1$, and the chance of survival in an encounter depends on $1 - P_k$. I am explicitly assuming here that $P_k = 1$, and the chance of survival in an encounter depends on $1 - P_d$. To minimise P_d, it pays to disperse. The extent of the advantage will depend on the opportunities for concealment offered by local geography.

The Advantage to Defender or Attacker

We come now to the question whether rising accuracy (carrying with it a rising kill probability) redounds to the benefit of the attacker or the defender.
We shall make the following assumptions:

a) There are two nations that are identical in every respect, except that one is attacking the other, trying to seize territory; the other is defending its territory, trying to frustrate the attack. The size, shape, population, terrain and every other geographical features of the two countries are assumed to be the same, and so are the size and characteristics of their armed forces. The object of these strong assumptions of symmetry is to isolate the variables with which we are concerned: who is attacking/defending and the kill probability. The nation that is defender in the war may be attacker (in the sense of the word with which we are concerned) in particular engagements or campaigns: he may counter-attack.
b) Technical means of observation, command and control are making it easier to detect and identify targets and direct fire at them, the more so the larger and more conspicuous are the targets to the eye or sensor.

I shall first consider single-target weapons.
As we have seen, high kill probabilities have two effects: there is a premium on shooting first; and there is a high reward to superiority of numbers in an open shoot-out. It follows that with high accuracy two considerations (which are not obviously reconcilable) will be important:

a) to shoot first;
b) to achieve superiority if there is an open shoot-out - though not overwhelming superiority: with high accuracy, moderate superiority pays off fast and will suffice: but it is vital not to risk moderate inferiority, except insofar as other factors compensate for it.

We shall consider first the question whether attacker or defender gains from the premium on the first shot; then whether attacker or defender gains from the high reward to superiority.

The First-Shot Premium

Who gains from the first-shot premium depends on the possibilities for concealment and protection afforded by the

terrain and by the man-made structures and diggings on it.
Concealment and protection help the defender; lack of it
helps the attacker. The point can best be expounded by
considering extreme cases.

Suppose first there is no possibility of concealment or
protection for a combination of two reasons:

a) the ground is bare and flat and there is no man-made cover
   or protection;
b) surveillance systems are such that each side can observe
   the men and weapons of the other side and direct accurate
   fire at them.

In these conditions, which amount to a high-tech confrontation on a concrete direct - or a high-tech confrontation at
sea with surface vessels - whoever shoots first can pick off
his opponent's forces with his opening shots. In the extreme
theoretical case, where the kill probability of all weapons
was one and each side had weapons in sufficient quantity and
of sufficient range to be able to cover all his opponents
forces, whichever side shot first would eliminate all his
opponents forces; he would wipe them out in his opening
salvo; there would be a huge advantage to firing first: in
other words, a great advantage to the attacker. The case is
analogous to the argument in the nuclear realm: if there are
vulnerable weapon systems, for example land-based missile
silos, there is an advantage to shooting first and a
temptation to attack pre-emptively. That temptation may
become acute and hence difficult, if not impossible, to
avoid, as regards surface ships.

Consider now the opposite conditions, namely that there are
rich possibilities of concealment and protection because:

a) the terrain (rural and urban) offers much cover; and/or
b) surveillance systems are of limited capability.

In these conditions the attacker cannot pick off his
opponent before he advances. He must advance and seek him
out. In advancing, he will reveal himself or his vehicle to
the defender. The defender, who has stayed concealed, can
then be the first to fire and pick off his opponent. He gains
the first shot premium.

Of course, the attacker may try to conceal himself by the
use of smoke or electronic counter-measures to upset
communications and sensors. But anything the attacker can do
in that line of business the defender can do too. There is
symmetry. But as regards revealing yourself in order to
advance, there is asymmetry. Whoever is on the attack - or

counter-attack - must reveal himself in a manner that is not necessary to the defender.

This proposition applies to an engagement with good cover/ limited surveillance, up to the moment of the defender's first shot. What happens after that?

Shooting gives away the position of directly-fired weapons. (We shall ignore for the moment weapons triggered by remote control or 'trip wires', that is any trigger activated automatically by the approach of a person, vehicle or other weapon, for example mines, booby traps or homing devices activated by sensors). So, as the defenders fire more shots and reveal their positions, whilst the attacker's positions remain known as a result of their movement and firing, the position will tend to become **symmetrical**: both will tend to have an equal knowledge of the positions of the other. At this stage there seems no reason why there should be an advantage to defender or attacker, except insofar as the defender may have better protection, for example, through prepared earthworks and trenches, and will have better knowledge of the terrain. In other words, there are always the classical advantages enjoyed by the defender. But leaving these aside, there seems to be a phase of symmetry once the defender has revealed his position by firing.

At that stage, each side can move so as to seek concealment and protection or to disengage. But whatever the outcome of the local engagement, the attacker must advance again (until the day when his opponent decides to offer no more resistance). In advancing he will again reveal himself and make himself vulnerable to first shots by the defender - if the defender has adopted a dispersed defence in depth that takes advantage of the cover which, **ex hypothesi**, is available.

In sum, if there is good cover, the defender, by means of a dispersed defence in depth, can repeatedly enjoy the first-shot premium.

The High Reward to Superiority

We turn now to the question whether the attacker or defender gains from the high reward to superiority in an open engagement that goes with high accuracy. The short answer is that there appears to be no general reason why attacker or defender should gain more from this effect.

The reason is this. The advantage should go to that side which achieves superiority in the open, whether in one big engagement or many small ones. But there is no general reason to suppose that in any engagement, the attacker - or counter-attacker - is any more likely to do so than the defender. True, the attacker has the initiative in the limited sense that he can choose the time of attack and what forces he uses. But the defender, by the very disposition of his forces and resources, dictates what must be attacked; and he can seek to out-manoeuvre the attacker, for example, leading him into a trap where he, the defender, enjoys a greater concentration of force (due allowance being made for the classical advantages of defence). In open warfare where concentrations of force are used, each side must guess at the plans of the other and seek to out-manoeuvre him. There is no means of saying who in general will be more successful at achieving local superiority.

What can be said, I think, is that high accuracy makes open warfare, where each side seeks to win by superiority, more risky than it was with low accuracy. As is evident from the numerical examples discussed earlier, small differences in numbers will bring rapid victory to the side that is numerically superior; the possibility of redressing the balance by reinforcement will be correspondingly small.

There is also a powerful reason why it may be increasingly dangerous to concentrate your forces in pursuit of numerical superiority. It lies in the increasing potency of multi-target weapons. Nuclear weapons are an example, but there are political constraints on their use and few powers possess them. The smart non-nuclear weapons with guided sub-munitions, which we are now promised, are another matter. There are going to be no obvious constraints on their use.

Multi-target Weapons

Let us consider the effect of potent multi-target weapons in the two sets of conditions we examined earlier - no possibility of concealment and protection, and a rich possibility thereof.

In the first case (no concealment) effective multi-target weapons are another means by which he who shoots first can knock out his visible and vulnerable opponent. If single-target weapons were alone sufficient for this task, multi-target weapons would be technically redundant but might be cheaper, that is, there would be another way to do the job but one that might be more expensive. By adding to the certainty that a first strike would demolish the enemy's forces, multi-target weapons when combined with single-target weapons would add to the temptation to shoot first and the pressure to do so for fear your opponent will yield to the same temptation.

In the second case (rich possibilities of concealment) multi-target weapons appear to redound to the advantage of whichever side is more dispersed; and that would seem to be the defender.

The first step in the argument is that if one side's forces are concentrated, they offer a richer target to the opponent's multi-target weapons - and are also more likely to be detected - than if they are dispersed. If they are dispersed and concealed, multi-target weapons (which include area weapons as well as weapons with aimed sub-munitions) can be used only to fire indiscriminately into areas into which you wish to advance, a usage that is inefficient in terms of the number of enemy forces you are likely to hit, and one which may also be politically counter-productive, in that you will destroy assets you might otherwise take intact and you may arouse political opposition against the wholesale slaughter and destruction you inflict on your opponent.

The second step in the argument is that it is the attacker who will have the strongest incentive to concentrate his forces, and who therefore stands to lose most from the vulnerability of concentrated forces to multi-target weapons. The essential point here, on which this argument stands or falls, is that it is not attractive to an attacker to disperse his forces and engage in widespread fighting in which his opponent's forces, if dispersed, repeatedly enjoy the first-shot premium. If the attacker concentrates his forces, his opponent will still enjoy that advantage **vis-a-vis** the concentrated attacking force as it advances and encounters successive units of dispersed defenders. But the attacker may hope to overwhelm the defenders by concentrated use of area weapons on the area into which he advances.

There is no comparable temptation to concentrate for the defender. He will want to be able to apply concentrated **fire**, probably with multi-target weapons, to destroy and break-up the concentrated force of the attacker. But to concentrate **fire** does not require that the weapons delivering that fire be concentrated. The advance of technology means that weapons which are kept dispersed and concealed - notably rockets but also, for example, helicopters and vertical take-off aircraft - can be used from many distant points to produce concentrated fire on any selected target.

We have now pursued the analysis as far as we can. But there is an important qualification to be made.

So far we have assumed that technical advances in accuracy and lethality produce a high kill probability per shot for single-target weapons; and that multi-target weapons are advancing too.

There can be little doubt that the **trend** of technology is going that way. But counter-measures that impede reconnaissance, communication and guidance systems are coming along too. The implication is that the performance of weapons

systems and of the armed forces using them is becoming more
variable (according to who is winning the counter-measures
game) and more unpredictable (insofar as you cannot know in
advance who is leading at the game). A question that matters
here is whether there is any reason why an attacker or
defender should be more successful at counter-measures. I can
see none, but I am no expert in that subject. I have not
explored the question how the choice of strategy by defender
and attacker, in particular, whether to disperse or
concentrate, should be influenced by **uncertainty** as to
the relative performance of the weapons of the two sides.

Conclusion

As accuracy rises, it is increasingly important to be the
first to shoot. The law that it pays to concentrate for the
sake of numerical superiority ceases to be generally valid:
it may pay to disperse, so as to be concealed and hence be in
a position to shoot first.

Whether the attacker or defender will gain from high
accuracy (and high kill probabilities per shot) depends on
the terrain and on the efficiency of target surveillance.
Those two factors determine whether it is the attacker or
defender who enjoys the advantage of shooting first. If the
terrain offers little cover and/or the means of surveillance
are efficient, the advantage goes to the one who chooses to
shoot first, that is, the attacker. Where the terrain offers
good cover and/or the means of surveillance are poor, the
advantage will go to the defender.

The oceans (as regards surface ships) and the desert areas
of the Middle East look like places where accuracy might help
the attacker. Europe - though the extent of cover varies -
looks like an area where accuracy might help the defender.

References

1. See, for example, 'Diminishing the Nuclear Threat: NATO's
   Defence and New Technology', British Atlantic
   Committee, 1984, pp.30-3.
2. cf. M. Howard, 'Men Against Fire: Expectations of War in
   1914', and S. Van Evera, 'The Cult of the Offensive and
   the Origins of the First World War', International
   Security, (Summer 1984) pp.41-57, 58-107.
3. F.W. Lanchester, 'Aircraft in Warfare', The Dawn of the
   Fourth Arm, (London: Constable, 1916) Chapter V.

11 Pros and Cons of a Chemical Weapon-Free Zone in Europe: The Genesis of a Concept

Karlheinz Lohs

Introduction

Now as before, a comprehensive and worldwide ban on development, manufacture, stockpiling and use of chemical weapons appears to be out of reach. The talks in the Geneva Committee on Disarmament have been dragging on for years and have produced a multitude of documents which describe the opposing positions taken by the countries of NATO and the Warsaw Treaty, and the various opinions of non-aligned nations.

Parallel to the negotiations of government representatives in the Palais des Nations in Geneva, discussions have taken place at the non-governmental level for more than ten years now (in the Pugwash Workshops, for example) on ways of banning chemical weapons. Elsewhere, non-governmental organisations have also dealt with the subject and published relevant material, as have international peace research institutes. Most prominent in the latter group is the Stockholm International Peace Research Institute (SIPRI), which deserves credit for working over many years towards the prohibition of this group of mass extermination weapons.

It is now more than 70 years since modern chemical warfare became a military reality. On 22 April 1915 the Imperial German troops used chlorine gas on a large scale near Ypres, Belgium, thus initiating the race for ever more perfect means of mass murder by chemicals, which has continued to this very day.

About sixty years ago, in 1925, the Geneva Protocol for the Prohibition of the Use in War of Chemical and Biological Weapons was signed. Most industrial countries and many developing nations have acceded (the USA, however, did this after a delay of 50 years, in 1975, that is, after the end of the Vietnam war in which it used herbicidal and harassing anti-personnel warfare agents on a considerable scale, with effects on humans and the environment lasting to this day).

It is impractical to elaborate here on the history of chemical warfare agents and the diverse efforts which have been made to achieve a worldwide ban on chemical weapons. The reader is referred to the relevant literature.

From the wide-ranging discussion which is currently under way, on how to put a ban on chemical weapons, the question of creating chemical weapon-free zones (CWFZ) will be singled out for consideration in this paper. This question has become very topical particularly with regard to the situation in Europe, and I discussed it frequently in Pugwash and SIPRI Symposia.

Chronology of the Previous Discussion of CWFZ

The Palme Commission, named after its chairman, Swedish Prime Minister Olof Palme, began its work in Vienna in September 1980. Its report, published in 1982, described, among other things, the dangers of chemical war, and went on to propose a zone in Europe which would be free from chemical weapons, as follows[1]:

> The Commission calls for the establishment of a chemical-weapon-free zone in Europe, beginning with Central Europe. The agreement would include a declaration of the whereabouts of existing depots and stockpiles in Europe, adequate means to verify their destruction, and procedures for monitoring compliance on a continuing basis, including a few on-site inspections on a challenge basis. The training of troops in the offensive use of chemical weapons also would be prohibited.
> There is an immediate need to initiate a downward turn in the arms spiral. We have, therefore, proposed a set of short- and medium-term measures. The short-term measures could, and should, be implemented within the next two years; the medium-term measures within the next five years.
> Short-term measures. Agreement on the establishment of a chemical-weapon-free zone in Europe.
> Medium-term measures. Conclusion of a comprehensive chemical weapons disarmament treaty banning the production and stockpiling of all such weapons and the destruction of existing stock and production facilities.

This idea of creating a chemical weapon-free zone, which the Palme Commission spelled out for the first time, had earlier been voiced in the discussions of the Pugwash Workshop on Chemical Weapons (1978/79) and its working group on chemical weapons. The formulation in the report of the

Palme Commission has been widely reported.

Even before the Palme report was published, protests took place in the Federal Republic of Germany against US Army depots of chemical warfare agents in that country, and the German Federation of Trade Unions (DGB) called for the liberation of Europe from chemical weapons[2].

Julius Lehlbach, chairman of the DGB in the state of Rhineland-Palatinate, emerged as the spokesman of a movement for a Europe free from chemical weapons. This movement has since spread, and I will refer to more of Lehlbach's initiatives later. Willi Brandt made a clear statement in favour of a CWFZ at Ludwigshafen on 7 February 1983. A similar stand against the deployment of chemical weapons in Britain has been taken by that country's Labour Party. The question of a CWFZ was also discussed during a hearing before the US Congress and was positively received[3].

On 5 November 1982 the proposal of the Palme Commission was welcomed, before the 37th UN General Assembly by Harry Ott, the German Democratic Republic Ambassador to the United Nations and Deputy Foreign Minister. This made the government of the GDR the first to issue a statement endorsing the idea voiced by the Palme Commission.

In January 1983 the Prague Declaration of the Warsaw Treaty nations clearly favoured the liberation of Europe from chemical weapons.

At a round-table discussion which dealt with the qualitative arms race held by the World Federation of Scientific Workers at Schmöckwitz, GDR, near Berlin in April 1983, the necessity for a chemical weapon-free zone was for the first time put before a large forum of scientists from East and West.

In a paper submitted to the 'National scientists conference to save the world from the threat of nuclear war and to assure disarmament and peace', of the Soviet Academy of Science, which took place in Moscow on 17-19 May 1983, I strongly supported the idea of a chemical weapon-free zone and explained the specific situation with regard to the deployment of US depots of chemical warfare agents on the western border of the GDR.

A similar statement was made to a scientific symposium organised by the Karl Marx University of Leipzig, with the participation of UNESCO, on 3-4 May 1983[4].

In June 1983 a special conference on 'Chemical Weapons and Arms Control - Views from Europe' was held in Rome where a detailed - not entirely positive assessment - was given of the Palme Commission's proposal to create a chemical weapon-free zone[5]. The results are discussed below.

At the International Pugwash Conference which took place in

Warsaw in August 1982 the idea of a chemical weapon-free zone was also welcomed. This had been preceded by discussions in the Pugwash Workshops on the prohibition of chemical weapons which also dealt with the problem of a chemical weapon-free zone.

During the International Conference for Common Security which was organised by SIPRI under the auspices of the Swedish government in Stockholm in September 1983, I reviewed the aims of a chemical weapon-free zone and thus initiated a wider discussion among the participants, who included scientists and governmental representatives from the Warsaw Treaty countries, NATO, and the non-aligned nations.

The year 1984 saw a considerable revival of the discussion about creating a chemical weapon-free zone. Early that year, on 10 January, the Warsaw Treaty nations appealed to the NATO countries to liberate Europe from chemical weapons. A few days later, on 23 January, Julius Lehlbach wrote identical letters to Helmut Kohl, Chancellor of the Federal Republic of Germany, and to Erich Honecker, the Chairman of the State Council of the German Democratic Republic, referring to a resolution adopted by the 12th Federal Congress of his organisation, which demanded the removal of chemical weapons from the FRG. Honecker answered immediately and, in a letter dated 15 February, declared the full support of the GDR for either worldwide or regional steps which would liquidate chemical weapons. Lehlbach is still waiting for a similar response from Kohl. In an indirect reaction, the FRG Chancellor merely let it be known that he was in favour of a worldwide ban on chemical weapons. He did not mention the creation of a chemical weapon-free zone in Europe but had government officials tell the press on his behalf that the FRG government had no say in the US depots of chemical warfare agents in his country because they were part of NATO 'defence concept'.

In March 1984 a meeting took place in Berlin (GDR) between Honecker and Hans-Jochen Vogel, chairman of the parliamentary group of the Social Democratic Party of Germany (SPD) in the Bundestag of the FRG. In the course of the discussion Vogel proposed talks by experts from the SPD and the Socialist Unity Party of Germany (SED) about the creation of a chemical weapon-free zone. Honecker agreed to this, and delegations of experts from the two parties held their first discussions in Berlin as early as July 1984. A second round took place in Bonn on 20-21 September; a third was held, again in Berlin, on 5-6 December 1984; a fourth in Bonn on 28 February - 2 March 1985; and the fifth in Berlin on 11 April 1985.

Events were also organised in the two German states in 1984

in which scientists discussed the idea of a chemical weapon-free zone and declared their support for related initiatives. Thus a colloquium, convened at the GDR Academy of Sciences by the country's Committee for Scientific Aspects of Securing Peace and Disarmament on 17 April 1984, received widespread attention because it highlighted the need for a ban on chemical weapons and the usefulness of a chemical weapon-free zone in Europe from various angles, including those of the natural and social sciences. Of equal import was a congress of scientists in the FRG which was held at the Johannes Gutenberg University in Mainz on 18 November 1984 on 'Responsiblity for Peace'. It vividly described the dangers of biological and chemical weapons, and one of its conclusions was the demand to create a chemical weapon-free zone. Among the speakers at the congress was the abovementioned Lehlbach who had, in the meantime, received support for a CWFZ in reply to a letter he had sent to Gustav Husak, the President of Czechoslovakia.

Earlier, meetings to discuss the CWFZ concept had been held in a number of other European countries. Mention should be made in this connection of a round-table discussion on 'The prohibition of chemical weapons in Europe and worldwide' which took place in the series of 'Vienna Meetings' on 2 June 1984 at the initiative of the International Institute for Peace in Vienna, and of the International Pugwash Conference held at Björkliden, Sweden, in 1984 which heard papers and discussions of the concept[6]. In late autumn of 1984 a series of lectures was held at the Free University in West Berlin on 'Physical and Chemical Aspects of Modern Arms Technology'. Among these was a lecture by Professor Ferdinand Hucho of the University's Institute of Biochemistry in support of a CWFZ[7].

Other efforts made in 1984 towards establishing a CWFZ included two exchanges of letters. The first of these occurred in May, when Petra Kelly, a Green Party MP in the FRG Bundestag, wrote to Konstantin Chernenko, General Secretary of the CPSU Central Committee and Chairman of the Presidium of the Supreme Soviet, to express deep concern at the possible use of nuclear, chemical and other means of mass destruction against targets in the Federal Republic of Germany. According to TASS, Chernenko replied on 29 May 1984 that he shared this concern, but that the FRG would be safe from a Soviet response if it ceased to be a deployment zone against the socialist countries. The Soviet leader said he was fully prepared to renounce first use, and introduce balanced steps towards the reduction of all kinds of conventional and mass-destruction weapons. On chemical weapons, Chernenko's letter said, among other things[8]:

... With equal resolution the Soviet Union is opposed to the use of chemical weapons at any time, and we have made concrete proposals to remove them from the arsenals completely. As a primary step the USSR and other socialist countries have proposed an agreement to liberate Europe from all kinds of chemical weapons...

The second important exchange of letters on this question took place shortly before Christmas 1984, between Julius Lehlbach and Konstantin Chernenko. Lehlbach had asked Chernenko the specific question as to whether the Soviet Union would consent to a chemical weapon-free zone in Europe. Chernenko replied that his country was prepared to commit itself to respecting such a zone and declared the readiness of the Soviet Union and the other socialist countries to enter into an exchange of views on this question with the NATO states and with all other interested European countries at any time.

In view of these diverse initiatives undertaken in 1984 one cannot help but find it worrying that no official statement from the FRG government exists on the question of a CWFZ. It is interesting to note, however, that Jürgen Todenhöfer, the disarmament spokesman of the CDU/CSU parliamentary group in the Bundestag, said the following on the subject in Bonn on 5 April 1984[9]:

... The world needs no chemical weapons for deterrence. What is true worldwide, naturally applies also to Europe. This is why the creation of a Europe which is verifiably free from chemical weapons could contribute towards a world-wide ban on all chemical weapons...

This statement at least shows that the idea of a CWFZ has not been completely ignored, even by the governing parties of the FRG, and that some thinking has begun. This is regard-less of the fact that Volker Rühe, the deputy chairman of the CDU/CSU parliamentary group, spoke out against the talks about a CWFZ between the SPD and the SED, and against the concept of a CWFZ, in the group's press bulletin on 20 September 1984[10].

Rolf Ekeus, who heads the Swedish delegation at the Geneva Committee on Disarmament (CD) and chairs the CD **ad hoc** Committee for Chemical Weapons, referred in detail to the CWFZ concept in a paper entitled 'How to ban chemical weapons', which he read as part of the second public SIPRI Lecture on the occasion of the Conference for Confidence-and-Security-Building, in Europe on 5 December 1984[11]. Later I will deal with his arguments in more detail.

Looking back at the year 1984 one might justly say that it gave more weight to the idea of creating a chemical weapon-free zone in the disarmament policy concepts of the European states, a fact reflected not least in the discussions at the Stockholm Conference on Confidence-and-Security-Building in Europe.

Under the headline 'No time must be lost', the Soviet Army newspaper **Krasnaya Zvezda** (Red Star) published an article at the beginning of 1985 which said, among other things[12]:

To free the world from chemical weapons is one of the most topical tasks in the area of arms, these weapons of mass destruction constitute a grave danger for mankind... The Soviet Union ... is prepared to approach the problem of liberating mankind from chemical weapons both in a global and partial sense... This is particularly urgent for the Federal Republic of Germany which has 10 000 tonnes of chemical warfare agents on its territory. It is topical also for the neighbours of the FRG because the use of chemical weapons on the densely populated territory of Europe would have particularly grave consequences for the civilian population... The Soviet Union will continue to do everything in its power to help establish a chemical-weapon-free zone in Europe...

During a symposium on 'Banning chemical weapons: An Exploration of Alternatives' organized by the Quaker United Nations Office, Geneva, held 8-10 March 1985, the pros and cons of a CWFZ were also discussed very intensively.

On 18 March 1985, the Ambassador of the GDR to the Stockholm Conference of Confidence-and-Security-Building in Europe, Günter Bühring, explored the position of the government of the GDR on a CWFZ[13].

Among other themes, the 6th Symposium of 'Leipziger Wissenschaftler für den Frieden', on 19 March 1985 focussed on a CWFZ in terms of natural science and international law[14].

Arguments in Favour of a CWFZ

When it is accepted that the establishment of a CWFZ in Europe would be no more (and no less) than a step towards the worldwide prohibition of all types and systems of chemical weapons, which remains as topical as ever, then it will be appreciated that a chemical **cordon sanitaire** in Europe would be an extraordinary signal and example to the rest of the world. Of course, the chemical weapons to be removed from the declared zone would continue to exist outside it, and no disarmament in the literal sense would be achieved. Nevertheless, an impetus would clearly be given to the talks about a comprehensive ban on chemical weapons, which have been dragging on for decades and have stagnated at times. In addition, the people living in this zone would enjoy greater security in a dual sense. First, the continuous hazard of technical defects and other incalculable factors which exist even in peacetime, would be removed (such as intervention by terrorists and external factors, including planes crashing into depots, and natural disasters). Second, there would be no danger of chemical war breaking out from within such a zone, and no chemical warfare agents could be released inadvertently through the action of other means of warfare, as would be the case simply when conventional munitions are fired into chemical weapon depots.

It is important to note that, as a result of the geographical separation brought about by a CWFZ, tactical chemical weapons could not be brought into play at the start of a possible war between East and West.

This enhanced security in a CWFZ would definitely promote confidence-building among states belonging to different social systems located in the zone and beyond. The general psychological effect should not be underestimated. Moreover, there is a technical aspect to disarmament which favours a CWFZ. This is the necessary verification which would be easier to implement in the case of a CWFZ than in the event of a worldwide ban on the development, production, stockpiling and use of chemical weapons. Last, but not least, the experience gained in verifying the CWFZ could directly and indirectly benefit future agreements on the comprehensive prohibition of all chemical weapons.

There are many more arguments in favour of a CWFZ. The establishment of such a zone would prove the sovereignty of the states belonging to it, encouraging their people to strengthen democracy and pursue peace in an active way. This in turn would have an effect on the political 'manners' of these countries toward others.

There can be no doubt that the opponents of a CWFZ are very well aware of these and other arguments in support of such a zone. Leaving aside those opponents who are against all peace promoting measures as a matter of principle, or base their case purely on political ignorance, a number of counter arguments still remain which must be dealt with by anyone seriously concerned with the subject.

Arguments Against a CWFZ

In dealing with arguments against a CWFZ, I would like to

refer to the very substantial statements made by Johan Lundin[15] at the above-mentioned conference in Rome, to Julian Perry Robinson's contributions[16] at the same conference and to the SIPRI Lecture by Ambassador Rolf Ekeus in Stockholm[11], mentioned earlier. Together, the three present the major counter-arguments and outstanding questions in regard to a CWFZ.

Both Lundin and Ekeus are first concerned with definitions, such as 'free' in a CWFZ: free for what period? free only in peacetime or also in time of war? free from a country's own chemical weapons or also those of its allies? I believe that these questions have been answered a long time ago because those who have to date seriously discussed the CWFZ concept have made it very clear that such a zone must be kept free from all kinds of chemical weapons, no matter who owns them; for all time, that is, in peace and war.

Lundin asks many questions about the concept of the zone and whether the chemical weapons in a particular zone will be destroyed or only removed, whether the zone is not more than a corridor in actual fact, whether it will remain in existence in time of war, and so on.

In my opinion, the scope of the zone cannot be defined in advance because this will depend on the particular states which are prepared to join it. These might be, for example, the countries involved in the Vienna M(B)FR talks; alternatively a small zone could be initiated in Central Europe beginning with the GDR, the FRG and Czechoslovakia. There is no reason why the initial zone could not be extended to other European nations and beyond, and it would obviously be superseded at once by a worldwide prohibition of chemical weapons.

Lundin's reservations concerning the participation of France in a CWFZ are certainly justified. As a country which is widely assumed to own chemical weapons (made domestically), France could not remove them from its territory without destroying them, which would then become the condition for implementing a CWFZ there. This would necessarily take longer than in other countries which are merely deployment areas and where the weapons need only be transported beyond the national borders. Lundin's question about the timetable leading to the implementation of the CWFZ is not really a counter-argument. This planning will depend on the technical conditions for the removal or destruction in situ, and on the specific agreements made by the countries forming the CWFZ. A period of two to three years would appear necessary between the conclusion of a treaty among these countries and the implementation of the resulting commitments; one might even add one or two additional years. The Palme Commission

estimated that medium-term measures would take five years.
There can be no doubt that verification problems represent
a major aspect of chemical weapon-free zones. Unlike Lundin,
however, I believe that the entire apparatus required for a
worldwide comprehensive ban on the development, production,
stockpiling and use of chemical weapons will not be needed.
A country joining a CWFZ will have to give verifiable proof
that it has no chemical weapons on its territory, that is,
that any chemical weapons once owned by it have been removed
or destroyed and will not be returned or allowed through its
territory again. To this end a national inspection system
must exist which has international credibility and which can
be checked by international means, if doubts arise.

The entire problem of verification was dealt with in detail
by one of my co-workers, Ralf Trapp, at the beginning of
1985[17]. A more critical view in this respect is given by
Arthur H. Westing[18].

Under the specific conditions of Europe, with a densely
populated territory and a complex industrial structure, and
with a vigilant work force, it is practically impossible for
a country to declare itself a CWFZ and still produce and
stockpile chemical weapons secretly. Anyone who doubts this
can have had no experience with stockpiles of chemical
warfare agents and will therefore be unaware of the necessary
related safety precautions and other technical handling
conditions.

There is also the question of whether precautions against
chemical weapons should be taken in a CWFZ. It should be left
to the member states to decide if and to what extent they
might wish to instruct their armed forces and populations
regarding protective measures against these weapons.

However, one cannot agree with Lundin when he says[15]:
'The problems would be still larger for a chemical-weapons-
free zone, since it could not be completely excluded that
chemical weapons eventually were to be used'.

With these kinds of doubts one could, in the last analysis,
question any agreement on arms limitation and disarmament
because there will always be countries which do not accede to
or which transgress an agreement, and might therefore (at
least in theory) act as aggressors against others. The system
of arms limitation and disarmament agreements concluded after
World War II has impressively proven its peace-stabilising
effect, even though such arrangements will be necessarily
imperfect and have not yet been joined or ratified by all the
world's countries.

Among the counter-arguments, the question is raised of why
Europe is singled out for a CWFZ. Priority for Europe can be
justified for a number of reasons: it is the site of con-

frontation between NATO and the Warsaw Treaty Organisation; large chemical weapon stockpiles are known to be present in the region, especially in the FRG; it is a region of high population density.

One cannot completely ignore the argument that a CWFZ in Europe or elsewhere would increase the risk of chemical weapons being used in areas outside the zone which might possibly receive the chemical weapons removed from the CWFZ. Countries fearing such a development would be well advised to join the zone or to make a binding declaration that they neither own chemical weapons nor wish to receive them. In this respect, the countries of the CWFZ might well encourage the governments of other nations also to renounce chemical weapons and thus greatly promote the entire process of moving toward a worldwide ban on chemical weapons.

The counter-argument that the Geneva Conference on Disarmament (CD) is overstrained by talks about a CWFZ, and therefore prevented from its work on a worldwide convention banning chemical weapons, is not convincing simply because one can go about negotiating and concluding CWFZ agreements in different ways. In this respect Lundin gives a quite acceptable summary of the CWFZ problem when he writes[15]:

... On the other hand, one should recognise already now the important political impact that the suggestion by the Palme Commission and by other parties has on public opinion. One should thus carefully consider what approaches might exist which could both preserve the option to institute in the future, when necessary, a chemical-weapons-free zone in Europe and preserve the possibility to obtain, as soon as possible, a comprehensive convention on chemical weapons in the CD.

One possible approach might be that the CD or the UN General Assembly recognised the importance of the suggestion by the Palme Commission and other parties and asked interested parties in Europe to declare their possession or non-possession of chemical weapons and where they were deployed or stockpiled. The parties could also declare their willingness to destroy the weapons where they existed and offer other parties possibilities to visit such destruction efforts. This would not cause concern in countries outside the zone which might fear redeployment of chemical weapons from Europe into areas in their own vicinity. An additional possibility might be that countries who feel that they would like to be part of such a zone, and which had chemical weapons on their territory placed there by other states, asked these states to withdraw the weapons as soon as possible and under observable forms.

Concluding Remarks

The discussion about the pros and cons of a CWFZ in Europe is
continuing, and there can be no doubt that the idea is gaining ground and taking shape. It is becoming more difficult
every year for advocates of an all-out confrontation course
to maintain their position, which is hostile to detente, and
to nip in the bud any steps towards arms limitation and
disarmament by making maximum demands. It is quite obvious
that the establishment of a CWFZ in Europe would be far from
the comprehensive solution to the problem of chemical weapons
sought by the socialist countries, that is, a final worldwide
ban on the development, production, stockpiling and use of
all types and systems of chemical weapons. Even if this
comprehensive prohibition of chemical weapons were to come
about in one or two years' time, it would take approximately
another 10 years before all existing stocks of chemical
warfare agents had been destroyed. Experience has shown that
not all countries would be prepared to sign and ratify such a
ban immediately, and one must therefore allow for several
more years of mankind having to live with some chemical
weapons. What this means in reality is that we would have to
wait until the end of the century to see the threat to
mankind of chemical weapons eliminated.

On the other hand, establishing a CWFZ offers a chance for
Europe (and why not also for other continents and regions of
the world?) to drastically reduce the existing dangers
arising from the storage of chemical weapons in peacetime and
their possible use in times of conflict and war. Just as
doctors today would not refuse the partial cures for some
types of cancer on the ground that there is no general
protection or cure for this fatal disease, so the governments
should not miss the chance to make the CWFZ a political
reality. Now, as before, there is truth in the Confucian
saying that it is better to light one candle than to curse
the darkness.

References

1. Independent Commission on Disarmament and Security
   Issues under the Chairmanship of Olof Palme, Report,
   Common Security: A Programme for Disarmament (London, Pan
   Books, 1982) pp.151, 177-9.
2. H.G. Brauch, in Sozialdemokratisher Pressedienst, 37, (2
   February 1982) p.6.
3. J.F. Leonard, Statement, 13 July 1982, in Hearings on
   Foreign Policy and Arms Control, Implications on Chemical

Weapons, before a subcommittee of the Committee on Foreign Affairs, House of Representatives. US Government Printing Office, (Washington 1982) p.178; see also: United States, Organization of the Joint Chiefs of Staff, 'Chemical Warfare in Europe, circa 1986', Institute for Defense Analyses, (December 1981); c.f. United States Comptroller General, Report to the Committee on Foreign Affairs, House of Representatives 'Chemical Warfare: Many Unanswered Questions', Report GAO/JPE-83-6, (29 April 1983).

4. K. Lohs, 'On the Stationing of Chemical Weapons at the Border to the GDR', in Science, Culture and the Mass Media in the Struggle for Disarmament, International Scientific Symposium Leipzig, GDR, (Dresden, Zeit im Bild, 1983) pp.25-6.

5. Centro di Studi Strategici, 'Chemical Weapons and Arms Control. - Views from Europe', (Rome, June 1983).

6. K. Lohs and K. Meier, 'A Chemical-Weapon-Free Zone in Europe', in J. Rotblat and S. Hellman (eds) Nuclear Strategy and World Security (London: Macmillan, 1985) pp.202-6.

7. F. Hucho, 'Waffen unter Beschuss', in Tagesspiegel (Berlin-West, 9 December 1984).

8. TASS, (29 May 1984).

9. J. Todenhöfer, CDU/CSU-Pressedienst, (Bonn, 5 April 1984).

10. V. Rühe, DCU/CSU-Pressedienst, (Bonn, 20 September 1984).

11. R. Ekeus, 'How to ban chemical weapons', The second SIPRI public lecture, Stockholm, 5 December 1984, (Stockholm International Peace Research Institute, SIPRI 1984).

12. Red Star, (Moscow, 9 January 1985).

13. Neues Deutschland, (19 March 1985) p.1.

14. Neues Deutschland and Leipziger Volkszeitung, (20 March 1985).

15. S.J. Lundin, 'A Chemical Weapons Free Zone in Europe?: An Analysis', see ref. 13.

16. J.P. Robinson, 'Salient Features of the Current European Chemical Warfare Situation: The Concept of a Chemical Weapons-Free-Zone in Europe.' see ref. 13.

17. R. Trapp, 'Eine chemiewaffenfreie Zone in Europa - Gedanken zur Kontrollfrage' in Wissenschaft und Fortschritt vol.35 (1985) H.1, pp.2-5.

18. A.H. Westing, 'Ban chemical weapons in Europe', Bulletin of the Atomic Scientists vol.41 (1985) No.5, pp.17-19.

12 There Can Be No Place for Chemical Weapons on Earth

Alexander Fokin

The current situation is characterised by a serious increase of tension and dangerous conflicts that create an international situation which bodes ill for the peoples of the world.

This situation has generated and strengthened the danger that weapons of mass annihilation, including chemical weapons, may be used in conflicts.

The problem of chemical disarmament cannot be considered an easy one. But the experience of disarmament negotiations shows that a mutually acceptable solution can be found for any problem under discussion if all the participants in the discussion really seek to reach an agreement on the basis of the principle of equality and equal security.

The Soviet Union has always advocated and continues to advocate resolutely and consistently the comprehensive prohibition of chemical weapons, their complete withdrawal from the arsenals of states, and effective destruction of their stocks. It was among the first states to ratify the Geneva Protocol of 1925, and in 1927 it proposed in the Preparatory Commission of the League of Nations to supplement the prohibition of the use of chemical weapons with a ban on their production. It also actively participated in the talks on the prohibition of chemical weapons at the Conference on Disarmament in the 1930s. The Soviet Union's and other socialist countries' initiatives in the post-war period to achieve the earliest prohibition of chemical weapons are well-known. They include the Draft Convention on the Prohibition of the Development, Production and Stockpiling of Bacteriological (Biological) and Toxin Weapons and on Their Destruction of 1971, and the 1972 Draft Convention on Chemical Disarmament.

During 1976-1980, the Soviet Union participated in the Soviet-American bilateral talks to prepare a joint initiative on the prohibition of chemical weapons to be submitted to the UN Committee on Disarmament (the talks were discontinued in

1980 by the USA). In 1982, at the Second Special Session of the UN General Assembly on Disarmament the Soviet Union made a new initiative, submitting draft Basic Provisions of a Convention on the Prohibition, Production and Stockpiling of Chemical Weapons and on Their Destruction, a document indicating solutions to the entire problem. The document took into account the results achieved in the 1976–1980 Soviet-American talks, and the positions of many other states. Since then the Soviet Union has repeatedly developed this initiative, and has put forward many constructive proposals taking into account the progress at the talks on the prohibition of chemical weapons. They include a number of proposals on questions concerning the declaration and liquidation of stocks of chemical weapons and control over this process; and considerations regarding a special procedure for the destruction of stocks of chemical weapons which would ensure security and meet the interests of all states party to the proposed Convention, as well as other issues. Moreover, the Soviet Union and the other socialist countries believe it necessary to seize every opportunity to protect mankind from the danger of chemical war. That is, **inter alia**, the purpose of the proposal recently made by the member-states of the Warsaw Treaty Organisation to the NATO countries to free the European continent from chemical weapons.

The Soviet Union and the other socialist countries do not claim a monopoly on proposals concerning the prohibition of chemical weapons. Other countries have also submitted many documents on different aspects of the problem. The total number of such documents distributed in the Conference on Disarmament has already exceeded three hundred.

What impedes the talks, and why has an agreement on the prohibition of chemical weapons and their destruction not become a reality?

There is only one reason: the unwillingness on the part of the USA and its closest allies to reach agreement. While paying lip service to the importance of the talks, and sometimes presenting the state of affairs as quite encouraging, the USA is trying to place the matter in the context of sterile technical discussions by introducing clearly unrealistic and unacceptable proposals, primarily concerning questions of control. At the same time, it is alleged that the Soviet Union does not want control over the prohibition of chemical weapons and that this is the only obstacle to progress in accepting the Convention.

Contrary to these allegations, accepting control over disarmament measures is no major problem for the Soviet Union. Where control is really necessary the Soviet Union always comes out in favour of including appropriate provisions in the agreements. This applies also to the talks on the prohibition of chemical weapons.

The Soviet Union attaches no less importance than other states to effective control over the implementation of the proposed Convention. This is only natural, since every activity prohibited or limited by the Convention should be effectively controlled. To this end the Soviet Union has proposed and continues to propose a wide range of measures of control: national verification, the use of national technical means, on-site inspection by challenge, and international on-site systematic inspection.

A very important question is that of control over the destruction of stockpiles of chemical weapons at special facilities. As is known, in this particular case the Soviet Union was in favour of the use of systematic international inspections, with the number per year (quota) to be determined by the Consultative Committee for each individual facility on the basis of criteria agreed upon beforehand. Such a differentiated approach would make the parties to the proposed Convention fully confident that the accumulated stockpiles of chemical weapons are being, or have been, really destroyed.

In addition, displaying a genuine interest in the progress of the talks, the Soviet Union declared its readiness to accept a solution about control procedures which would ensure the effectiveness of the control from the beginning of the destruction to its completion, either by way of constant presence of international inspectors at such a special facility, or through a combination of systematic inspections at the facility (including its store of weapons) and the use of control instruments.

One might have expected that the USA would not give up this opportunity and would take its full part on the road to the agreement.

This did not happen, however. Events have shown that the present US Administration is in fact unwilling to accept the prohibition of chemical weapons or, for that matter, any other agreements in the sphere of disarmament. Previously, in order to frustrate the conclusion of the Convention on Chemical Disarmament, the USA insisted on a system of control under which other states would have had to admit, on first demand, foreign inspectors to any chemical plant, whether it was engaged in the production of chemical weapons or not. The Draft Convention introduced in late April 1984 contained the concept of 'inspection on standing invitation'. The USA suggested that states voluntarily declare beforehand that they would freely admit foreign inspectors 'to any place and at any time'. Vice-President Bush specified that foreign inspectors should have constant and unimpeded access only to plants that 'belong to governments or are controlled by governments'. In other words, everything is to be subjected to verification in socialist countries, while chemical companies in the USA and other capitalist countries would be free to produce anything including chemical weapons, while remaining outside control. Obviously, this proposal is divorced from reality and discriminates against countries with a system of state ownership or partially nationalised industry. The US draft has a number of other substantial defects. It plays down, in particular, such important questions as the prohibition of the use of herbicides and irritants during hostilities, and the prohibition of binary chemical weapons.

Therefore, at all international meetings which considered the question of chemical weapons it was the US position which was the main obstacle to the adoption of the Convention on Chemical Disarmament. Here is a typical example: of the 157 member-countries of the UN, the USA was the only one to openly oppose the will of the international community by voting against the adoption at the 36th Session of the UN General Assembly in 1981 of the resolution which called upon all states to abstain from the production and deployment of new types of chemical weapons and their stationing on the territory of those states that did not have them at that time.

Nothing has changed for the better since then in the policy of the US Administration. While paying lip service to the prohibition of chemical weapons, the US Administration is stepping up its preparations for the use of these weapons of mass annihilation in wartime. A decision was made to construct in Pine Bluff a plant to produce binary chemical shells and 'Big Eye' bombs. In the autumn of 1981 the US Congress planned to appropriate $455 million for chemical rearmament in 1982, $820 million in 1983, and $1.4 billion in 1988. The USA intends to spend around $10 billion on its programme of chemical rearmament. In the USA chemical weapons are developed and produced by some 90 State and private plants, including Dow and Union Carbide which for many years has been the Pentagon's biggest contractors for developing and producing components of chemical weapons. To develop new chemical warfare agents and means of delivery the USA actively employs the scientific and technical potential and industrial capacities of its NATO allies. New designs of chemical weapons are being intensively developed which are tested at numerous firing grounds under different climatic conditions.

In the 1960s, countries of Southeast Asia were turned into a vast proving ground where US chemical weapons were extensively used.

The war in Vietnam is called unprecedented because of the scale and duration of the use of chemical weapons. During 1961-1971, the US armed forces dropped on Vietnam's territory over 94 thousand tonne of herbicides specially designed for military applications, which destroyed forests and agricultural crops, and eight thousand tonne of toxic agents (CS and others).

Twenty five thousand km^2 of forests and 13 thousand km^2 of agricultural land were destroyed. Many thousands of people, mostly civilians, received lethal doses and died during the war. The long-term effects of these substances are still felt by the population of these Southeast Asian countries. Various impacts on nature have undermined the life support system of the population in this region for many years to come, have provoked profound environmental changes in Vietnam, Kampuchea and Laos, and have caused huge economic losses and irreparable harm to human health.

In attempts to justify the dimensions of the chemical war the US official quarters argued that only herbicides which were almost innocuous and widely applied in agriculture were used in Vietnam. However, it became known as far back as the 1950s that plants were contaminated with compounds containing chlorinated derivatives of phenolacetic acid accumulate substances which are toxic for warm-blooded animals. In the early 1960s information became available of the high toxicity of tetrachlorodibenzoparadioxine ('dioxine') and its high content in 'orange'-type compounds. It became clear after 1963, namely the catastrophe at the Phillips-Dufar plant in Holland which produced herbicides for the USA, that to lower the dioxine content in herbicide 2.4.5.-T it was necessary to introduce stringent controls over the production of 2.4.5.-trichlorophenol and additional operations to purify its fractions and the final product.

Even after 1967, when a wave of protest against the criminal war in Vietnam swept across the USA, when the danger to man and the environment of all the three herbicides used by the US army had been demonstrated, the scale of their use in Indochina did not diminish.

Assessing the purity of 2.4.5.-T used in Thailand in 1954-1964, scientists of the US National Academy of Sciences found that it contained 3-50 mg/kg of dioxine. These and other analytical data show that in 'orange'-type herbicides concentrations of this poison reached tens of mg/kg. This means that no less than 500-600 kg of dioxine were introduced into the environment of Vietnam with the 57 thousand tonne of the 'orange'-type herbicides officially authorised in the USA.

Nevertheless, to obtain a realistic assessment of the quantity of dioxine it is necessary to take into account the capacity of non-volatile derivatives of 2.4.5.-trichlorophenoxiacetic acid and trichlorophenol for transforming into dioxine when heated to high temperatures or burned under conditions of an oxygen deficit. As is known, the US troops widely used incendiary weapons, burned down vegetation over large territories, and bombed and shelled areas where herbicide mixtures were used. These were indeed conditions for the above mentioned transformations of the 'orange'-type compounds into dioxine. Under these conditions additional hundreds of kilogrammes of dioxine could appear right on the battlefields. No less than one tonne of dioxine might be the result of these activities, during 1961-1971, in Vietnam's natural environment. Recent direct measurements of dioxine content in soil bear out this assessment. Given the scale of contamination of the environment with this perfidious poison (the natural half-life of dioxine exceeds ten years) long-term consequences of chemical war should be considered a most serious problem.

The fact that trichlorophenol-based herbicides, supplied by transnational chemical companies to many countries of the Third World (especially in the tropics), can also disintegrate with the formation of dioxine, causes concern.

As is known, an appalling tragedy occurred in early December 1984 in Bhopal, India. According to official estimates, the leak of methylisocyanate at the chemical plant of the American company Union Carbide resulted in the death of over 2500 and acute poisoning of more than 50 000 Indians. Agricultural crops were contaminated in a radius of tens of kilometres around the town. One has to share the opinion of the Indian press and a number of Indian political figures that the Bhopal catastrophe was caused not only by violations of safety precautions by Union Carbide; according to Indian papers, doctors are afraid that the deaths were also caused by another, more toxic compound apart from methylisocyanate.

One more fact. In November 1984, information became available about long and massive use in the Amazon basin of 'orange' and 'white'-type herbicides supplied by Dow Chemical. This has resulted in mass poisoning of the indigenous population and destruction of vegetation.

Debates on chemical disarmament in the UN General Assembly show that consistent efforts to prohibit chemical weapons and destroy their stockpiles on a global scale do not preclude parallel measures which can and should be taken in individual geographical zones.

Regional measures which lead to the liquidation of a type

of weapon of mass annihilation will undoubtedly help to weaken the threat of war, strengthen confidence among states, and normalise the general political atmosphere.

Moreover, such measures can put under control the activities of transnational chemical companies in the countries of the Third World.

It is a well-known fact that on the initiative of the GDR and other socialist countries, as well as non-aligned nations, the UN General Assembly adopted resolutions that reflected the ideas of establishing nuclear weapon-free zones.

In his reply to a letter from West German trade unionist Julius Lehlbach, President Konstantin Chernenko said:

... the Soviet Union has long been proposing to outlaw chemical weapons, to remove them from the arsenals of states. We are prepared for a solution of this problem either on a global basis or step by step. As one of the first steps, the USSR and the other socialist countries proposed in January 1984 that agreement be reached on ridding Europe of all types of chemical weapons.

It follows from this proposal that obligations of states arising out of such agreement could include the following items: declaration of the deployment of these weapons where they do not exist at present; freezing these weapons; evacuation or destruction of the existing stockpiles of chemical weapons; refusal to produce, acquire, import and transfer them. Unlike global measures, implementation of partial regional measures affects a smaller number of states-parties to an agreement. For this reason they are easier to agree upon and implement.

As for the creation of chemical weapon-free zones, it appears advisable to proceed step by step, with due regard to all factors and circumstances. Parties to the understanding could agree upon mutually acceptable forms of control which would ensure effective implementation of obligations by all parties. Agreement to establish a chemical weapon-free zone can be reflected in a declaration or any other binding legal document, such as an agreement, treaty or convention.

While in no way undermining or replacing the talks of the Committee on Disarmament in Geneva, such local initiatives to limit, reduce and destroy chemical weapons would promote global efforts, and contribute to the earliest conclusion of an International Convention on the Prohibition of Chemical Weapons.

PART THREE
Security of the Developing Countries

13 Problems in Developing Countries that Affect World Peace

Franklin Long

Introduction

It is tempting to argue that problems in developing nations affecting world peace are pretty much the same as those in developed nations that also affect world peace. For is not human nature the same the world over? This approach will not do, however, since the political, economic and social differences among nations are very considerable. More to the point, perhaps, is the simple observation that developing nations commonly do have difficult and sometimes rather special problems that have in the past affected world peace and have the potential to do so in the future.

The following is a list of some of the major problems that many, and occasionally all, of the developing nations face:

1. Difficulty in raising standards of living towards those of the developed nations.
2. The existence within the countries of gross inequalities in income and opportunity - cities versus villages and the uneducated versus the educated.
3. Frequent absence of democracy or other ways to let citizens' voices be heard.
4. Inadequate procedures to adjudicate differences among nations.
5. Inadequate procedures for regional collaboration.
6. Interference by big powers in the political and economic development of the smaller or poorer nations.
7. Large commitments to military expenditure.

Basic Goals

The broader social concerns that underlie all of the items of this list are ones that the developing world shares with the developed world, namely concerns about social justice, independence and freedom. Achieving these basic goals has been a problem for virtually all of the peoples of the world. But the problems are more serious and the way more difficult for developing nations because they are comparatively poor. Moreover, roughly half of them are relatively new to statehood, many having become independent states only since the Second World War. For many of their peoples the simple struggle for livelihood is a difficult and burdensome problem. The fact that so many of the states are relatively new means that effective governments have often not yet been established, and in many cases, neither have effective and peaceful relations with neighbouring nations.

Another feature that exacerbates the problems which these countries face is the impact of the richer, often larger, nations of the developed world. Part of the problem is that these richer nations are simply **there**, so that the contrast between rich and poor remains evident. Occasionally the impact of the richer nations are malign. But even when they are well-meaning, they are frequently not very helpful.

Most of the developing nations of the world have made some progress in raising their **per capita** income, and in a few cases, notably in Asia, several of the once-poor nations have made remarkable economic progress. But for far too many the situation is closer to the following example: an average increase of four per cent per year in national GNP, combined with a population increase of $2\frac{1}{2}$ per cent per year to give a net **per capita** growth rate of only $1\frac{1}{2}$ per cent. Moreover most of this very limited growth may occur in the cities, leaving the hinterlands stagnant.

To be a small and poor nation in the late 20th Century means: great difficulty in attaining economic independence, with most trade and many prices effectively established by the richer nations; very inadequate access to modern technology, and extreme difficulty in developing a viable and effective capability in science; very great difficulty in establishing a nationwide education system that will produce the trained people that are needed. Even though the overriding problem is the existence of sharply lower standards of living than in the developed world, these other difficulties contribute to a pervasive sense of dissatisfaction which in turn leads to 'brain drain' of the trained people and emigration from the poorer to the richer nations, Algerians migrating to France and Mexicans to the United States are only two of many examples. Often it is not simply comparative poverty that leads to this dissatisfaction and emigration. It is the all too common gross inequalities in income and opportunity between groups within a poor nation. In many nations the inequalities are particularly great between cities and countryside, with the cities having both greater amenities and more opportunities. There are often also great inequalities between one segment of the population and another. The relative poverty of the original and ethnically distinct populations of many nations is an example.

How do these social and economic difficulties influence the maintenance of world peace? First, they affect the stability of governments, leading to dictatorial one-party states and, not infrequently, to military coups. A common result is instability in the relations among neighbouring nations, sometimes leading to war. The danger of war between neighbouring nations and the possibility of wars spreading are exacerbated by a variety of political difficulties and inadequacies. For many of the new nations, boundary problems constitute a continuing source of friction. This is notably true in Africa, where the boundaries established in the colonial era are often so arbitrary as to separate members of a single tribe, but it is also true in other areas of the world.

Compounding these problems of poor relations among the developing nations is the common inadequacy of procedures either for regional collaboration, which represents the positive aspect of the problem, or for adjudicating differences and conflicts among nations. Occasionally, organisations to enhance regional collaboration are vigorous and fruitful; the ASEAN Organisation in Southeast Asia is an example. The Organisation of African Unity is a much broader and more ambitious attempt to build regional collaboration, but - perhaps because of the great differences among African nations - it has so far tended to be more of a debating group than one that takes initiatives to foster collaboration and settle conflicts.

Finally, there is the widespread problem of extensive militarisation of the developing nations. The militarisation of the developing countries as a group has continued to increase, as shown by such data as expenditure on the military, sizes of armed forces, and imports of armaments from developed nations. Putting all of these things together means war. Indeed the most frequent and destructive wars since the Second World War have been those among developing nations. And wars continue.

The obvious international agency to play a major role in fostering regional collaboration and helping to adjudicate differences among nations is the United Nations. The benefits from UN programmes among developing nations have been substantial. At the same time, the overall weakness of the UN organisation itself, and the frequent lack of consensus within the General Assembly, have decreased its effectiveness in all of its activities.

Increasingly the world realises that wars among developing nations are both a demonstration of internal and regional tensions, and constitute a threat of a much broader impact on world peace. We increasingly realise that when combined with the tensions and confrontations that exist in the developed world, particularly between the superpowers, there is the continuing threat that a small war in any part of the world can become the initiator for a much greater and more devastating conflagration. The initial world apprehensions about the possibility that the continuing war between Iran and Iraq might become such a trigger is one illustration.

The Role and Responsibilities of the Developed World

Running like a dark thread through this picture of internal dissatisfaction and difficulty in the developing nations, leading to unrepresentative governments, to militarisation, and all too frequently to war, is the frequently baneful role of the richer nations. It is they that, almost as an aside from their own large military build-ups, provide modern armaments to poorer nations, sometimes to enhance their influence, other times for simple profit. It is also tensions and divisiveness among the developed nations that have seriously weakened the United Nations' ability to function as a strong presence for adjudication and peace.

The principal problem is, of course, the continuing tension and military competition between the United States and the Soviet Union.   Each of these superpowers has developed a set of allies, and each is concerned with enhancing its 'spheres of influence'. Selling arms to developing nations, often at concessional prices, is only one of the consequences. More broadly, the emphasis on military impacts and associations constitutes a severe distraction from and interference with the truly central problem of the developing world: how to improve standards of living, and enhance freedom and social justice.   Occasionally the impact of big powers is more direct and more devastating. The several-year old presence of Soviet troops in Afghanistan and the deadly struggles with dissident Afghans is one example. The continuing political and economic pressure of the United States on Nicaragua is another.

What is to be done? A first point is that there will be no miracles and no quick solutions. The militarisation of the developing nations (as well as of the developed nations) has been proceeding for decades, and will not be reversed quickly. Genuine tensions and problems do exist among many of the developing nations, and these will not be easily solved. Finally, the confrontation between the superpowers is now of long standing and will not be easily or quickly solved. But the important point is to make a start.

It is easy to point the finger at some of the unnecessary tensions, aggressive militarisation and adventuresome governments that exist in the developing nations, and urge that these nations work harder to solve their own problems and work more effectively among themselves to minimise the threat of war. However, a very large element of concern must be directed at developed nations. They have taken some responsibility for helping the progress of developing nations economically and politically. The effort, however, has been modest in size and considerably fragmented. Even worse, it has been substantially compromised by the confrontation between the superpowers and their separate searches for allies and spheres of influence. If, for example, the problem is to enhance the effectiveness of the United Nations, nothing would be more important than for constructive joint action by the superpowers. But, above all, it is these two nations in particular that must themselves make major moves toward world peace. If individual wars among the developing nations do end up spreading to world conflagration, it very likely will be because the initial trigger reacts on the existing tensions and military forces of the two superpowers.

In this difficult and troublesome situation of the combination of poor and rich nations and extensive militarisation, what can scientists do to enhance world peace? One response is to say that a group such as Pugwash has already done a good deal, and could reasonably continue along the paths it has been following. However, the urgency of the slow development of many countries and the many threats to world peace suggest that much more is needed. Perhaps the next step for us would be to try to lay out an explicit plan of action to focus on these twin problems and their interactions.

As a group consisting primarily of scientists, Pugwash might also give special attention to the problems of science, technology and science education in developing nations. These are not the only, and often not the primary, needs of poor nations, but they are areas where there is a world community, where collaboration is common, and where countries with different political and economic beliefs can work together. We should seek to identify the special needs of developing nations in these areas and identify principal areas where scientists and technologists of the developed world can effectively collaborate.

14 The Organisation of African Unity in Crisis Management in Africa

Ngung Mpwotsh

Security threats to the African continent mainly arise from the following types of conflict:

boundary and territorial conflicts (Ethiopia/Somalia);
civil wars and internal conflicts having international repercussions (Chad/Nigeria);
anti-colonial conflicts and national liberation struggles;
political and ideological conflicts (Uganda/Tanzania).

According to Article II of the Organisation of African Unity (OAU) the Organisation shall have the following purposes:

a) to promote the unity and solidarity of the African States;
b) to coordinate and intensify their cooperation and efforts to achieve a better life for the peoples of Africa;
c) to defend their sovereignty, their territorial integrity and independence;
d) to eradicate all forms of colonialism from Africa;
e) to promote international cooperation, having due regard to the Charter of the United Nations and the Universal Declaration of Human Rights.

Article III of the Charter states:

The Member States, in pursuit of the purposes stated in Article II, solemnly affirm and declare their adherence to the following principles:

1. The sovereign equality of all Member States.
2. Non-interference in the internal affairs of States.
3. Respect for the sovereignty and territorial integrity

of each State and for its inalienable right to independent existence.

4. Peaceful settlement of disputes by negotiation, mediation, conciliation or arbitration.

5. Unreserved condemnation, in all its forms, of political assassination as well as of subversive activities on the part of neighbouring States or on any other States.

6. Absolute dedication to the total emancipation of the African territories which are still dependent.

7. Affirmation of a policy of non-alignment with regard to all blocs.

In Article VII of the Charter the Founding Fathers created a Commission of Mediation, Conciliation and Arbitration as one of the Organisation's four principal institutions to enable Member States to settle all disputes among themselves by peaceful means, as they had pledged. The Commission comprising 21 African lawyers was never operational because of its unwieldy legalistic structure. Furthermore, Member States were reluctant to submit themselves to third party arbitration and procedures, and showed preference for a political as opposed to a juridical approach. There was the added question of the expenses involved in setting up such an organ. The practically defunct Commission, moreover, lacked supranational attributes, such as coercive powers since these would have been an infringement on the Charter principle of 'sovereign equality of Member States'.

While the highly politicised conflict management remained the preserve of the Assembly of Heads of State and Government, the need to deal urgently with crisis situations, and to take prompt and effective measures for the maintenance of peace and the prevention of the escalation of conflicts, was acutely felt. This need was all the more felt given the procedural and practical difficulties in convening at short notice emergency sessions of the Council of Ministers and the Assembly of Heads, since the holding of such extraordinary sessions called for the approval by two-thirds of the membership.

It was to that end that the establishment of an OAU Political Security Council was proposed by the Government of Sierra Leone in 1980. The objectives of the proposed Council were:

to deal urgently with crisis situations in Africa, that are likely to threaten peace and security and the stability of the continent;

to take prompt and effective measures for the maintenance of peace and prevent the escalation of conflicts, be they political or military.

Expert studies were undertaken by the General Secretariat in conjunction with UNITAR on the legal, political, military and financial implications of establishing such a Council. The studies were submitted to the **Ad Hoc** Ministerial Committee of Twelve which was established by Resolution CM/860; it was mandated to study the proposal and formulate appropriate recommendations to the Council of Ministers. The **Ad Hoc** Committee was of the general opinion that the establishment of such a Council was inopportune, and that instead the Commission of Mediation, Conciliation and Arbitration should be reactivated, thus avoiding the proliferation of institutions within the OAU.

In its Forty-first Ordinary Session in Addis Ababa, from 25 February to 4 March 1985, the Council of Ministers, after reviewing the reports and recommendations of the **Ad Hoc** Committee of Twelve, decided that it was 'premature and inopportune to establish a Political Security Council in the present political and economic situation', but requested 'the Committee on the review of the Charter of the Organisation of African Unity to seek appropriate ways and means enabling Africans to face situations of crisis in Africa'.

The Founding Fathers of the Organisation were well aware of the need for a collective security machinery that would 'safeguard and consolidate the hard-won independence as well as the sovereignty and territorial integrity of our States' and had set up a Defence Commission in Article XX of the Charter for that purpose. Yet, in the eight sessions of its 21 years of existence, the Defence Commission recommendations and proposals remain largely unimplemented, with only the principle of establishing an OAU Defence Force being retained. It should be mentioned in passing that the OAU does not have the powers to coerce its member states when they defy calls or procedures for peaceful settlement of disputes. In contrast, two other continental Organisations, the League of Arab States and the Organisation of American States, have provisions in their Charters and treaties that require them to take all necessary measures to re-establish or maintain peace and security between their members, or to enable them to determine measures to repulse aggression against their member states.

Since accession to independence, some OAU Member States have been plagued with internal strife, civil wars and internecine fighting. Cases in point include Zaire, Nigeria, Angola, Sudan, Ethiopia and Chad. While border disputes and clashes occurred among Member States, as instanced by Algeria -Morocco, Ethiopia-Somalia, Chad-Libya, Nigeria-Cameroon, to quote only but a few, what was the OAU's role in these conflicts? In the absence of a permanent crisis control mechanism, the OAU had to deal with these crises on an ad hoc basis as they arose and try to contain them before they escalated to endanger regional stability. To some extent, these efforts have been successful. Those Conciliation Commissions that have not yet completed their mandate still continue to meet. Mention should be made here of the role that is invariably played by neighbouring members states in the case of border disputes among member states. Mention should also be made of the peace-keeping forces sent to Chad as the only example when the OAU took such a step in seeking a solution to an internal crisis in a member state. In addition, the Current Chairman as well as the Bureau of the Assembly of Heads of State and Government also use their good offices when the need arises.

With regard to the anti-colonial conflicts and national liberation struggle, the OAU Liberation Committee has been effective in ensuring the continuity of the liberation wars against the racist South African regime. The OAU, however, has been ineffective in taking any meaningful counter-measures against the aggression, brigandry and destabilis-ation, which is being perpetrated against the Frontline States by the Apartheid regime.

The OAU has to date no permanent mechanism to deal with crises. This may be due to several factors, but the main contributing factor is lack of political will. As one of the leading Founding Fathers of the Organisation had occasion to observe, the Organisation of African Unity had been founded on idealism, with Member States pledged to 'co-ordinate and harmonise their general policies' including 'cooperation for defence and security'. But, as the distinguished leader remarked, circumstances have overtaken the ideals before they could be implemented, and Africa became a continent of fragmented sovereign states, each concerned with its sole national interests, to the detriment of the continental weal.

15 Southern Africa and the South Atlantic

Neil MacFarlane

Introduction

In placing the crisis in Southern Africa within the broader South Atlantic context, I wish to address four issues: the nature and sources of the crisis; the roles of the superpowers in it; the broader implications of the Southern African conflict for the South Atlantic region; and prospects for and methods of crisis control in the region. By Southern Africa, I mean the Republic of South Africa and those neighbouring states which are significantly affected by South African military activity and economic pressure, namely Mozambique, Zimbabwe, Swaziland, Lesotho, Botswana, Zambia, Angola, and Namibia. I take the concept of crisis control to include the prevention, limitation, and resolution of crisis.

The Problem and Its Sources

Most superficially, there are two related elements to the crisis in the region. The first is internal unrest in the Republic of South Africa, pitting an economically and politically disenfranchised black majority against a ruling white political and economic elite. This unrest takes the form of mass protest demonstrations, strikes by black workers, sabotage, bomb attacks, and assassination, all of which appear to be growing in frequency and intensity, as do repressive countermeasures on the part of security forces. This raises the prospect of gradual decay into domestic anarchy and revolution.

The roots of the political crisis in South Africa lie in the white minority's determination to defend the system of apartheid in rapidly changing internal and international conditions. Internally, the population balance is shifting rapidly against the whites, rendering the maintenance of the system in the face of majority resistance to it increasingly problematic. This is connected to a second factor - the politicisation of the majority, their growing consciousness of their political, economic, and social deprivation in the current system, of the unnatural character of that deprivation, and of the possibility of altering this un- acceptable state of affairs through concerted action. This decay in the internal situation is matched at the regional level by the gradual disappearance of South Africa's **cordon sanitaire** of white-dominated states to its north, and consequently, by the greater ease with which anti-government forces in South Africa can benefit from external support and sanctuary.

One subjective consequence of these internal and regional trends has been the gradual strengthening of a seige mental- ity on the part of the Afrikaner elite. This is manifested internally in highly repressive police actions, and regionally in repeated use of force against its neighbours. It is enhanced by the growing isolation of South Africa in the international community.

The second aspect of the crisis is economic decline and political decay elsewhere in the region, both of which have resulted in substantial political instability and human suffering. This element is closely linked to the situation within South Africa itself. Many of the economic and internal security problems faced by South Africa's neighbours are the result of military and economic pressure brought to bear upon these countries in order to minimise regional support for anti-government activities inside South Africa. Among the events that could be cited here are: South African incursions into Southern Angola; raids against targets deeper inside that country and against installations in Botswana, Lesotho, and Mozambique; and South Africa's financial, technical, and logistical support of the Mozambique National Resistance Movement (MNR).

However, South Africa is not the only source of crisis within the region. Many of the region's economic problems may be ascribed not to South African-sponsored sabotage or military activity, but to such factors as declining terms of trade for goods produced within the region, prolonged drought and its disastrous consequences for regional agriculture, and the poor performance of economic planners and policy-makers. Political instability is again the result not only of South African military intrusions and support for opposition groups, but also of the economic problems mentioned above, the failure of governments to pay sufficient attention to the needs of their peoples and to broaden their base of support among populations which are ethnically heterogeneous, and their often highly repressive policies towards disaffected individuals and groups.

The Role of the Superpowers

Many in the United States characterise the problem in Southern Africa primarily as one of Soviet and Cuban destabilis-
ation of the region. Likewise, many Soviet writers leave the
impression that the source of instability is Western support
of imperialism's local proxy - South Africa - as part of a
global attempt to contain or reverse the world revolutionary
process, the implication being that if the West desisted, the
white regime in South Africa would collapse and peace and
progress would flourish in the region as a whole. In my
opinion, the fundamental sources of crisis are overwhelmingly
local in origin (except perhaps in the sense that both the
white and most of the black populations of South Africa are
immigrants, and that in many respects the apartheid system
had its origins in the colonial period).

The role of the superpowers, and for that matter other
external factors is, by contrast, ancillary. The Soviet Union
and its allies have accelerated the development of the
liberation struggle in the region through the provision of
training and military assistance to the liberation movements.
But the basic source of that struggle lies in the desire of a
relatively small minority in South Africa to maintain a
highly exploitative and inhumane system of racial privilege
in the face of a deteriorating demographic balance and an
awakening black social and political consciousness. The
Western countries, in their slowness to impose an effective
arms embargo on South Africa and in their reluctance to adopt
meaningful economic sanctions, have perhaps made it easier
for the whites to avoid concessions. The same would apply to
the reported collaboration of the Soviet Union and South
Africa in the manipulation of prices in the diamond and gold
markets. But again, the basic problem lies in the political
structure established and maintained by a group which has
become used to privilege and which believes these privileges
to be a matter of divine right.

Indeed, what is striking about the **current** situation in
Southern Africa is the degree to which the superpowers are
not involved. Repeated South African raids against
Mozambique and Angola have failed to elicit any substantial
Soviet military response, despite the fact that such a
response could be relatively easily justified in terms of the
defence of a sovereign state's territorial integrity in the
face of aggression, and with reference to treaty instruments
linking Angola and Mozambique to the Soviet Union. What this
suggests is that Southern African issues are just not that
prominent on the Soviet policy-making agenda. The reasons for
this neglect are not difficult to discern: Poland,

Afghanistan, the domestic economic crisis, the leadership transition, the expense of other Third World commitments, the more militant posture of the current US administration and consequently the higher perceived risks associated with forwards policies in the Third World, and, finally, the low returns on previous investments in the region. In the latter vein, it is significant that despite Soviet requests for military facilities in Angola and Mozambique, neither country has come close to fully complying, with the result that the Soviet military presence in the region is minimal. (It is reported that both Angola and Mozambique have refused Soviet requests for basing privileges, though the Angolans provide Soviet naval vessels with port privileges and allow Soviet reconnaissance aircraft to use Angolan airfields). It appears, morever, that the principal obstacle to the emergence of a more clearly non-aligned foreign policy on the part of both Angola and Mozambique is an ideologically-derived American hostility towards self-styled 'Marxist-Leninist regimes'.

On the American side, there appears to be no significant military support for, or for that matter connection with, the South African regime. Even if the current administration sought to take a more active partisan (that is pro-South African) role in Southern African affairs - though I detect little interest on the part of the Reagan administration in so doing - the domestic political constraints would be prohibitive. Indeed, the current trend in US policy appears to be one of increasing dissociation from the Botha regime, given the latter's continuing unilateral use of force against targets in neighbouring states. One gets the impression that, 'strategic minerals' and Cape routes notwithstanding, Southern Africa is well down on the American list of priorities. The one thing that could change this would be a substantial increase in Soviet activity in the region. But this seems unlikely in the near future for the reasons noted earlier.

The third external role which should be mentioned is that of Cuba, which maintains a small number of military advisers in Mozambique and a relatively large group of regular forces in Angola. Here too, however, the Cuban presence is more a consequence of regional instability than a cause of it. Cuban troops are apparently stationed in Angola to serve as a deterrent to any serious attempt on the part of South Africa to unseat the MPLA regime, and to ensure that that regime does not fall prey to internal dissent, as nearly occurred in 1977. Cuban forces are relatively passive, avoiding sustained contact with the South Africans or with UNITA forces in the south and centre of the country. Both Angola and Cuba have displayed signs of a desire to reduce the Cuban military

presence in Angola, but are unwilling to jeopardise the
security of the regime in doing so.

The Implications for the South Atlantic Region

The assessment of the roles of external factors in the
Southern African conflict leads naturally to the consideration of the implications of the crisis for the South
Atlantic region as a whole. One of the more persistent
elements of South African diplomacy has been their effort to
convince other Western states of the value of their contribution to Western security in order that they might bolster
themselves against what they perceive to be Soviet-sponsored
regional and internal challenges through embedding South
Africa in a broader alliance framework.

One element of this strategy was the effort in the mid- and
late 1970s to construct a South Atlantic Treaty Organisation
(SATO)), which would bring together South Africa and conservative military regimes in Argentina, Uruguay, and Brazil into
a regional naval alliance to police the South Atlantic,
perhaps with informal American participation. This was a far
more credible option then than now, for a number of reasons.
Soviet and Cuban involvement in the Angolan War caused a
stirring of American interest, as the dimensions of the
Soviet-Cuban challenge to US interests in the region had not
fully emerged; as this involvement was accompanied by a
substantial upgrading in the Soviet naval presence off the
Western coast of Africa; and as the MPLA victory gave the
Soviets limited military access to support facilities in the
region, rendering the maintenance of a permanent presence in
the region easier. However, the passage of time has established the fact that there are fairly narrow limits on the
degree to which the Soviet Union is willing to involve itself
in conflicts in the region and to deploy substantial force
there. That is to say, the Soviet threat is less compelling
than it was. Moreover, as noted above, there are relatively
narrow limits on the extent to which Angola is willing to
serve as a platform for Soviet force projection in the
region. Again, the emergence of democratic civilian regimes
in Argentina and Brazil has reduced Latin American willingness to contemplate such a venture. And growing consciousness
within the United States of the intransigence of the South
African regime has strengthened the domestic constraint on
American security cooperation with South Africa. South
Africa, to judge from its defence policies, has accurately
assessed these trends and is increasingly determined to
satisfy its security needs unilaterally. At present, therefore, while events in Southern Africa have to an extent

provided an entry for Soviet forces into the region and have thus altered the military balance in the region, the consequences for the South Atlantic as a whole are rather limited. There is little prospect in current conditions for superpower confrontation in the South Atlantic growing out of the crisis in Southern Africa.

This could change. In my view, the security forces of South Africa have both the will and the capacity to contain both internal and external challenges to the apartheid system (see Table 1), while the regime may be capable of defusing some of the internal pressure through cosmetic reform of the apartheid system and through partial satisfaction of many of the economic demands of more active black forces such as the trade union movement. Moreover, I expect that the South Africans will eventually deal with the Namibia problem by cutting their losses and allowing self-determination. Indeed, such a concession might improve their external and internal security situations. But in the long run, in the face of a continuing Afrikaner unwillingness to accede to the political demands of the black majority, it is difficult to imagine how South Africa can avoid the eventual emergence of a revolutionary situation. Serious instability inside South Africa raises the prospect of superpower confrontation in Southern Africa and in the South Atlantic, as naval lines of communication would be essential to intervention, and as naval forces of both sides would enter the region in support of intervention or in order to display political will.

Crisis Control in Southern Africa

Such considerations render the matter of crisis control in Southern Africa a matter of serious concern in the East-West and South Atlantic contexts. The fact that the origins of the crisis are local suggests that it is local actors who have the power to resolve it. Short of a massive police action to suppress South Africa, outside actors have only a limited capacity to resolve these conflicts. This is particularly true given the near self-sufficiency of South Africa's defence establishment (see Annex). Indeed, it may well be that a bloody denouement within South Africa itself is unavoidable, for reasons suggested above. From the point of view of the outsider, the question of crisis control in this region is, therefore, one of determining ways in which the crisis can be contained within South Africa itself, how its effects on other regional actors can be minimised, and how superpower confrontation over Southern African issues can be avoided.

These are complex issues, and it is impossible to give them

Table 1
A. The Balance of Power in Southern Africa

	Population (million)	GDP ($ billion)	DE ($ million)	AF
Angola	7.8	4	800	43000
Botswana	0.92	1	26.6	3000
Mozambique	12	2.95	196.7	15650
South Africa	26.8	76.58	2700	83400
Zambia	6.6	3.84	325.9	14300
Zimbabwe	8.3	5.78	336	41300

GDP: Gross Domestic Product
DE: Defence Expenditure
AF: Armed Forces

B. The Military Balance in Southern Africa

	Combat Aircraft	Naval Vessels	Tanks	AC/APC/ICV
Angola	64	30	495	350
Botswana	5	–	–	50
Mozambique	35	15	285	235
South Africa	304	56	250	3100
Zambia	44	–	34	143
Zimbabwe	35	–	48	153

AC: Armoured Cars
APC: Armoured Personnel Carriers
ICV: Infantry Combat Vehicles

Note: These figures are somewhat misleading as they ignore
qualitative differences in weapons systems and differences in
maintenance systems. It is safe to assume, however, that, in
addition to the quantitative advantage, South African weapons
systems are generally of better quality, are better maintained, and better supplied with spares.

Source: The Military Balance (1984-85), (London: IISS, 1984).

full treatment here. It will suffice to offer a short 'wish
list' of actions which could be taken by the superpowers and
by the Lusophone states which might at least reduce the
impact of the crisis on the front-line states and the probability of competitive superpower involvement.

1. At the level of the superpowers, the exchanges of views on the Southern African situation should continue on a more frequent basis in order to minimise the possibility of misperception of Soviet or American policy in the region.

2. Ideally, the superpowers could agree on military non-involvement in the regional crisis, that is to say, non-use of the regular forces of either superpower in regional conflict. (This would not exclude continuing military assistance to the liberation movements in Namibia and South Africa; the East-West dimension of the liberation struggle would, however, be reduced if sources of such assistance were diversified and if this assistance were more closely controlled by the front line states and/or the Organisation of African Unity.) Given the limited extent to which the interests of the two are on the line in this region, this is not beyond the realms of possibility.

3. The United States should respond more forcefully to South African force projection in the region in an attempt to convince the South Africans that there are diplomatic and economic prices to be paid for the unilateral use of force against their neighbours. One relatively easy step in this context would be recognition of the Launda regime in retaliation for continuing South African raids against Angola. The United States might offer security assistance to Mozambique in response to South African support of the MNR in violation of the Nkomati Accords. The economic sanctions now being contemplated in Congress might have some use in this regard as well. This too is not as unrealistic as it might seem. There is evidence that the Reagan administration is becoming increasingly aware of the limitations on 'constructive engagement' as an approach to the crisis in Southern Africa and of the growing domestic unpopularity of the policy.

4. While I personally believe the linking of the Cuban presence in Angola to the question of South African withdrawal from Namibia to be unwise, there is no question that this presence renders American diplomacy in the region far less flexible than it might otherwise be. This raises the question of whether it might not be possible to satisfy Angola's security needs through a replacement of Cuban forces with a more neutral military force. Portugal could have a role to play here, though the return of Portuguese forces so soon after the liberation is problematic. Alternatively, Brazilian forces could play this role.

There is a significant economic dimension to crisis control as well. I mentioned earlier that South African military activity has had significant economic consequences for neighbouring states such as Angola and Mozambique, while the economic dependence of a number of the front line states on South Africa gives South Africa great flexibility in its dealings with other regional actors. These effects could be reduced through the provision of assistance in reconstruction and in the strengthening of infrastructural links which would bypass South Africa and facilitate the economic integration of other states in the region.

These measures by no means constitute a means of resolving the various conflicts in the region. They would, however, go some distance towards reducing their pernicious effects and the potential of regional conflict in Southern Africa to disturb world order.

Annex

South Africa has responded to its growing difficulty in importing arms by developing one of the most comprehensive and advanced indigenous arms production in the Third World. South Africa is virtually self-sufficient in small arms and small arms ammunition production. It produces its own armoured cars (the Eland) and armoured personnel carriers (the Hippo and Rhino), principally under French licence. The Atlas aircraft factories, again under French licence, manufacture Mirage jets, Alouette and Super Frelon, and Puma helicopters, and Cactus missiles. Under Italian licence, it produces Impala jets. Much of the engine manufacture for these aircraft is also done locally. The South African ship-building industry is now producing Israeli-designed fast attack craft armed with Gabriel missiles. Although the limitations on South African arms production - principally dependence on foreign licencing of technology and foreign supply of a number of critical components in air engine and avionics manufacture - should not be ignored, Pretoria clearly has the only substantial modern arms production capacity in the region.

16 Central America: Present and Future

Angel Ruiz-Zuniga

Introduction

For Ronald Reagan's administration, the Central American region has become one of the main foci of political attention. In dealing with the problems of the region, a whole battalion of diplomats, with differing attitudes and political options, has come and gone within a span of a few years. It all began with Alexander Haig and a hard line that hoped to force a quick ending. Following him was Thomas Enders (Under Secretary for Interamerican Affairs), who considered El Salvador a central nerve: use of military force was not enough, political negotiation was also necessary. Jeane Kirkpatrick's criticism helped throw out Enders, and her own recommendations, which appeared in the presidential briefings of 27 April 1983 to a joint Congressional session, generated a new political tone. American policy was then moved from the State Department to the National Security Council under William Clark; Enders and Dean Hinton were relieved of their duties.

Later, Clark moved to the Department of Interior and United States policy returned to the State Department, with Robert McFarlane as National Security Advisor, Thomas Pickering as Ambassador to El Salvador, and Langhorne Motley as Under Secretary of Interamerican Affairs. All were nominees of Secretary of State George Shultz.

The reason for all this shifting about in the Reagan administration bureaucracy lies in the difficulty of resolving the Central American crisis, which the United States Government considers to affect its national security. For the Reagan administration, the political evolution of Sandinista Nicaragua represents the threat of a 'New Cuba' allied with the Communist bloc right in the backyard of the United States. Through the eyes of the administration, Sandinista consolidation means danger of a leftist uprising throughout the entire region that could come as close as

Mexico. Consequently, its policy has been directed towards impeding such consolidation. It has been aimed at fomenting the deterioration of the Sandinista regime at every level (economic, political and military) and particularly at military harassment, by unabashedly supporting the anti-Sandinistas operating out of Honduras and Costa Rica, in search of the best opportunity with the most favourable conditions for an eventual overthrow of the Sandinistas. The implications of this policy bring dangers which threaten world peace by encroachment into the international political arena. To understand these implications better, we must clarify to what extent this is purely an East-West conflict.

Basis of Nicaraguan Revolution

The Central American conflict revolves essentially around Nicaragua and El Salvador, although the same problems affect the rest of the region as well. Nevertheless, Nicaragua is the real Gordian knot. With the downfall of Somozo's dictatorship, the Nicaraguan revolutionary eruption paved the way for a combination of East-West conflict (insofar as the Sandinista leaders have been trained by the Communist bloc, especially Cuba, and enjoy its support, although they declare Nicaragua to be non-aligned), with a deepening North-South conflict (due to the US policy of economic and political colonisation of the region, with marine invasions and the sustenance of bloody dictatorial regimes, for the benefit of North American multinationals). Both conflicts are profoundly interrelated. The basic origin underlying both is the social condition of poverty and repression, which engenders rebellion; and anti-American sentiment, linked with seeking support from Socialist countries, has been motivated by US policies that supports these conditions. In but a few years, two hundred thousand Central Americans have died and one million have been uprooted from their homes. To this has to be added the thirteen million desperately poor people in the region who barely survive (approaching 60 per cent of the population).

The Nicaraguan revolution generated a propagating wave of support for 'popular' movements in the rest of Central America; not only in El Salvador, but also in Guatemala and even Costa Rica. Nevertheless, El Salvador was a special case because the Romero dictatorship was then in an advanced state of decomposition. 1979-1980, for example, saw large demonstrations in El Salvador, and popular pressure eventually led to Romero's fall and to changes in government policy. This upsurge was in no way provoked by logistical military interference from Nicaragua (a country which,

emerging from a costly bloody civil war, was hardly in condition to do this). Rather, it was inspired by moral support
and encouragement from Nicaragua showing that the overthrow
of social and political oppression was possible.
The Nicaraguan revolution, and the general effervescence
among the masses of Central America, occurred at a moment of
international upheavals. The overthrow of the Shah of Iran;
major strikes in Colombia and Brazil; huge anti-nuclear,
Green and pacifist, movements in Europe (expressed in electoral gains for Social Democrats in some countries); and the
burgeoning growth of the gigantic union Solidarity in Poland,
are some examples. The moment also coincided with the last
part of Jimmy Carter's Presidential term, and his 'soft
line'. This favourable historic conjuncture did not last
long, however.
The international situation has since been changing in the
opposite direction. Poland experienced a **coup d'etat** and
the defeat of Solidarity; Western Europe saw the failure of
the pacifist and anti-nuclear movements, along with electoral
advances by the right; unpopular policies were applied in
Social Democratic France; and the Middle East experienced an
Israeli invasion of the Lebanon and the massacre of the
Palestinians. And, one must add, a new US administration with
aggressive foreign and defence policies came into office. The
only region still experiencing mass uprisings is South
America but their future in the midst of a strong international rightist wave is not too promising. In short, we
see an advance of conservative forces throughout the world at
nearly every level, including morally and culturally.

El Salvador
_____

In 1980-1981 in El Salvador, the political organisations now
grouped together under the Frente Democratico Revolucionario-
Farabundo Marti de Liberacion National (FDR-FMLN) squandered
the best moment - in terms of the low prestige of the
Salvadorean regime and the popular support enjoyed by their
organisations - to launch an insurrection to take power.
Archbishop Romero's death did not become the angry human sea
that characterised the response to Pedro Joaquin Chamorro's
death in Nicaragua. Since then (and in line with the new
international political situation), the progress of the
conflict has gone badly for the guerrillas, despite the
weakness of the Salvadorean regime (just barely being kept
afloat by US economic, military, and political aid). The
guerrillas have reached a point of social and political
isolation. Broad sectors of Salvadorean society have
supported various elections; this was a hard blow to the

Left, obliged to distance itself from decisive urban centres. The guerrillas of El Salvador, despite all their military manoeuvres and attacks, are plainly incapable of achieving either military or political defeat of the regime. But by the same token, neither can the government militarily defeat the guerrillas, in the short term. The FDR-FMLN can only strive for a long-term defensive strategy to give them time to take advantage, sometime in the future, of the social and political crises of an economically supported regime. Meanwhile, they represent no major threat to the United States. For the US administration, then, everything centres on Nicaragua, and the Sandinista power.

Role of the Contras

US support of the contras is not going to defeat the Sandinistas, simply because the contras are in no condition to achieve it. As a report in **Time** indicates[1]: 'The overall reality, however, has not changed; the **contras** right now are too small in number and too ill equipped to threaten the Sandinistas seriously, but they are also too stubborn to give up'.

This situation, however, is not merely a product of the contras' lack of equipment and their financial problems. The North-South conflict weighs heavily. The Sandinistas received the support of the Nicaraguan masses to lead them out of poverty and tyranny. The Nicaraguan people chose the Frente Sandinista de Liberacion Nacional (FSLN) because, needing a political instrument in their struggle against Somoza, they had nothing better at hand (neither on the Left nor on the Right) than the FSLN. But it was the United States which created and supported Somoza for years. One cannot erase overnight the anti-American sentiment that this policy generated in Nicaraguans; so soon after the fall of Somoza, they are not going to change their minds and listen to those who contributed decisively to their poverty and oppression. The FSLN continues in power, not only on account of its military might, nor because it has usurped power from other 'democratic' sectors, nor even because of Cuban-Soviet support. Rather it is because Nicaraguans are not going to turn away from the FSLN in the face of the United States and the contras, the majority of whom are former supporters of Somoza. But this does not mean that they are uniformly in agreement, or happy with the Sandinistas.

Overthrowing the Sandinistas in the near future would only be possible by a massive military intervention in Nicaragua, whether by a combination of various Latin American armies or from the United States. The military and political activities of the contras impose only a limited strain on Sandinista power. That the Reagan administration is willing to invade Nicaragua is not the problem. The problem is whether doing so is politically feasible. Militarily, the US Army could destroy the Sandinista Army (which itself is not negligible, with a hundred thousand men). But considering the Sandinistas' smart trench strategy in the cities, this could only be done on the basis of a gigantic urban massacre. Would it be feasible to repeat the Nazi German treatment of the Warsaw ghetto? It is hard to believe this happening in current world political conditions (bad as they are), but we can never completely exclude the possibility of this, or some variant of it.

American Policy at Crossroads

It is necessary to point out that although anti-war, Salvadorean solidarity, and Nicaraguan solidarity movements have been on the wane these last few years, the Vietnam syndrome has not completely disappeared from American consciousness. This too is a formidable restraint on adventuristic military initiatives by the Reagan administration. Grenada was a special case. Apart from the smallness of the country, Reagan staged a quick and effective (and low-cost) intervention, in the midst of political cannibalism between marxist groups and general disorder that not only failed to arouse disapproval but even won the support of US public opinion.

It is not even clear that a military invasion of Nicaragua would put an end to the political instability in Central America. There is no guarantee that it would be a quick job, effective and cheap, with the intervening troops leaving the region within a few months. The prospect of a prolonged involvement (with a steadily increasing number of casualties and the economic burden in the face of permanent resistance, could revive dormant anti-war sentiments, precipitating severe political difficulties in the United States.

The crossroads where the US administration finds itself today is thus plain: whether to launch this 'adventure', a military invasion against all sense of political prudence, or not to. If not, and still not accepting the Sandinista regime, the administration can only support a policy of military harassment (with no short-term prospects of success) and economic boycott (which the Cuban experience showed to have little effectiveness). With this option the Sandinistas would manage to stay in power, in better or worse conditions. As George Church[2] correctly pointed out, between the US alternatives in Nicaragua:

One is to accept a Marxist government, and Washington is not in the mood to do that. Last week the United States broke off talks with the Sandinistas and walked out of World Court hearings over the Nicaraguan complaint against the United States for its support of the contras. The other alternative of backing Nicaragua's neighbors is an effort to 'contain' the Sandinistas but this could go on for decades.

The absence of a military invasion of Nicaragua could also represent a time bomb in Central America: it would mean that the United States is not in a political condition to support its allies, come what may. The governing social groups (and other social sectors too) in Honduras, El Salvador, Guatemala, and Costa Rica might come to this sobering conclusion; and fear could become a political factor leading to blunders, or it could precipitate dangerous crises in the region. The Reagan administration has had to walk a very thin line in relation to the confidence of its allies.

The bilateral talks in Manzanillo (promoted by Mexico), whose terms were not made public but towards which US hostility was noticeably toned down (during the first few weeks of 1985); the nod of favour to Contadora; and the latest restructuring of the US diplomatic corps in the region; all this, added to the controversy in 1984 regarding aid to the contras, generated a cloud of scepticism and fear among the Central American Right. The administration was obliged to send down some high-ranking officials in January 1985 to assuage the worries of its allies: Vice President George Bush travelled (and will return) to Honduras, and McFarlane passed through all of Central America.

Without a military invasion against the Sandinistas, US policy as seen in the rupture at Manzanillo, in pressure on Congress to approve covert aid to the contras, in military operations held jointly with Central American armies, and in all the anti-Sandinista propaganda - apart from aiming at the deterioration of the Sandinistas - is essentially an attempt to preserve the confidence of its regional allies.

Neither the Kissinger Report, nor the Jackson legislation with its strategy of economic aid alongside military aid, could overcome the disagreement concerning a military invasion. Opponents of invasion would reject any proposal for greater military involvement in the region. The Democrats, who control the House of Representatives, opposed the approval of military funds (no doubt for electoral convenience). The project languishes. The American political climate neither favours an invasion nor seems too happy with covert aid to the anti-Sandinistas. Moreover, a whole series

of major American politicians have taken a stand against this
covert aid, as well as generally against military involvement
in the region.

For their part, the Sandinistas have made several gestures
which have benefitted them in world opinion, something which
is not without influence within the United States. Subsequent
to the CIA mining of Nicaraguan ports, the Reagan
administration lost credibility when the United States
withdrew from the World Court in The Hague. Nicaragua's
November elections (despite all their defects, limitations,
and so late in coming) conferred a measure of democratic
legitimacy on the Sandinistas. Similarily advantageous to the
Sandinistas' world image have been the departure of one
hundred Cuban military advisors from Nicaragua, the offer to
stop Soviet arm imports, Daniel Ortega's proposed amnesty,
and the freeing of Urbina Lara, who had sought asylum in the
Costa Rican embassy. All this surely weighs in the decisions
of the US Congress.

The Contadora group (constituted 9 January 1983), whose
political heart is Mexico, has sought a negotiated political
solution to preserve peace in the region. Such a formula
would necessarily include stability of the Sandinista regime
and a status quo unfavourable to the United States. From
the beginning, the Right in Central America has been clear
about this, and it has fought back from various angles. The
United States, powerless to oppose Contadora's efforts in a
public and decisive manner, has tried to put obstacles in the
way by using its regional allies, and pretexts such as arose
out of Urbina Lara's capture. Ultimately though, it is not a
feasible mechanism because nearly all political factors push
towards a negotiated solution.

Honduras and Costa Rica

The main allies of US policy in Central America have been
Honduras and Costa Rica. Honduras is the main base for the
anti-Sandinistas; the Nicaraguan Democratic Front (FDN)
represents the central bastion of military pressure on
Nicaragua. Honduras has always been a strategic country in
Central America (geographically and politically). It is
precisely because it knows this that Honduras has been trying
to blackmail the United States into augmenting the military
and economic aid it receives.

The political base of support for the anti-Sandinistas is
in Costa Rica. The leaders of all the groups either live in
or pass through San Jose. The local press is always full of
paid advertisements from all these groups, joining in chorus
with the national Right, especially in its attacks on the

Sandinistas, on Contadora, on US politicians who are not in favour of a 'rapid solution', and even on the Reagan administration when the Right becomes distrustful of it. The policy of Luis Alberto Monge's government has been to stay neutral, uninvolved, and to try to keep the peace. Nonetheless, various sources have reported the presence of counter-revolutionary encampments in the northern part of the country, where there are also said to be contra recruitment and training centres. The local Right both inside and outside the government party, has become a powerful group urging the severance of relations with Nicaragua and calling for greater involvement in the conflict. US pressure on the government (especially when Curtin Windsor was US Ambassador to Costa Rica) has also been very strong. Nevertheless, it is improbable that Costa Rica will involve itself more in the conflict. The most important role that Costa Rica plays in this chess game is perhaps as a stable, democratic mirror vis-a-vis Nicaragua, and as a privileged ally of the United States. From the very beginning, the Monge administration tried to assert the global prestige of Costa Rica's democratic tradition as part of the political and ideological attack on Nicaragua, and in support of US foreign policy. In this the Monge administration probably saw possibilities for winning some sort of political backing so that the country's creditors would take it easy on Costa Rica; it is looking for a way out of the gigantic economic crisis strangling the country ever since the administration of Rodrigo Carazo.

US Aid to Contras

Even if the policy of economic pressure and military harassment does not challenge Sandinista power in the short term, it nevertheless presents a danger that a better path towards a more effective political and military US intervention may be found in the middle or long term. Furthermore, the Sandinistas fear that extreme poverty (the minimum salary is five dollars a month), economic stagnation, and the political, military, and economic measures necessitated by the military pressure of the contras (40 per cent of the Nicaraguan budget is earmarked for defence), will undermine their social base of support. These considerations explain why the $14 000 000 of contra aid is so important, although the specific amount involved is less important than the approval of what would be a permanent source of covert aid to the anti-Sandinistas.

For the contras themselves, the covert aid is also decisive, considering that they have gone practically a full year without funding, apart from support from private individuals

and organisations. The debate over covert aid is a debate
over the contras' future. In the manoeuvre to present a more
attractive face for the debate, the various contra groups
have sought some form of unity.

The decision over covert aid represents an element of
distortion of the truths, political determinants, and choices
of all the protagonists in the Central America drama. All
have called upon their best resources, and best cosmetics,
hoping to come out ahead when the decision is made over the
future of one group of Nicaraguans or another - which, as is
customary, will be made far from their own country, in
Washington. The outcome is hard to forecast. The aid was
conditionally approved in October 1984; reapproval counts on
the support (and even more: on a campaign to identify the
contras with the patriotic heroes of the US War of Independence) of an administration whose general direction has been
amply ratified by the election of November 1984. Moreover,
the international political climate favours the conservatives. Nevertheless, the opposition is by no means small,
and no one wants to get messed up in a spiralling military
involvement in Central America. If the aid is not approved,
Reagan will look for a way to continue the policy which
enables him to maintain the pressure on the Sandinistas and
keep his allies' confidence at the same time.

Salvadorean Guerrillas

In El Salvador, with the isolation of Salvadorean guerrillas,
the far Right occupies a very large political space despite a
Christian Democrat electoral majority. Conversations and
negotiations between Jose Napoleon Duarte's government and
the FDR-FMLN do not have a very encouraging future: they are
founded on shifting sands. On the one hand, the guerrillas
would benefit from a political pact that would not disarm
them. It would offer them the possibility to survive and to
recover a lost urban social base. But neither D'Abuisson's
Right nor, ultimately, Duarte are going to accept a pact with
these conditions. Basically, the Christian Democrat peace
initiatives sought to generate a better international image
in order to win economic and military aid with which to
stabilise their position and try to crush the guerrillas.
The peace initiatives were a clever political manoeuvre on
Duarte's part, something the FDR-FMLN could not turn down
but which would yield nothing. For their part, should the
guerrillas lay down their arms they would simply lose all
prospects of achieving anything. On these terms, an
agreement that might lead to a definitive peace is impossible. Everything seems to lead to a constant state of war

without a decisive character.

Without doubt, the future of the Salvadorean guerrillas is linked to that of Nicaragua. In this whole situation, the policy of the Soviet Union and of Cuba is no small factor. Pro-Soviet organisations in the region have generally defended not an orientation towards a takeover of power and the installation of socialism, but rather towards the edification of local pressure groups in tune with Soviet needs, somewhat corresponding to the lines dividing the world into spheres of influence as symbolised by the Yalta and Potsdam Conferences of 1945. After the triumph of the July 26 Movement in Cuba, a series of political-military groups formed in Central America, and throughout Latin America, seeking power via guerrilla warfare (the 'lesson' of the Cuban revolution) and opposing pro-Soviet communist parties (as 'reformists'). Nevertheless, with time Cuba has come to link its policy to that of the Soviet Union. The Cuban leaders have rethought not only guerrilla strategy, but even the kind of political and economic organisation to promote for other Latin American countries. This has become evident in the attitudes and movements of Latin American pro-Castro groups, from Guatemala to Colombia to Peru (including Nicaragua). All these changes are in search of a strategy that would permit Cuba to defend its political power without losing too much of its regional influence or its manoeuvring capacity.

The Sandinistas have been the only group after Cuba to succeed in seizing power by commanding a mass revolution. Among marxist groups, however, the new Nicaraguan revolution has awakened new yearnings for power. In fact, some pressures against the classic communist line have provoked party splits. Thus in 1984 the Costa Rican Communist Party, the People's Vanguard Party - one of Latin America's most monolithic - broke into two hostile camps (although both unrepentantly pro-Soviet). Still, it seems that the dominant criterion in the high echelons of Soviet-Cuban policy is that of concentration of effort to attain stability for Nicaragua, although without becoming totally involved. Sandinista leaders are not going to get from Moscow a greater commitment than the present one: arms, ideological-propangandistic defence, and some 'technicians' from Eastern Europe. The Soviets are too far away, the Cubans perhaps too near. What has been attempted is the instrumentation of various marxist groups in the area in defence of Nicaragua, recalling **mutatis mutandis** Soviet foreign policy towards the Comintern during the period of 'socialism in only one country'. The policies of these groups would emphasise Sandinista needs over and above the needs and political

dynamics of any other country in the region. The FSLN itself
would assume direct responsibility for setting the political
line for these groups. In effect, Managua has practically
become a political 'oracle' for all Central American marxist
groups (whether pro-Soviet or pro-Castro).

Future of Central American Conflict

The future of the Central American conflict is totally
uncertain. And yet, the historically determinant political
and military options were set ever since the FSLN took power.
If the United States invades and crushes the FSLN and the
people who support them, that will initiate a new period for
the entire region. A thick cloud of repression and misery
would settle for many years, even though all centres of
resistance would not necessarily be eliminated. It would be a
profound tragedy, to be counted among the worst that humanity
has yet borne (and an act to be condemned by the clearest
humanist consciences of our species). On the other hand, if
there is no invasion and the Sandinista power stabilises
(despite military harrassment and boycotts), the prospects
for Nicaraguan social organisation are not likely to be very
far from those of the Socialist countries. Tendencies present
since their original formation would lead them to reproduce
the communist political and economic model. This is seen
already in the role of the State and of the FSLN in social
life, as well as in Sandinista political attitudes towards
freedom of association and expression at every level.   In
fact, it is practically certain that the present existence of
a mixed economy, an electoral system, and a whole series of
typically capitalist measures, are merely responses to the
strains of the different situation of political and military
pressure. Nonetheless, today Nicaragua is not a Communist
regime, nor a totalitarian dictatorship. It has advantages
not seen in Communist countries[3]. The tendencies
mentioned are not yet a living reality.
    To the lack of points of view other than a marxist one, the
Sandinistas further add major weaknesses in administration
and policy: tremendous empiricism in governmental decisions;
a lack of tact, and a rude attitude in relations with
relatively adverse countries and political sectors. The
Sandinista's coarse manner with the Catholic Church, whose
earthly power is very important, has permitted the Right to
use it to the detriment of the Nicaraguan revolution. The
operation to discredit the priest Bismarck Carballo was a
political error that created major tensions with the
Nicaraguan Catholic Church. The pamphleteering political act
staged at the open air mass given by Pope John Paul II in

Managua had similar consequences[4]. In the same way, the decision to arrest Urbina Lara (affecting even the right to asylum), as well as the way the business was handled up to his being set free, constituted a series of gigantic political errors. The Central American Right knew how to utilise the matter as a pretext to generate an important anti-Sandinista wave that reached as far as the Contadora group, whose efforts were consequently debilitated. The decision not to allow Arturo Cruz into the country with his peace proposal was also a stupid reply to what was essentially a manoeuvre on the part of the anti-Sandinista opposition for the benefit of the US Congressional debate over covert aid. These mistakes are adding up; they give pretexts for the anti-Sandinistas and contribute to undermining sympathy and solidarity with Nicaragua.

One can also consider the contradictions present within the heart of the FSLN as a latent weakness in the Sandinistas. It is possible to trace differing positions and lines among the various members of the National Directorate. It should not be forgotten that the present leadership is a product of the fusion of three political factions (Terceristas, Guerra Prolongada and Tendencia Proletaria) which put aside their mutual hostilities practically only after the defeat of Somoza. This 'invisible' factor is not simply a matter of different positions arising among the Commandantes and of general disarray; it could bring back factional political lines in the future.

Despite the lack of a new (non-marxist) political and ideological perspective, and despite all the Sandinistas' errors and political weaknesses, the Nicaraguan revolution has awakened a wave of sympathy and hope in some North American and European quarters, although not as great and enthusiastic a wave as the Cuban revolution aroused in the 1960s. This has translated into a solidarity movement that weighs in the future of Central America.

The political difficulties of a massive military intervention to destroy the Sandinistas in Nicaragua make one think that US policy should stick to a war of words with an economic boycott and military pressure via the contras. If this path is chosen, it will only be able to yield what the Reagan administration claims it wants: permanent pressure to negotiate some reform in Nicaragua's political and economic structure, perhaps delaying the emergence of a classical Communist regime. For their part, the Soviets, Cubans, and Sandinistas are interested first and foremost in preserving a specific form of social and economic organisation. In this situation we could anticipate permanent political and military conflict, but without it necessarily producing a broader conflagration with greater political consequences for world peace. Still, this does not say everything: there are more elements of macropolitics to consider apart from the politics of confrontation.

Conclusion

The complex social conditions and the economic crisis strangling Central America will become another time bomb if no deeper solution is found. Costa Rica's crisis has barely been semi-controlled by the traditional electoral machine and by an influx of US economic aid, but poverty is growing to threatening proportions. In Honduras a germinating seed of social activity has yet to be smothered by military negotiations with the United States. The Salvadorean regime depends economically and militarily on US aid. In Guatemala a terrible silent war has been smouldering for many long years, and there are no visible prospects for a stable future. Is the Reagan administration prepared to maintain the economic and social hardships (albeit 'artifically') at a 'controllable' level? Resolving the East-West conflict in Central America is not enough to resolve the latent crisis in the region. Would the United States be willing to grant 'privileged' status to Central America and absorb the burden of providing massive economic aid (as with Israel)? Or would it return to 'control' via bloody dictators, when everything in Latin America points the other way? All indications are that the United States is in no condition to go either one way or the other.

Whatever the outcome, Central America has been added to – and will not be deleted from – the list of priority concerns of the United States, and of the world. In the short term, it looks unlikely that this situation will generate an East-West conflict of great proportions. The Soviet Union more or less respects the US sphere of influence and is not going to risk everything for Nicaragua; nor will Cuba. On the contrary, they are exercising great prudence. But in Central America a time bomb goes on ticking, one which seems to mark not so much the present conflict as a new explosion which could be the spark to ignite the whole world.

References

1. Time, 24 December 1984.
2. Time, 28 January 1985.
3. See M. Niedergang in Le Monde, 3 and 4 May 1984.
4. The Times, 8 November 1984.

17 Self-Determination, Non-Intervention and the Case of Nicaragua

Alfonso Garcia-Robles

Introduction

To define international law applicable to the matter of Nicaragua it is sufficient if we review a selection of international instruments such as the Charter of the United Nations, the two International Covenants on Human Rights and the Charter of the Organization of American States - all of them treaties - and some fundamental declarations of the General Assembly of the United Nations which, because of their rank, possess an undeniable legal value. Undoubtedly, self-determination and non-intervention are closely linked: for it would be impossible to conceive the exercise of self-determination should intervention be held to be permitted. Nevertheless, following the method used in most cases by competent international organs which have dealt with this matter, both principles will be examined separately, starting with self-determination.

Self-Determination of Peoples in the United Nations System

The Charter of the United Nations attaches great importance to the principle of self-determination by proclaiming in Paragraph 2 of Article 1 that one of the purposes of the Organization is 'to develop friendly relations among nations based on respect for the principle of equal rights and self-determination of peoples'. Later, in Article 55, the Charter quite rightly states that one of the means for the realisation of that purpose is to promote 'universal respect for, and observance of, human rights and fundamental freedoms for all'.

It is therefore not strange that the first Paragraph of Article 1 of both the International Covenant on Economic, Social and Cultural Rights and the International Covenant on Civil and Political Rights, adopted by the General Assembly on 16 December 1966 in Resolution 2200 (XXI), reads as follows: 'All peoples have the right to self-determination. By virtue of that right they freely determine their political status and freely pursue their economic, social and cultural development'.

The year before the approval of the two International Covenants on Human Rights, the General Assembly had adopted a Declaration on Non-Intervention. This will be examined more fully in a later part of this chapter, but in the present context it is important to note that in respect to self-determination it stated: 'All States shall respect the right of peoples and nations, to be freely exercised without any foreign pressure, and with absolute respect for human rights and fundamental freedoms'.

Four years after the adoption of the Covenants, during the session marking the twenty-fifth anniversary of the United Nations, the General Assembly adopted the 'Declaration on Principles of International Law concerning Friendly Relations and Co-operation among States in accordance with the Charter of the United Nations', in which, with regard to the 'principle of equal rights and self-determination of peoples', it proclaimed, inter alia that:

By virtue of the principle of equal rights and self-determination of peoples enshrined in the Charter of the United Nations, all peoples have the right freely to determine, without external interference, their political status and to pursue their economic, social and cultural development, and every State has the duty to respect this right in accordance with the provisions of the Charter.

Every State has the duty to promote, though joint and separate action, realization of the principle of equal rights and self-determination of peoples, in accordance with the provisions of the Charter, and to render assistance to the United Nations in carrying out the responsibilities entrusted to it by the Charter regarding the implementation of the principle, in order:
(a) To promote friendly relations and co-operation among States: and
(b) To bring a speedy end to colonialism, having due regard to the freely expressed will of the peoples concerned:
and bearing in mind that subjection of peoples to alien subjugation, domination and exploitation constitutes a violation of the principle, as well as a denial of fundamental human rights, and is contrary to the Charter.

That same year, 1970, the jubilee of the Organization, the Assembly adopted a 'Declaration on the Strengthening of

International Security', in which all States were urged to abide strictly in their international relations by the purposes and principles of the Charter, among which was expressly mentioned 'the principle of equal rights and self-determination of peoples'.

Self-determination of peoples with regard to their economic development was already included, in general terms, in the International Covenant on Economic, Social and Cultural Rights, whose Article 1, Paragraph 2, establishes that 'The peoples may, for their own ends, freely dispose of their natural wealth and resources without prejudice to any obligations arising out of international economic cooperation, based upon the principle of mutual benefit, and international law'. These provisions were to be strengthened and broadened by those of the 'Declaration on the Establishment of a New International Economic Order', adopted on 1 May 1974 at the Sixth Special Session of the General Assembly, and those of the Charter of Economic Rights and Duties of States, which the Assembly adopted in Resolution 3281 (XXIX) of 12 December 1974.

In the aforementioned Declaration the Assembly proclaimed that the new international economic order should be founded on 'full respect' for certain principles, among which it specified 'self-determination of all peoples', and, since peoples act in the international scene through their respective States, 'full permanent sovereignty of every State over its natural resources and all economic activities'. The Declaration also included the following passage:

> In order to safeguard these resources, each State is entitled to exercise effective control over them and their exploitation which means suitable to its own situation, including the right to nationalization or transfer of ownership to its nationals, this right being an expression of the full permanent sovereignty of the State. No State may be subjected to economic, political or any other type of coercion to prevent the free and full exercise of this inalienable right.

As for the Charter of Economic Rights and Duties of States, after affirming in Article 1 that 'every State has the sovereign and inalienable right to choose its economic system - in accordance with the will of its people, without outside interference, coercion or threat in any form whatsoever', it asserts the following in Article 2:

1. Every State has and shall freely exercise full permanent

sovereignty, including possession, use and disposal, over all its wealth, natural resources and economic activities.

2. Each State has the right:

(a) To regulate and exercise authority over foreign investment within its national jurisdiction in accordance with its laws and regulations and in conformity with its national objectives and priorities. No State shall be compelled to grant preferential treatment to foreign investment;

(b) To regulate and supervise the activities of transnational corporations within its national jurisdiction and take measures to ensure that such activities comply with its laws, rules and regulations and conform with its economic and social policies. Transnational corporations shall not intervene in the internal affairs of a host State. Every State should, with full regard for its sovereign rights, co-operate with other States in the exercise of the right set forth in this subparagraph;

(c) To nationalize, expropriate or transfer ownership of foreign property, in which case appropriate compensation should be paid by the State adopting such measures, taking into account its relevant laws and regulations and all circumstances that the State considers pertinent. In any case where the question of compensation gives rise to a controversy, it shall be settled under the domestic law of the nationalizing State and by its tribunals, unless it is freely and mutually agreed by all States concerned that other peaceful means be sought on the basis of the sovereign equality of States and in accordance with the principle of free choice of means.

As regards the right of peoples to decide freely on what best suits them for their social development, this is also dealt with in general terms in the aforementioned International Covenant. The main instrument adopted by the United Nations on the subject is, however, the 'Declaration on Social Progress and Development', Annex to Resolution 2542 (XXIV) of 11 December 1969. Here mention will be made of only a few of its numerous provisions, those embodied in its articles 1, 2, 7 and 9:

All peoples and all human beings, without distinction as to race, colour, sex, language, religion, nationality, ethnic origin, family or social status, or political or other conviction, shall have the right to live in dignity and freedom and to enjoy the fruits of social progress and should, on their part, contribute to it.

Social progress and development shall be founded on respect for the dignity and value of the human person and shall ensure the promotion of human rights and social justice...

The rapid expansion of national income and wealth and their equitable distribution among all members of society are fundamental to all social progress, and they should therefore be in the forefront of the preoccupations of every State and Government.

The improvement in the position of the developing countries in international trade resulting, among other things, from the achievement of favourable terms of trade and of equitable and remunerative prices at which developing countries market their products is necessary in order to make it possible to increase national income and in order to advance social development.

Social progress and development are the common concerns of the international community, which shall supplement, by concerted international action, national efforts to raise the living standards of peoples.

Social progress and economic growth require recognition of the common interest of all nations in the exploration, conservation, use and exploitation, exclusively for peaceful purposes and in the interests of all mankind, of those areas of the environment such as outer space and the sea-bed and ocean floor and the subsoil thereof, beyond the limits of national jurisdiction, in accordance with the purposes and principles of the Charter of the United Nations.

Finally, there is the best-known United Nations instrument relating to self-determination: Declaration 1514 (XV). A passionate statement made before the General Assembly by the then Prime Minister of the Soviet Union, Nikita Khrushchev, as well as a subsequent draft submitted by 43 Asian and African States and adopted on 14 December 1960 by 90 votes in favour, none against and 9 abstentions, played a decisive role in its formulation and adoption. It is worth stressing that its official title is 'Declaration on the Granting of Independence to Colonial Countries and Peoples'. It thus dealt mainly with the need to put a quick and unconditional end to colonialism in all its forms and to ensure the exercise of independence to non-self-governing territories. The Declaration, nevertheless, also contained provisions applicable to 'all peoples' and not only those under foreign rule, such as paragraph 2 of its operative part, which is almost identical to what would become the first paragraph of the two Covenants on Human Rights, as well as its second preambular paragraph, in which the Assembly declared itself to be

Conscious of the need for the creation of conditions of stability and well-being and peaceful and friendly relations based on respect for the principles of equal rights and self-determination of all peoples, and of universal respect for, and observance of, human rights and fundamental freedoms for all without distinction as to race, sex, language or religion.

Non-Intervention

Next it is necessary to examine the genesis of the main norms applicable on non-intervention, both in the inter-American and in the international spheres.

I will begin by recalling what I stated on 6 December 1965 before the First Committee of the General Assembly during the consideration of the draft that was to become the first resolution adopted by the United Nations on the subject: Resolution 2131 (XX), in whose elaboration I had the privilege to participate directly. I said on that occasion:

The principle of non-intervention has been given its most perfect definition in America from the standpoint of the legal-technical approach. This indeed could not be otherwise if due account is taken of the many aspects of intervention to which the Latin American States were subjected ever since they emerged to independent life. The attribute of sovereignty came to us in the midst of the nineteenth century, at a time when the so-called community of civilized nations had arrogated to itself the right to intervene lawfully, in accordance with the theoreticians of that era, whenever any of the circumstances included in a long catalogue of possibilities occurred.

A review confined to the immediate antecedents of such a definition should begin with a memorable polemic which took place at the sixth Inter-American Conference held in Havana in 1928. Although inconclusive in its results, it made possible that the principle of non-intervention be finally enshrined in the Convention on the Rights and Duties of States, opened for signature in 1933 at the seventh conference in Montevideo, although it was still limited by a reservation of the United States. This reservation was to

disappear three years later in the Additional Protocol on
non-intervention, adopted unanimously at the Inter-American
Conference on Consolidation of Peace.

The principle was solemnly reiterated in the so-called
'Declaration of Mexico', adopted in Chapultepec in 1945, and
it attained the full rank of a constitutional norm in 1948
when it was embodied in Articles 15 and 16 of the Charter of
the Organization of American States. The complete text of
those articles, which became Articles 18 and 19 after the
Charter was amended by the Buenos Aires Protocol in 1967, is
as follows:

Article 18. No State or group of States has the right to
intervene, directly or indirectly, for any reason whatever,
in the internal or external affairs of any other State. The
foregoing principle prohibits not only armed force but also
any other form of interference or attempted threat against
the personality of the State or against its political,
economic, and cultural elements.

Article 19. No State may use or encourage the use of
coercive measures of an economic or political character in
order to force the sovereign will of another State and
obtain from it advantages of any kind.

When the United Nations was created in 1945, it was not
possible to include in its Charter provisions similar to
those just quoted. The only form of intervention which was
expressly prohibited was that of the Organization itself:
Paragraph 7 of Article 2 establishes that 'nothing contained
in the present Charter shall authorise the United Nations to
intervene in matters which are essentially within the
domestic jurisdiction of any State...'.

Twenty years were to elapse before the General Assembly
could fill this lacuna by adopting on 21 December 1965 the
'Declaration on the Inadmissibility of Intervention in the
Domestic Affairs of States and the Protection of their
Independence and Sovereignty'. The first paragraph of the
Declaration, almost identical to Article 18 of the Charter of
the Organization of American States, is the following:

No State has the right to intervene, directly or
indirectly, for any reason whatever, in the internal or
external affairs of any other State. Consequently, armed
intervention and all other forms of interference or
attempted threats against the personality of the State or
against its political, economic and cultural elements are
condemned.

The second paragraph faithfully reflects Article 19 of the Inter-American instrument, although in this case, it has a broader scope, since it covers certain aspects which that article does not contemplate. The paragraph states the following:

No State may use or encourage the use of economic, political or any other type of measures to coerce another state in order to obtain from it the subordination of the exercise of its sovereign rights or to secure from it advantages of any kind. Also, no State shall organize, assist, foment, finance, incite or tolerate subversive, terrorist or armed activities directed towards the violent overthrow of the regime of another State, or interfere in civil strife in another State.

Furthermore, paragraph 5 of the Declaration adds the following: 'Every State has an inalienable right to choose its political, economic, social and cultural systems, without interference in any form by another State'.

Five years later, in one of the main instruments with which the Assembly wished to commemorate the jubilee of the Organization, the 'Declaration on Principles of International Law concerning Friendly Relations and Co-operation among States in accordance with the Charter of the United Nations', adopted on 24 October 1970, these provisions were repeated almost verbatim.

On the occasion of the twenty-fifth anniversary of the United Nations, the Assembly also adopted, on 16 December 1970, the 'Declaration on the Strengthening of International Security' which was referred to earlier in the context of the principle of self-determination. In Paragraph 4, the Assembly solemnly reaffirmed 'that States must fully respect the sovereignty of other States and the right of peoples to determine their own destinies, free of external intervention, coercion or constraint, especially involving the threat or use of force, overt or covert, and refrain from any attempt aimed at the partial or total disruption of the national unity and territorial integrity of any other State or country'.

To conclude this series of quotations with one from an instrument of similar rank, it is appropriate to recall that the Charter of Economic Rights and Duties of States, adopted by the Assembly on 12 December 1974, after expressly including non-intervention among the 'fundamentals of international economic relations', stipulated in its Article 32 that 'no State may use or encourage the use of economic, political or any other type of measures to coerce another

State in order to obtain from it the subordination of the exercise of its sovereign rights.

Nicaragua: A Case in Point

After having briefly examined the evolution and current status of those two fundamental principles of international law - self-determination and non-intervention - we may now turn to a case in point: Nicaragua. I have two reasons for choosing this particular example. In the first place, I consider that the covert war which for some time has been waged against Nicaragua constitutes one of the clearest systematic violations of both the principle of self-determination and that of non-intervention. Secondly, the international community has pronounced itself on this issue through three of the main organs of the United Nations: the Security Council, the General Assembly and the International Court of Justice.

Here it is not intended to dwell upon the origins of the present Central American conflict, nor on the specific internal situation of Nicaragua. Neither will a catalogue be provided of the numerous hostile actions carried out against its sovereignty in flagrant violation of its right to self-determination and the fundamental principle of non-intervention. Nor is it intended to analyse the relevant proceedings of the Security Council and the General Assembly since their respective resolutions, which are annexed, are self-explanatory. In this chapter it will suffice to briefly review what the highest international jurisdictional organ - the International Court of Justice - had to say when the case was brought before it.

On 9 April 1984 the Government of Nicaragua filed in the Registry of the Court at The Hague an application for instituting proceedings requesting the Court to adjudge and declare, **inter alia**:

(a) That the United States, in recruiting, training, arming, equipping, financing, supplying and otherwise encouraging, supporting, aiding, and directing military and paramilitary actions in and against Nicaragua, has violated and is violating its express charter and treaty obligations to Nicaragua and, in particular, its charter and treaty obligations under:
- Article 2(4) of the United Nations Charter:
- Articles 18 and 20 of the Charter of the Organization of American States:
- Article 8 of the Convention on Rights and Duties of States:

- Article 1, Third of the Convention on Rights and Duties of the States in the Event of Civil Strife.

(b) That the United States, in breach of its obligation under general and customary international law, has violated and is violating the sovereignty of Nicaragua by:

- armed attacks against Nicaragua by air, land and sea;
- incursions into Nicaraguan territoral waters;
- aerial trespass into Nicaraguan airspace;
- efforts by direct and indirect means to coerce and intimidate the Government of Nicaragua.

(c) That the United States, in breach of its obligation under general and customary international law, has used and is using force and the threat of force against Nicaragua.

(d) That the United States, in breach of its obligation under general and customary international law, has intervened and is intervening in the internal affairs of Nicaragua.

(e) That the United States, in breach of its obligation under general and customary international law, has infringed and is infringing the freedom of the high seas and interrupting peaceful maritime commerce.

(f) That the United States, in breach of its obligation under general and customary international law, has killed, wounded and kidnapped and is killing, wounding and kidnapping citizens of Nicaragua.

Furthermore, the Government of Nicaragua, 'because of the importance and urgency of the matters raised' in its suit, and 'in order to avoid further loss of life and destruction of property pending a final determination', requested the Court to indicate the following provisional measures of protection:

- That the United States should immediately cease and desist from providing, directly or indirectly, any support - including training, arms, ammunition, supplies, assistance, finances, direction or any other form of support - to any nation, group, organization, movement or individual engaged in planning to engage in military or paramilitary activities in or against

Nicaragua;

- That the United States should immediately cease and desist from any military or paramilitary activity by its own officials, agents or forces in or against Nicaragua and from any other use or threat of force in its relations with Nicaragua.

For its part the Government of the United States did not attempt to address the substance of the issue. Instead it 'indicated its firm conviction that the Court was without jurisdiction to deal with the Application, and was a **fortiori** without jurisdiction to indicate the provisional measures requested by Nicaragua, and requested the Court to remove the case from the list'. This 'lack of jurisdiction **in limine**' raised by the United States 'as a plea in bar of fundamental importance' and based on technicalities such as the contention that 'the declaration which Nicaragua made on 24 September 1929 purporting to accept the Optional Clause never entered into force' and that, consequently, 'Nicaragua never accepted the compulsory jurisdiction of the Permanent Court', only served one purpose: to delay the proceedings.

Furthermore, the United States alleged that the indication of provisional measures by the Court 'could irreparably prejudice the interests of a number of States and seriously interfere with the negotiations being conducted pursuant to the Contadora process', and, finally, contended that:

Nicaragua's Application appears on its face to request a definitive legal determination regarding an alleged illegal use of armed force in the midst of on-going hostilites. In the circumstances of this case, where the United Nations and the Organization of American States have approved the Contadora process, such questions regarding the use of force during hostilities are more properly committed to resolution by the political organs of the United Nations and of the Organization of American States ...

On 10 May 1984, the Court, without prejudging the question of its jurisdiction to deal with the case, issued an Order in which it unanimously rejected 'the request made by the United States of America that the proceedings on the Application filed by the Republic of Nicaragua on 9 April 1984, and on the request filed the same day by the Republic of Nicaragua for the indication of provisional measures, be terminated by the removal of the case from the list...'.

It also unanimously indicated:

Pending its final decision in the proceedings instituted on 9 April 1984 by the Republic of Nicaragua against the United States of America, the following provisional measures:

1. Unanimously,

   The United States of America should immediately cease and refrain from any action restricting, blocking or endangering access to or from Nicaraguan ports, and, in particular, the laying of mines;

2. By fourteen votes to one,

   The right to sovereignty and to political independence possessed by the Republic of Nicaragua, like any other State of the region or of the world, should be fully respected and should not in any way be jeopardized by any military and paramilitary activities which are prohibited by the principles of international law, in particular the principle that States should refrain in their international relations from the threat or use of force against the territorial integrity or the political independence of any State, and the principle concerning the duty not to intervene in matters within the domestic jurisdiction of a State, principles embodied in the United Nations Charter and the Charter of the Organization of American States.

3. Unanimously,

   The Governments of the United States of America and the Republic of Nicaragua should each of them ensure that no action of any kind is taken which might aggravate or extend the dispute submitted to the Court.

4. Unanimously,

   The Governments of the United States of America and the Republic of Nicaragua should each of them ensure that no action is taken which might prejudice the rights of the other Party in respect of the carrying out of whatever decision the Court may render in the case...

The only dissenting vote on provisional measure 2 was cast by the American Judge, Stephen M. Schwebel.

Finally, in that same Order, the Court:

Unanimously,

Decides further that, until the Court delivers its final judgment in the present case, it will keep matters covered by this Order continuously under review;

Unanimously,

Decides that the written proceedings shall first be addressed to the questions of the jurisdiction of the Court to entertain the dispute and of the admissibility of the Application;

And reserves the fixing of the time-limits for the said written proceedings, and the subsequent procedure, for further decision.

The question of the jurisdiction of the Court was examined at length between May and November 1984. On 26 November the Court issued a Judgment in which inter alia, it found 'by fifteen votes to one, that it has jurisdiction to entertain the case...'.

The single dissenting vote was again cast by Judge Schwebel.

The case of Nicaragua remains before the Court, which is now examining the substance of the matter. The United States, however, holds the view that 'the Court is without jurisdiction to entertain the dispute and that the Nicaraguan Application of 9 April 1984 is inadmissible'. Accordingly, 'the United States intends not to participate in any further proceedings in connection with this case'.

In spite of the negative attitude of the Government of the United States during the proceedings, it is important to stress, in my opinon, that the International Court of Justice, in its Order of 10 May 1984 quoted above, indicated that the right to sovereignty and political independence of any State

should be fully respected and should not in any way be jeopardized by any military and paramilitary activities which are prohibited by the principles of international law, in particular the principle that States should refrain in their international relations from the threat or use of force against the territorial integrity or the political independence of any State, and the principle concerning the duty not to intervene in matters within the domestic jurisdiction of a State, principles embodied in the United

Nations Charter and the Charter of the Organization of American States'.

It thus gave to the principle of non-intervention a full jurisdictional character.

Annex 1

RESOLUTION 530 (1983) ADOPTED UNANIMOUSLY BY THE SECURITY COUNCIL OF THE UNITED NATIONS ON THE QUESTION OF CENTRAL AMERICA 19 MAY 1983

Resolution 530 (1983)

The Security Council

Having heard the statements of the Minister for External Relations of the Republic of Nicaragua,

Having also heard the statements of the representatives of various States Members of the United Nations in the course of the debate,

Deeply concerned, on the one hand, at the situation prevailing on and inside the northern border of Nicaragua and, on the other hand, at the consequent danger of a military confrontation between Honduras and Nicaragua, which could further aggravate the existing critical situation in Central America,

Recalling all the relevant principles of the Charter of the United Nations, particularly the obligation of States to settle their disputes exclusively by peaceful means, not to resort to the threat or use of force and to respect the self-determination of peoples and the sovereign independence of all States,

Noting the widespread desire expressed by the States concerned to achieve solutions to the differences between them,

Commending the appeal of the Contadora Group of countries, Colombia, Mexico, Panama and Venezuela, in its 12 May 1983 communique, that the deliberations of the Council should strengthen the principles of self-determination and non-interference in the affairs of other States, the obligation not to allow the territory of a State to be used for committing acts of aggression against other States, the peaceful settlement of disputes and the prohibition of the threat or use of force to resolve conflict,

Considering the broad support expressed for the efforts of the Contadora Group to achieve solutions to the problems that affect Central American countries and to secure a stable and lasting peace in the region,

1. **Reaffirms** the right of Nicaragua and of all the other countries of the area to live in peace and security, free from outside interference;

2. **Commends** the efforts of the Contadora Group and urges the pursuit of those efforts;

3. **Appeals urgently** to the interested States to co-operate fully with the Contadora Group, through a frank and constructive dialogue, so as to resolve their differences;

4. **Urges** the Contadora Group to spare no effort to find solutions to the problems of the region and to keep the Security Council informed of the results of these efforts;

5. **Requests** the Secretary-General to keep the Council informed of the development of the situation and of the implementation of the present resolution.

Annex 2

RESOLUTION 38/10   ADOPTED UNANIMOUSLY BY THE GENERAL ASSEMBLY OF THE UNITED NATIONS ON 11 NOVEMBER 1983

The Situation In Central America: threats to international peace and security and peace initiatives

The General Assembly

Recalling Security Council resolutions 530 (1983) of 19 May 1983 in which the Council encouraged the efforts of the Contadora Group and appealed urgently to all interested States in and outside the region to co-operate fully with the

Group, through a frank and constructive dialogue, so as to resolve their differences,

Reaffirming the purposes and principles of the Charter of the United Nations relating to the duty of all States to refrain from the threat or use of force against the sovereignty, territorial integrity or political independence of any State,

Also reaffirming the inalienable right of all peoples to decide on their own form of government and to choose their own economic, political and social system free from all foreign intervention, coercion or limitation,

Considering that the internal conflicts in the countries of Central America stem from the economic, political and social conditions obtaining in each of those countries and that they should not, therefore, be placed in the context of East-West confrontations,

Deeply concerned at the worsening of tensions and conflicts in Central America and the increase in outside interference and acts of aggression against the countries of the region, which endanger international peace and security,

Mindful of the necessity of promoting the achievement of peace on a sound basis, which would make possible a genuine democratic process, respect for human rights, and economic and social development,

Noting with deep concern that in recent weeks armed incidents, border clashes, acts of terrorism and sabotage, traffic in arms and destabilizing actions in and against countries of the region have increased in number and intensity,

Noting with great concern the military presence of countries from outside the region, the carrying out of overt and covert actions, and the use of neighbouring territories to engage in destabilizing actions, which have served to heighten tensions in the region,

Deeply concerned at the prolongation of the armed conflict in countries of Central America, which has been aggravated by increasing foreign intervention,

Bearing in mind the progress achieved in the meetings that the Ministers for Foreign Affairs of the Contadora Group have held with the Foreign Ministers of Costa Rica, El Salvador, Guatemala, Honduras and Nicaragua in identifying issues of concern and proposing appropriate procedures for the consideration of those issues,

Recalling the Cancun Declaration on Peace in Central America issued by the Presidents of Colombia, Mexico, Panama and Venezuela on 17 July 1983, which contains an appeal for political commitments on the part of countries situated in and outside the region with the aim of achieving lasting peace in the area,

Bearing in mind the Cancun Declaration and the endorsement by the States of Central America of a Document of Objectives, which provides a basis for an agreement on the negotiations, that should be initiated at the earliest possible date with the aim of drawing up agreements and adopting the necessary procedures for formalizing the commitments and ensuring appropriate systems of control and verification,

Appreciating the broad international support expressed for the efforts of the Contadora Group to secure a peaceful and negotiated settlement of the conflicts affecting the region,

1. **Reaffirms** the right of all the countries of the region to live in peace and to decide their own future, free from all outside interference or intervention, whatever pretext may be adduced or whatever the circumstances in which they may be committed;

2. **Affirms** that respect for the sovereignty and independence of all States of the region is essential to ensure the security and peaceful coexistence of the Central American States;

3. **Condemns** the acts of aggression against the sovereignty, independence and territorial integrity of the States of the region, which have caused losses in human life and irreparable damage to their economies, thereby preventing them from meeting the economic and social development needs of their peoples; especially serious in this context are:
(a) The attacks launched from outside Nicaragua against that country's strategic installations, such as airports and seaports, energy storage facilities and other targets whose destruction seriously affects the country's economic life and endangers densely populated areas;

(b) The continued losses in human life in El Salvador and Honduras, the destruction of important public works and losses in production;

(c) The increase in the number of refugees in several countries of the region;

4. **Urges** the States of the region and other States to desist from or to refrain from initiating, military operations intended to exert political pressure, which aggravate the situation in the region and hamper the efforts to promote negotiations that the Contadora Group is undertaking with the agreement of the Governments of Central America;

5. **Notes with satisfaction** that the countries of the region have agreed to take measures leading to the establishment and, where appropriate, the improvement of democratic, representative and pluralistic systems which will guarantee effective popular participation in decision-making and ensure the free access of various currents of opinion to honest and periodic electoral processes based on the full observance of civil rights;

6. **Expresses its firmest support** for the Contadora Group and urges it to persevere in its efforts, which enjoy the effective support of the international community and the forthright co-operation of the interested countries in or outside the region;

7. **Welcomes with satisfaction** the Cancun Declaration of the Presidents of Colombia, Mexico, Panama and Venezuela and the Document of Objectives endorsed by the Governments of Costa Rica, El Salvador, Guatemala, Honduras and Nicaragua, which contains the basis for the start of negotiations to ensure harmonious coexistence in Central America;

8. **Requests** the Secretary-General, in pursuance of Security Council resolution 530 (1983), to keep the Council regularly informed of the development of the situation and of the implementation of the present resolution;

9. **Requests** the Secretary-General to submit a report to the General Assembly at its thirty-ninth session on the implementation of the present resolution;

10. **Decides** to keep under review the situation in Central America, threats to security which may occur in the region and the progress of peace initiatives.

18 US Security Interests in Central America

Tommie Sue Montgomery

Escalating US involvement in Central America raises a series of questions about real security interests in the region: whether current policies are, in fact, serving those interests; the costs of continuing to pursue these policies; and whether alternative policies might, in fact better serve legitimate US security interests. First, it is essential to have a precise sense of the importance to the United States of the region, in national terms, because that determines what the United States is prepared to expend in resources to defend those interests. When the 'Our-national-security-interests-are-at-stake-in-the-region' argument is invoked, as it regularly is by the Ronald Reagan administration, it is usually justified by arguments about dominoes; sea lanes; foreign military bases; the Panama Canal; refugees; proximity; contingency planning; and/or preemptive action.

The argument relating to **dominoes** is that one revolution (in Nicaragua) will inevitably lead to other revolutions in El Salvador, Honduras, Guatemala, Mexico, ending with the last domino, the United States. Hence, our national interest demands that we eliminate the domino that started it all: Nicaragua. Certainly those who assert that the Reagan administration does not have, as its ultimate objective, the overthrow of the Nicaraguan Government, are not listening to the President and his subordinates. As far back as 1981, for example, Robert McFarlane said, privately, 'We have no intention of coexisting with the Sandinista government'.

A further argument relates to **sea lanes.** According to one scenario, if there is a conventional war in Europe, the United States must resupply its and NATO forces, much of which would come out of Gulf ports. Cuba, it is argued, could impede this traffic. Similarly, the sea lanes leading to the Panama Canal could be blocked if there are additional, hostile governments in the region.

With respect to **the Panama Canal** it is argued that

revolutionary governments in the region pose a threat. One scenario is that MiGs based in Nicaragua could attack and destroy the Canal.

In the matter of **foreign military bases** we are told that it is not in the interest of the United States to allow their construction in the region. This argument assumes that Nicaragua is willing to permit the construction of such bases on its soil, and that a revolutionary government in El Salvador or Guatemala would be similarly disposed.

We are also frequently told that the issue of **refugees** is vital. It is assumed that if revolutionary governments come to power, the United States will be innundated with refugees fleeing the tyranny of totalitarian regimes.

The question of **proximity** is another significant point. The US public is periodically reminded that San Salvador is closer to Washington than is San Francisco.

A further issue concerns **contingency planning.** An argument, regularly invoked by administration insiders, asserts that Pentagon and other contingency planners have more important areas of the world to worry about and that Central America is an unnecessary distraction from the Middle East, the Soviet Union and so on. A long as there are leftist governments in the region, contingency planners will have to spend time that could be better spent elsewhere developing scenarios for conflict in the isthmus.

Finally there is the case for **preemptive action.** In some quarters it is held that the United States should control the situation now, that is overthrow the Sandinistas and prevent a victory of the FDR/FMLN in El Salvador so that it will not have to worry about the sea lanes, the refugees, the canal, the foreign military bases, and the dominoes in the future.

These arguments will now be subjected to brief analysis. With respect to the argument about **dominoes,** history told 20 years ago that if Vietnam fell, the whole of Southeast Asia would follow, and the wave of revolution would sweep into south Asia, ultimately consuming India and Pakistan, on its march to the Middle East and Africa. But as a recent Washington Post headline announced: 'Asia's dominoes didn't fall. They got rich instead'.

The Mexican revolution was not repeated for almost 50 years. A second Mexican revolution depends on how the Mexicans handle their continuing economic crisis and how they conduct their foreign policy, which has domestic implications - not on what happens in countries to their south.

The Cuban revolution occurred a half century after Mexico and it was another 20 years until Nicaragua. In El Salvador the rise of the contemporary revolutionary organisations was very much a response to conditions inside that country, not to the fact that the FSLN had been formed eight years earlier. The first Salvadorean uprising in this century occurred in 1932, when Fidel Castro was still in short pants. It was preceded by a series of peasant uprisings in the Nineteenth Century, well before Karl Marx became a household name. If Nicaragua and Cuba disappeared tomorrow, the revolutionary movements in El Salvador and Guatemala would continue.

Next let us consider the matter of **sea lanes**. If there were a war in Europe, which does not become nuclear, Cuba, with about 200 MiGs, could, theoretically, impede US shipping. Given the size of the US defence budget, however, if the US Air Force is not capable of taking out every Cuban air base and closing every Cuban harbour in six hours, it is incompetent. If Cuba's two old diesel attack submarines pose a threat, the US Navy is incompetent, and the increases in defence spending that Reagan is requesting are insufficient to correct the weakness.

As for **the Panama Canal**, if the Soviets and Cubans want to close it, does it make more sense to 'subvert' Central America - a costly and extremely risky policy - in order to establish bases from which the Canal could be attacked? Or would it be more efficient to send in frogmen with sachel bombs? Or to lob a mortar or two into one of the locks? The argument that Nicaragua's acquisition of MiG 23s poses a threat to the Canal is similarly frivolous. MiG 23s could reach the Canal from Nicaragua - barely - but the Nicaraguans do not have any, and they said, back in December 1983, that they would not acquire any.

Turning to the case of **foreign military bases,** we must ask whether the Nicaraguans are suicidal. Are they willing to risk national destruction to allow Cuba or the Soviet Union to construct military bases in the country? The same question may also be raised about the Salvadorean revolutionary leaders. Have these people spent years in the mountains, living in extraordinarily difficult conditions, or years in exile to follow a policy that they know will bring immediate and massive US retaliation? There is no evidence that they are so irrational; indeed there is quite a record, in both cases, that they recognise - and acknowledge - that the USA has legitimate security interests in the region. They are not prepared to risk annihilation by pursuing such a policy.

We must next consider the matter of **refugees.** According to America's Watch, the UN High Commissioner for Refugees, and other human rights organisations that compile data on refugees, 25 per cent of El Salvador's population - more than one million people - are in refugee camps in Central America, in refugee camps or internally displaced inside El Salvador, or living in Mexico and the United States. It is generally accepted that there may be as many as half-million Salvadoreans in the United States - at least half of whom have arrived since 1980. The refugees, then, have already left. Except for the relatively small Miami enclaves of wealthy Central Americans, the vast majority of the Salvadoreans and Guatemalans have not fled a Communist, totalitarian government, but right-wing military dictatorships or military-dominated civilian governments. After five years and hundreds of interviews and informal conversations, it is clear to me that the Salvadorean refugees with whom I have talked, from Costa Rica to the United States, would head home tomorrow if a political solution were achieved that incorporated the FDR and FMLN. While Nicaraguans have left their country since the revolution, their numbers in both relative and absolute terms are far lower than either the numbers of those who left before the revolution, or those who have left El Salvador. In short, human rights violations in Central American countries allied with the United States (with the exception of Costa Rica) are much worse than in Nicaragua.

Then there is the argument about **proximity**. Implicit in this is the notion that the nearness of Central America **ipso facto** involves critical security considerations that, in turn, give the United States the right to control internal domestic developments in those countries. But proximity acquires significance only to the extent that concrete US interests, such as preventing construction of Soviet bases, become a factor.

As for the matter of **contingency planning**, the argument that the mere presence of leftist governments in the region will absorb, **ad infinitum**, too much attention by too many contingency planners may be countered by asking: has China claimed as much attention from planners in the last decade as it did between 1949 and 1972? The answer is no. Similarly, peaceful resolution of the conflict in Central America and normalisation of relations between the United States and Nicaragua and Cuba, would reduce demands on strategists.

Finally, there is the **preemptive** argument. It is held that the policy now being followed costs less than the policy the United States would have to follow if it lets events run their course. To meet that argument we may recall some history: the United States gave trainers to the South Vietnamese so that it would not have to send American boys to fight a war!

In sum, the arguments which are generally advanced to support US policy, suggest that the security threat to the United States from Central America is pretty thin. It is therefore difficult to make a case that the vital interests of the United States are at stake in the outcome of the Central American conflicts.

It is important, however, to stress that the United States does have national security interests in the region. It has an interest in ensuring the security of the Panama Canal; in political stability in Mexico; in keeping the shipping lanes open; in keeping foreign military bases out of the region; in socio-economic conditions in the region that significantly reduce the number of refugees making their way across the Rio Grande/Rio Bravo.

But what policy is most likely to ensure that these interests are protected? How much is the United States willing to pay, in military, economic and political terms to achieve its goals? How much it will have to pay to control the outcome of the crisis in Central America is a function of what the situation in the region is - or perhaps, a function of what official US perception of the situation is. It is clear that the cost is already very high, especially relative to the lack of progress in military terms in El Salvador (in spite of President Jose Napoleon Duarte's electoral successes). The relative success of US policy can be measured in the following. In 1979 there were only a few hundred guerrillas scattered in the mountains of northern and eastern El Salvador. Today there are over 10 000 - according to US government estimates. In 1979 they controlled no territory. Now on any given day, they control between 25 and 35 per cent of national territory. In Nicaragua, the contras are obviously not capable of defeating the Sandinistas and there are growing indications that the Nicaraguan government is gaining the upper hand. The cost in Honduras is taking the form of a growing national reaction to the US presence. In Guatemala there is a Thirty Years War characterised by cycles in which guerrilla resurgence is followed by massive army repression, which is, in turn, followed by bigger and stronger guerrilla resurgence. In short, the cost of controlling the outcome in Central America is very high - higher than the United States is currently paying, especially if it wants to get rid of Sandinistas, and certainly if it wants to defeat militarily the FMLN in El Salvador. There is also the cost at home: the political consensus in favour of the current policy is stretched to the breaking point and is reflected in Congress' refusal to approve continuation of aid to the contras.

It will not damage US credibility as a nation to settle for half-a-loaf. The problem is that, in trying to get the whole loaf, the United States risks getting nothing at all - which would indeed be a major blow to its credibility. US

credibility is in jeopardy in Western Europe when they think
the United States is getting itself into another Vietnam. US
credibility is also at stake when Latin Americans think the
North Americans prefer to use military means to solve
essentially political and economic problems - and when they
are unwilling to support regional efforts, such as those of
Contadora, to achieve a peaceful solution.

US policy, rather than weaning Nicaragua from Cuba and the
Soviet Union has, demonstrably, had the reverse effect. As
the United States has increased military pressure, Nicaragua
has turned to the Socialist bloc for military supplies. The
Sandinistas, it should be recalled, asked the Carter administration for military aid shortly after they took power in
1979, and were refused. Where else were they going to go?

In the case of Nicaragua the US has two choices. It can
through negotiations reach a **modus vivendi** which takes US
interests into account: stopping the arms flow across
borders; limiting the size of armies in the area; withdrawing
Cuban and Soviet - and US - military personnel in the region.
All these things are attainable - and verifiable. The Cubans
have indicated their willingness to go along with such an
arrangement. The second choice is to continue current policy:
Reagan says the Nicaraguans cannot be trusted and therefore
'the structure of the current government' must be changed.
The contras cannot do it. Yet the US administration seems to
think that a little more economic, military, and/or political
pressure will get rid of the Sandinistas. The Nicaraguans are
not fools: they recognise who has power in the hemisphere.
They are prepared to negotiate and reach an accommodation.
But they are not prepared to surrender. That, it seems, is
what the US administration wants them to do. In the bilateral
Manzanillo talks, the United States, in effect, said 'OK,
you have to get rid of all Soviet and Cuban military
personnel, and then we'll take that into consideration'. No
quid pro quo was offered. That is not the way for one
sovereign nation to deal with another, but that has been the
US administration's pattern of behaviour towards Nicaragua
since 1981.

When the United States confronted Nicaragua in late 1980
and early 1981 with evidence of arms shipments to the
Salvadorean insurgents, they stopped the shipments. In April
1981 the US administration stated that there had been no
evidence of arms trafficking for several weeks and that other
forms of support had been curtailed. But, the administration
added, the supplies **may** be going through other channels,
although there is no evidence - and cut off all economic
assistance. The Sandinistas, by acceding to the US demands
in 1981, acknowledged that they value a relationship with

the United States. But the US response, as Alexander Haig has indicated, was in effect: you're heeding our warning, which means you are in a weak position, and therefore we are going to tighten the screws.

This scenario was replayed after Foreign Minister Miguel D'Escoto submitted a series of draft treaties that, among other things, would have banned foreign bases and offensive weaponry. In January 1984, Assistant Secretary of State Langhorn Motley rejected these proposals in a speech. In February the CIA mined Nicaraguan harbours.

With regard to Cuba, Fidel Castro, on 28th July 1983, said that Cuba would be willing to consider pulling its military forces out of Nicaragua if the United States pulls out of El Salvador. One would have thought that the US administration would have taken this as a cue. Indeed, on 4 August 1983, Secretary of State George Shultz assured Congressional leaders that Castro's offer would be seriously explored. But on 13 August Reagan said that the United States would do nothing because he did not think Castro serious.

The Salvadorean FDR/FMLN leaders have also expressed their willingness to negotiate with the United States over similar security interests. But those offers have also been ignored.

In each case the United States never bothered to find out how serious the Nicaraguans, Cubans, or Salvadoreans were. It has continued to up the military ante while paying lip service to the need for a political solution. It seems clear that the current policy does not serve US interests or national security. By opting for military solutions to problems that are inherently political, economic, and social, costs can only rise and returns diminish. The logic of US policy, in Nicaragua and El Salvador, leads inexorably to the commitment of US troops. What will the United States do if the contras are decimated by the Nicaraguan army, or if the Salvadorean army begins to unravel?

The United States cannot have it both ways. It cannot continue to support, indeed underwrite, insurgency in Nicaragua and oppose it in El Salvador. It cannot continue to insist that the Nicaraguan government negotiate with the contras, while opposing similar negotiations between the Salvadorean government and the FDR/FMLN. It cannot denounce elections in Nicaragua, where one opposition party refused to participate, as fraudulent, while celebrating elections in El Salvador where all opposition to the left of the political centre was prevented by violence from participating. The United States cannot have it both ways because it will not work. A policy so rent with contradictions is as doomed to failure as US policy was in Vietnam twenty years ago.

PART FOUR
Economic Prospects for the Developing Countries

19 The World Economy in 1985: Its Prospects for the Rest of the Eighties and the North–South Problem

Miguel Wionczek

Introduction

The purpose of this paper is to give an account of the current state of the world's economy, as well as its future prospects up to the end of the present decade. In conditions of extreme uncertainty in this respect, it is particularly important to obtain a realistic view of possible developments in the industrial North during the years to come. What happens in this part of the world economy will undoubtedly determine the economic future of the rest of the planet, and particularly that of the so-called peripheral economies: those of under-developed countries in Latin America, Africa and Asia.

Although detailed and fully authoritative analyses of the current situation in the world economy are not yet available, there are many partial reports originating from such international organisations as the World Bank, the International Monetary Fund, the General Agreement on Tariffs and Trade, and the United Nations Conference on Trade and Development, amongst others, which cover 1984 and the first few months of 1985. These documents, together with the international financial press, provide a breadth of information which permits two key questions to be posed.

First, have we seen by the mid-1985 the end of the short but dynamic economic recovery of the United States in the two previous years, a recovery which, contrary to the tendency of the 1970s and the early 1980s, was not accompanied or followed by a parallel or subsequent recovery of the other industrialised market economies (with the exception of Japan)? Secondly, what kind of policies would the group of industrialised countries need to pursue to ensure a collective and sustained recovery from a crisis which was not halted or even alleviated by the 1983-1984 economic boom in the United States, a recovery which would provide the minimal conditions for developing countries to escape from the crisis in which they have been submerged since the beginning of the 1970s?

There is a growing body of opinion which maintains, even in traditional neoclassical economic circles, that since the end of the 1960s it has not been possible to analyse or comprehend the behaviour of the world economy in terms of the business cycle, and that we are in fact faced with the interaction of two distinct phenomena: a generalised structural crisis and an acute series of cyclical oscillations superposed on the former. The seriousness of the general situation is aggravated by the fact that in industrialised market economies, in the so-called peripheral economies, and even in socialist economies, also affected by the crisis, diagnoses of roots of economic disequilibria are erroneous, and the policies devised to combat them are in general either irrelevant or have adverse effects.

The Battered United States Economy in 1985

During the last quarter of a century, the United States economy has suffered five economic recessions of varying duration and intensity: from April 1960 to February 1961, from December 1969 to November 1970, from November 1973 to March 1975, from January to June 1980 and, finally, from July 1981 to November 1982. If these cyclical imbalances are analysed in terms of three indicators (duration, drop in industrial production and peaks in unemployment), the two most severe ones were about 1973-1975 and 1981-1982. The latter, which coincided with the initial year of President Ronald Reagan's first term of office, not only lasted sixteen months but was characterised by a drop in industrial production of more than 12 per cent and an unemployment level which at one moment reached almost 11 per cent of the labour force. On taking up office, Reagan himself declared in a televised speech, in early 1981, that he was sorry to say that 'we are in the worst economic situation since the times of the Great Depression'.

Partisans of 'Reaganomics' insist that the cyclical recovery of the United States economy, which began in the winter of 1981-1982 and apparently ended just before the 1984 elections, can be largely attributed to the deep tax reduction decreed by Congress in 1981 under the pressure of the Executive, and to the restrictive monetary policies of the Federal Reserve System in force from 1982 to 1984. Without denying the dynamism of the economy during these three years (the GNP growth rate from the second quarter of 1983 up to the first half of 1984 was above 6 per cent, and during the period from the spring of 1983 to the winter of

1983-1984 exceeded 8 per cent annually in real terms), critics and adversaries of Reagan's economic policies maintain that the costs have been much higher than the benefits, in spite of the considerable slowing of the inflationary process and the drop in unemployment.

In fact, the most important thing the Republican adminis-tration did in 1981-1984 was to reduce taxes; while it drastically increased military spending, it compensated for this by severe cuts in social programmes. The consequences of this set of policies, which seriously widened the gap between the living standards of the rich and the majority of the United States population, have begun to be felt and will be felt more and more in the near future. For the moment, nearly all the achievements of the 'New Deal' of the 1930s and 1940s have been lost, the country is facing budgetary and foreign trade deficits of unmanageable proportions even in the middle term, monetary policies have diverted national savings away from production enterprise towards financial speculation, and the country has become the world's greatest debtor with a foreign debt calculated at $800 000 million and a domestic debt of $1.3 trillion. The accumulation of nuclear and conventional arms has contributed nothing to national security, and the monetary and financial policies of the United States weakened, beyond reasonable limits, the international financial system, turning the industrialised North Atlantic allies of the United States into its greatest creditors, and the poor Third World into its debtor, hovering on the brink of bankruptcy.

After Reagan's re-election, even some distinguished co-authors of 'Reaganomics' started insisting that only a substantial reversal of economic policies can save the United States from very serious internal problems and the world economy from a general collapse.

These interesting, although partially contradictory, opinions of the most distinguished US economists, represent-atives of a wide range of positions from pure monetarism to a revised Keynesianism, have one thing in common: they accepted implicitly in the autumn of 1984 that the 'miracle' boom of 1983-1984 was over. Their views were shared by many other United States academics and businessmen. In short, in late 1984 there were three groups of economic forecasters in the country. The first, which is relatively small, comprised the adherents of Reaganomics and was predicting a GNP growth rate on the order of 5.5 per cent for 1985; the second, the largest, which included such people as Paul A. Samuelson, spoke of a growth rate on the order of 4 per cent; the third maintained that the economic situation was so complicated, and the behaviour of the President so unpredictable, that anything could happen in 1985 and 1986, short of a repeat of the Great Depression of the 1930s, although they could envisage a new serious recession like those of 1973-1975 and 1981-1982 taking place. Both the most cautious and the most pessimistic economists insisted, though, that another Great Depression could not happen, simply by virtue of the fact that the United States Government had means of averting a collapse and if necessary would act in that sense. However, numerous econometric predictions foresaw growth rates in the United States dropping in the rest of the 1980s to an average of 3.5 to 4.0 per cent anually. These predictions seem to be being fulfilled starting in mid-1985.

It is worth recalling that during the 1984 presidential campaign the problem of protectionism, which is a worldwide phenomenon though centred in the United States, was hardly mentioned. Similarly, post-electoral debates on the future of the US economy contained no reference to the relationship between the monumental budgetary deficit and military spending. Nearly all schools of thought in the area of economic policies accepted the constant growth of the latter as an axiom. Curiously enough, defence spending expansion was questioned in 1984 and continued to be questioned in 1985 by some military figures from the Pentagon rather than by economic specialists. It is therefore worth quoting one of the few exceptions to this rule, an opinion expressed in the **New York Times**. In an article which appeared, apparently by sheer coincidence, the day after the November 1984 elections, Jonathan Fuerbringer argued[1]:

...some economists believe that the rate of military spending will probably decrease and that strengthening of the military will not contribute as much in the future to economic growth as it did in the past. Some economists maintain that the large federal deficits, caused partially by the boom in military spending, will keep interest rates high in 1985, thus producing a slower growth in many industries and neutralizing that part of the growth impetus deriving from the financing of the arms race.

The same author reminded us that, while the military budgets acted between 1960 and 1982 as a stimulus for the United States economy, defence spending has recently become an inhibiting factor. The growth in military spending which started at the end of the 1970s during the last phase of the Carter administration, and which was accelerated by Reagan, helped to mitigate the 1981-1982 recession. During the 21 months of unexpectedly vigorous overall growth after the winter of 1982, the military budget increased at a rate

comparable to the overall GNP. Experts in the US Department
of Commerce insisted, though, that this latter growth phase
of the military budget, although, insignificant, was not a
crucial factor in the 1983-1984 boom. The reason given was
the growing control of inflationary pressures arising in the
military sector (which continues to expand despite having a
smaller share in the GNP than during the Vietnam war). While
it is justifiable, in this new situation, to state that
military spending played only a limited part in the 1983-1984
boom, it is also valid to argue that, given the case of a
substantial slowing down in the economic growth of the United
States in 1985 and the prospects for stagnation during the
rest of the 1980s, such spending could not be a compensating
factor, since it would only cause new inflationary pressures
and additional increases in budget deficits.

The Start of the New US Economic Recession in 1985

Despite the optimism generated in Western industrialised
economies as a whole by the unexpected strength of the United
States' economic recovery from early 1983 to late 1984, the
supposed success of 'Reaganomics' was very short-lived. As
early as July 1984, **The Economist**, the well-informed and
influential British weekly, ventured this opinion[2]:

The greatest threat to world economy is a recession
provoked by high-cost money policies which could start
during the next twelve months. Such an event would have
serious consequences for European countries, whose
unemployment rates continue to increase slowly, as well as
for Latin-American debtors, who need a boom in their export
markets based on low-cost money. It would also negatively
affect Americans, who have just experienced twelve months
of the most rapid economic growth of the last decade.

According to this same non-American source, the world
economy could be prevented from falling into another crisis
if the United States immediately relaxed its monetary
policies and applied the most stringent fiscal measures after
the 1984 elections. Otherwise, the situation will become most
serious, since the short-lived boom of the United States
economy has largely been based on the constant and growing
flow of savings from Western European countries (and the rest
of the capitalist world) towards the United States to finance
its continuing fiscal and trade deficits. According to
The Economist, these flows of foreign capital and the US
policy of high-cost money, resulting from the 'permissive-
ness' of its fiscal policy, make it extremely difficult,

if not impossible, for the rest of the North Atlantic industrial economies to recover; and they also create serious side-effects in international commerce, particularly the world market for raw materials. Instead of adopting a series of expansionist policies and thus paving the way for its own recovery, Western Europe has been obliged to strengthen its restrictive monetary policies which abort any sign of emergence from the crisis. Furthermore, developing countries have become even greater victims of these restrictive policies applied throughout the industrial world. Their trading situation vis-à-vis developed countries has notably deteriorated in 1984 and the same trend became even more acute in 1985.

The concern expressed by **The Economist** half way through 1984 was echoed even more energetically by the main economic commentator of **The New York Times**, Leonard Silk, shortly before the 1984 elections. This very widely-read writer came to the conclusion that a new recession in the United States was highly probable in 1985 or 1986. In reference to the behaviour of the US major economic indicators in the autumn of 1984, Silk stated a few days before the presidential elections[3]:

The tremendous budgetary deficit could jeopardize and paralyze fiscal policy after the elections, whatever their results. A recession could mean an increase in this deficit of US $300 000 to $400 000 million; a deficit of this size would impede any fiscal measure applied to combat recession through increasing spending or cutting taxes, and the fear of a recession could dissuade the White House and Congress from decisive action to cut the budgetary deficit. A deep recession in the United States would have dangerous international repercussions. It would cause a slowing or a drop in foreign investment in this country, as a result of diminishing profits and a drop in dollar exchange rates. Decreases in the influx of capital would in turn result in scarcity of funds necessary both to finance the budgetary and trade deficits of the United States, and private investment in its new productive capacity. Diminishing flows of foreign savings would increase real interest rates. Although a decline in the value of the dollar would allow a reduction in the trade deficit, which is currently reaching unprecedented annual levels of $130 000 million, it would at the same time cause a decrease in foreign exports and would aggravate the problems of the heavily-indebted developing countries, thus worsening in the final analysis the position of American banks.

In mid-1985 even many optimists seem to agree that the new economic recession will hit the country with full force in 1986.

The US trade deficit for 1985, according to the US Department of Commerce, may well reach a record of $160 billion ($123 billion in 1984), while the size of the budget deficit in the fiscal year ending in September 1985 was estimated within the range of $200 - 250 billion. Even such a publicly prudent person as Paul A. Volcker, chairman of the Federal Reserve Board, warned during his Congressional testimony in mid-July 1985 that 'we are piling up debts abroad in amounts unparalleled in our history' and 'when we are living on this much borrowed money, we are also living on borrowed time'[4].

A growing number of academic economists, and some central bankers as well, believe that the United States cannot solve on its own the triple problem of a growing budget deficit, a widening trade deficit and of a dollar overvalued by some 40 per cent. They complain, on the other hand, that the US partners in Western Europe and Japan are not particularly helpful. Under such circumstances, reflecting the general climate of uncertainty, concern and confusion spreading in the United States, one reads in the most influential US newspapers and financial journals an increasing number of articles asking a question whether the country is headed for a 1929-style crash and noting that although 'a lot has changed since then, but there are still some disturbing parallels'[5].

The discoveries of some of the similarities between the 1920s and the 1980s are quite startling. First, both decades followed periods of extremely high inflation and later witnessed high real interest rates and low inflation. Moreover, in the 1920s, as today, the dollar was one of the strongest currencies. Secondly, then as now, there was slow economic growth, marked by extreme weakness in some sectors and strength in others. Presently, many economic experts and commentators describe the United States as a 'double-tier' economy with deeply depressed sectors like agriculture and traditional manufacturing along with dynamic sectors based on high-technology catering largely to the arms industry. Thirdly, protectionism raised its head in the Congress in the 1920s and resulted in the 1930 passage of the Smoot-Hawley Tariff Act, which set off a wave of retaliations abroad. In the 1980s the US protectionism takes the form of non-tariff restrictions and 'voluntary' import quotas in most major industrial branches. Fourthly, the expanding strains in the present US financial system - the Continental Illinois National Bank, the Ohio and Maryland state savings and loans institutions, and the collapse of some Government bond firms are reminiscent of the precarious conditions of many US banks in the 1920s. Fifthly, a real estate boom in the early part of the 1920s was followed by a crash in real estate prices; the beginning of a similar pattern can be detected in the 1980s. Sixthly, the excessive speculations with stocks and other financial instruments terminated with the stock market crash of 1929; while – this time – the stock market boom started in 1982 still continues, many experts are concerned over the increased use of credit to finance investment and the appearance of highly speculative investment instruments. Finally, as in the 1920s, there is in the 1980s the accelerated trend towards the deregulation of all sort of economic and financial activities aimed at releasing **market forces.**

All these developments considered jointly strongly suggest that the US economy is getting sicker and sicker year after year, that, 'Reaganomics' are failing on all fronts, and as one of the New York economic consultants put it in July 1985, 'the bad news is that the odds are pretty good that in the late 80s or 90s we will have a real depression'[6].

Conditions in the Other Industrialised   Countries

In the World Bank and GATT reports, published in autumn 1984, there was a noticeable effort to refrain from being overly pessimistic in relation to prospects for the industrialised part of the world economy for the remainder of the 1980s. However, data from OECD sources and West European research centres published in the first half of 1985 provided sufficient basis for the conclusion that, independently of what might or might not happen with regard to Washington's fiscal and monetary policies, the economies of the rest of the industrialised world, with the exception of Japan, will grow at low rates not exceeding much those predicted in late 1984. Only in Japan was the economy growing in mid-1985 at over 8 per cent annually. In other words, there are no exceptions for a strong West European economic recovery in 1985. The partial reports available from the European Economic Community Commission in Brussels predict for 1985 an average annual growth rate in the ten member countries of about 3 per cent - slightly over that registered in 1984 (2.3 per cent). It could not be a surprise to anybody that the present 'eurosclerosis' is making it progressively more difficult to solve the growing intra-European economic conflicts, both within and around the EEC, or to design some sort of joint economic policy vis-a-vis the United States and Japan.

The complete failure of the annual meeting of the heads of the ten EEC member states, held in Milan at the end of June 1985, provides the most recent evidence in that respect. Moreover, the signs multiply that the entry of Spain and Portugal into the European Common Market will complicate matters further rather than simplify them. Leaving aside conventional analyses of the reasons for the persistent economic stagnation in Western Europe, such as inflexible labour markets and excessive real wages, an alleged fall in the rate of return on investment and the technological weaknesses[7], there are much deeper political and economic reasons for the EEC countries' refusals to take the advice from the United States that it is their turn to become the 'growth locomotive' for the whole North Atlantic area by putting in force large tax cuts. Finance ministries and central banks in Western Europe (as well as in Japan) seem to be concerned much less with sustaining economic growth and increasing global demand by tax cutting than with excessive national debt burden which must be contained at almost any cost. They place the blame for this situation on a decade of experimenting with ideas about demand management policies mostly imported from the United States and Great Britain[8].

It is further pointed out, particularly in West Germany (and also in Japan), that while the outstanding US gross government debt stabilised between 1970 and 1983 in terms of its ratio to the GNP, it increased very substantially in many OECD countries in the same terms because of the US-originated world-wide policy of high interest rates. According to many West Europeans, it is not a good idea for a country to borrow at real interest rates much higher than their expected economic growth, because debts compound automatically into an ever-larger share of national income and in a longer-run lead to national bankruptcy or uncontrollable inflation or both. These arguments contain a severe indirect criticism both of the United States and of other developed countries. As long as they continue to prevail in the treasuries and central banks of many OECD countries, the 1985 steep decline in the US economic growth rate cannot be expected to be compensated by the growth of the rest of the industrialised market economies.

The Socialist Economies

Unlike the tendencies observed in Western Europe, economic recovery in the Eastern bloc is proceeding at a reasonable albeit still slow rate. Both in the Soviet Union and in the other socialist countries, goals set at the end of 1983 for production and national income were surpassed in 1984. The average 1984 growth rate for the area was at around 4.5 per cent and in 1985 it may exceed 5 per cent, after the low of around 2.5 per cent recorded in 1982. Economic development in Eastern Europe is stronger in the Soviet Union and in the least industrialised countries (Romania, Bulgaria) than in the more developed ones (GDR, Hungary and Czechoslovakia). This divergent tendency would suggest that the drawbacks of centralised planning are felt more in the industrialised and diversified Socialist economies than in the others. If this proved to be true, it would give further support to the thesis sustained by the 'liberal' wing of economists in socialist countries: that the major structural obstacle in the centrally-planned economies is the rigidity of the planning process itself, which does not fit any longer the diversification of the productive system.

The Peripheries of the World Economy

Information on the behaviour of the peripheral economies in 1985 is still scarce because of the delays in data gathering, elaboration and diffusion. Thus it is that, in the case of Latin America, the last two annual reports published respectively by the UN Economic Commission in Latin America (ECLA) and by the Inter-American Development Bank give no final data for 1984, much less predictions for 1985. Both studies confirm that the cost of adjusting to IMF guidelines has been particularly high for the region in terms of economic growth and social welfare, even though some progress has been made in slowing the high rates of inflation, and in external debt renegotiation in most countries. Apparently, in some of the larger republics, such as Brazil and Mexico, 1984 saw a recommencement of economic growth. The Brazilian economy grew at 3 to 4 per cent, and that of Mexico at an even higher rate in 1984, while Argentina's GNP remained stationary in real terms. In the first half of 1985 however, economic conditions in most of Latin America started deteriorating again, in oil exporting countries as the result of the decline of international oil prices, in oil importing countries because of the continued deterioration of their terms of trade and growing protectionism in industrial countries against Latin American manufacturers' exports. In the region as a whole, imports continued to decline because of the heavy burden of servicing external debt.

Information from Africa shows that except for the oil producing countries of the north of the continent, the region's economy continues to deteriorate dramatically. Among the most important reasons for such deterioration are: the drop in external demand and prices for raw materials, the considerable decrease in flow of aid and foreign investment and the adverse climatic conditions in the countries to the south of the Sahara which have caused a serious famine in Western, Central and Eastern Africa. In such critical circumstances, it is difficult to foresee an economic recovery of Africa. The United States apparently continues to be indifferent to the constant deterioration in the economic and social conditions of the continent, and continues to oppose increasing substantially economic aid to Africa because of alleged lack of financial resources. As elsewhere in the developing world the United States takes the position that African countries should try to resolve their problems by working harder and broadening their private sector, as the key to a long-term economic recovery.

Asia seems to have fared better than Africa and even Latin America. The Chinese economy continues to grow at an annual rate of 10 per cent and India's at over 6 per cent. However, as a result of the persistent difficulties of the industrialised nations, the economic growth rate is slowing down even in relatively prosperous South-East Asia, the region comprising the Association of South-East Asian Nations (ASEAN) and South Korea. The Singapore economy, which in the past was constantly used as the example of the 'free-market miracle' in Asia, just stopped expanding suddenly in early 1985, for the first time in 20 years.

To sum up, the possibilities for economic recovery in Latin America and Africa, and for sustained growth in Asia (except Japan, China and Soviet Asia) are minimal in view of the end of the spectacular 1983-1984 boom in the US economy and the continuing 'eurosclerosis' on the other side of the North Atlantic. This sclerosis will not be over before the end of the 1980s at the earliest. Such is the opinion, at least, of research centres in the six major countries of the EEC (Great Britain, France, West Germany, Italy, the Netherlands and Belgium) as expressed already in mid-1984 in a special report by the **The Economist**[9]. These findings are confirmed in the **UN World Economic Survey 1985**.

Short and Mid-Term World Prospects

All these indications of the behaviour of the industrial market economy countries, again with the exception of Japan, explain why in a wide range of international organisations, from the bastions of traditional neoclassical wisdom (the World Bank, the OECD and GATT) to the various agencies and regional commissions of the United Nations, concern increases over the economic future of the industrialised North. This

concern is reflected in less dynamic forecasts of growth
rates for the world economy not only for the rest of the
1980s but for the 1990s as well.

Moreover, it has become clear that, for structural reasons
(this term was absent just five years ago from the vocabulary
of the neoclassical economists and the institutions such as
the World Bank, the OECD and GATT), the last economic boom in
the United States did not make out of this country a suitable
longer-haul 'locomotive' for development in other industrialised countries, and that there are no candidates to take upon
themselves the US role. A growing number of experts in
international organisations are more and more of the opinion
- expressed in 'alternative' economic and financial scenarios
- that nothing is certain any longer in the short and middle
terms, and that we cannot exclude the possibility that
things will get worse before they get better. The
question of a possible date for the beginning of a longer-
term improvement is passed over in silence, and there is an
implicit rather than explicit reasoning that the uncertainty
and complexity of all kinds of events make it impossible to
foresee the future, even in the short term.

One may conclude this part of the analysis with the
following general forecast: the Western European economies
will be the most affected by the persistence in the more and
more complicated world of conventional economic policies
focussing on the supposed danger of inflation, even if they
achieve the objective of 'monetary stability' (6 per cent
average annual inflation). In the six major member countries
of the EEC, stagnation between 1984 and 1990 will express
itself in GNP annual growth rates equal to the ones during
1975-1983 (2.0 - 2.5 per cent) and in the persistence of
unemployment of over 10 per cent of the labour force (6.8 per
cent between 1975 and 1983). This will happen despite (or
rather, because of) the 'heroic' efforts to cut budgets and
public spending in the EEC; cuts in fiscal deficits from 5
per cent of the GNP in 1983 to 4 per cent in 1990, and in
public spending from 50.5 per cent of the GNP in 1983 to 49
per cent at the end of the decade. The 'stagflation'
predicted in Europe will have an additional cost: it seems
that Western Europe will continue to lose world markets for
its manufactured goods, to Japan in particular, as a
consequence of high public spending, lack of flexibility in
labour markets and delays in the adoption and spread of new
technology which are a drawback to the competitiveness of
European manufacturing, and will continue to be so at least
until 1990. After that date - as in any fairy tale situation
- the situation might well get better to some extent, unless
the US economy runs into a very deep economic crisis before

the end of the 1980s. If this should happen all the bets in favour of the slow recovery of the industrial market economies sometime before the end of the present century would be off.

Apart from the case of the United States examined at the beginning of this section, Japan is the only industrial market-economy country whose economic prospects appear excellent despite the last three years of relative slowing in growth rates. According to the estimates of the Economic Planning Agency in that country, its GNP grew somewhat over 5 per cent in 1984, as a result of a 10.3 per cent growth in manufacturing industry, 8.5 per cent in private investment, 3.6 per cent in personal consumption, 4 per cent in housing, and 1.7 per cent in public spending. Inflation rates dropped once again (to 0.6 per cent in wholesale prices, and 2.6 per cent in consumer prices). The current account of the balance of payments showed in 1984 a surplus of $33 000 million, $10 000 million more than in 1983. All these figures considerably exceeded official projections made in early 1984 and have allowed Japan to free itself to a certain extent from its restrictive import and foreign capital policies. In other words, the Japanese economy is in no danger of a sclerosis of the kind prevalent in Europe, even though it forms part of the industrialised North. Bearing in mind that, in overall terms, Japan's economic policies have for several decades run completely contrary to those of Western Europe, it is easy to come to the conclusion that the so-called 'eurosclerosis' foreseen for the rest of the 1980s is a result of internal policies rather than of the world economic situation. The fact that because of the absence of excessive military spending on technologicallybackward stagnant industries, Japan is not facing the three main bottlenecks observed in Europe (high public spending, a rigid labour market and relative technological backwardness) indicates to anybody not lacking in commonsense that conventional economic policies in force in Western Europe can in no way be seen as a suitable remedy to the structural problems of highly industrialised economies. Neither can the trick be done by the opposite set of conventional economic policies, known as 'Reaganomics', practiced in the United States and consisting of record high expenditures on arms, the dismantling of practically anything left from the welfare state, and the defence of the overvalued dollar exchange rate.

World Trade

Even for GATT, an international organisation which can in no way be considered a source of heterodox analysis, the current

situation and prospects for world commerce contain few
optimistic elements. GATT's report on international trade in
1983-1984[10], published in Geneva in early autumn 1984 and
based on the still partial data available for the first half
of 1984, suggested that world commerce measured in dollars
grew that year at close to 9 per cent after a very slight
recovery in 1983 and the shrinkage recorded in 1982. However,
the report emphasised that the recovery continued to be very
uneven, was due principally to US imports reflecting largely
the dollar overvaluation, and has not been propagated
internationally to the extent of previous cyclical post-war
trade recoveries. Among the various explanations for this new
phenomenon that GATT specialists offered, of particular
importance were: first, the commercial policies of the major
industrialised countries other than the United States, and
second, the fragmentation of the world market caused by the
persistent and ever-growing presence of discriminatory
protectionist measures everywhere in the industrialised part
of the world economy.

Paradoxically, even though world commerce grew in 1984 at
an unusually high rate of 9 per cent, commercial transactions
were concentrated in the exchange of manufactured goods
between industrial countries, despite the degree of discriminatory protectionism mentioned above. The extent and depth
of this can be seen, for example, in the fact that in the
last few years at least a third of the United States market
for manufactured goods has been covered by the so-called
voluntary quotas and other quantitative restrictions. The
similar proportion of exports of the developing countries to
the United States are affected by all sorts of non-tariff
restrictions. As a reflection of this state of affairs, the
international financial press started using lately, for the
first time since the 1930s, the expression: the 'American
fortress'[11].

With respect to the concentration of the 1984 recovery in
international commerce in the exchange of manufactured goods
among the countries of the industrialised North, GATT
observed that the weak response of markets for basic products
to the economic recovery of the United States and the
sustained growth of Japan can be attributed, among other
factors, to weak demand in industrial countries and high
interest rates, which constitute an additional obstacle to
the replenishment of basic product inventories. However, this
disappointing and very harmful situation for developing areas
reflected - according to GATT - changes of a structural
nature and, in particular, the fact that the economic
recovery in the United States in 1983-84 and the stagnation
of many other industrial countries was characterised by a

displacement of economic structures towards service activities. Finally, the adoption of new technologies in the dynamic modern manufacturing sector favoured processes of conservation and replacement of both energy and raw materials.

There is no doubt that the events described are seriously affecting the developing world, both the so-called newly-industrialised countries attempting to export manufactured goods to the industrialised North, and the producers of raw materials. Complete accounting of world trade became complicated by the extremely rapid growth of barter and multiple forms of so-called **counter-trade** resulting from acute financial and payment problems at the national and regional levels. GATT itself estimated that the very complicated formulas for barter which partially result in repayment with goods, as well as operations which involve chains of countries, accounted for close to 10 per cent of the value of overall world trade, that is something like $200 000 million annually. Counter-trade, which until a few years ago was almost exclusively practised in transactions between Socialist and market-economy countries, has now spread to a large part of the trade between industrialised countries and the Third World. In Western Europe there were between 250 and 300 public and private intermediary organisations and companies involved in the most elaborate and complex forms of barter. There was also a growing participation in this type of commercial transactions by the major US, British, Swiss and other banks.

Primary Commodity Trade

The cyclical recoveries of the world economy in the 1960s and 1970s were accompanied by a more than proportional recovery in prices for raw materials. For example, while industrial production in OECD countries rose 7 per cent from October 1972 to March 1974, international indices for prices of raw materials (with the exclusion of oil) rose 97 per cent. In the two years of most rapid growth in the industrial economies during the 1970s (from mid-1975 to mid-1977) industrial production in OECD countries rose 15 per cent, and the price indices for raw materials 59 per cent. However, there was no such trend in 1983-1984. In the summer of 1984, when the United States economy was growing at an annual rate of 7.5 per cent, the Japanese economy at 5 per cent, and the European one at nearly 2.5 per cent, the international indices for prices of raw materials, after a slight recuperation in 1983, dropped considerably from the levels recorded in May 1984. The average drop recorded was of the order of 8 per cent. The prices of eight raw materials fell 10 per cent, coffee prices 10 per cent, cotton 14 per cent, sugar 24 per cent and prices of various metals at even higher percentages. The drop in primary commodities prices has continued ever since.

The agricultural products sector offers a disastrous perspective primarily because of increased supply in North America and Western Europe, rather than as a result of a drop in international demand. The metals sector shows a similar situation, in this case because of a widespread drop in demand due to changing technology. To appreciate the magnitude of this latter phenomenon, it should be noted that, according to very recent studies by the OECD, the use of copper per unit of the GNP has dropped 20 per cent since 1973, the use of nickel 30 per cent and tin 40 per cent. Even aluminium, which in the 1960s substituted for many traditional metals on the international market, has been a victim of technological change. A quarter of all the aluminium sold presently on the US market originates from recycled aluminium.

The World Hydrocarbons Market

The situation prevailing in the raw materials market has its counterpart in the growing uncertainty of international trade in petroleum crude and petroleum products, which together represent over a third of world trade. The oil market is in a state of extremely fragile equilibrium, given the constant reduction in demand in the industrialised economies of the North and the growing supply in producing countries, the list of which is lengthening all the time. The defence of oil prices organised by the OPEC member countries is crumbling, despite their recent decisions to further reduce crude production and exports which have been more and more displaced by oil producing outside the OPEC area. The refining and petrochemical industries are experiencing a deep crisis at a world level, and the entry of Middle East and North African countries into these two fields creates further complications in the oil market. While there is no reason to share the philosophy of the International Energy Agency (IEA), made up of the major oil importers among the market-economy industrialised countries, its executive director, Helga Steeg, was correct in her statement that OPEC's decisions in late 1984 and in early 1985 to cut back exports by close to 20 per cent did not solve the problem of the growing imbalance between supply and demand for this major energy source.

The additional declines in crude oil prices, will no doubt create serious difficulties for the world economy on various counts. First, the developing oil-producing countries, including Saudi Arabia, are beginning to feel the negative effects of difficulties observed in the market concerning their plans for development and capital goods imports. The possibilities for Latin American oil exporters to overcome their financial crises, largely related to the size of their foreign debt, are becoming more and more uncertain. Finally, despite the fact that the probable drop in international oil prices could improve somewhat the trade position of the industrialised countries which are net importers of this hydrocarbon, such gains will possibly be nullified by reductions in their export trade with the oil-producing sector of the world economy.

International Financial Problems

The extreme degree of instability in the international financial system has increased even more in 1984 and the first half of 1985, because of the complete lack of interest on the part of the United States and some of its industrial allies in reforming the statutes and policies of the IMF and increasing the World Bank's resources. On the eve of the annual meeting of the Bank and the Fund in September 1984, the so-called Group of Ten (which in fact has eleven members, given the recent incorporation of Switzerland) issued a communique expressing their full support for the continuation of the particularly strict policies of the IMF with respect to financial aid for the Third World. The eleven most important industrial market-economy countries agreed also that aid from the Fund to its members should be gradually reduced in the course of the next few years. The only concession of the Group of Ten to developing countries, obviously dictated by tactical reasons and void of real content, was the British proposal calling for a special meeting of finance ministers in spring of 1985 to examine long-term attitudes with respect to the Third World's debt and the part played by international financial institutions in settling it[12]. The meeting did not result, however, in any measure alleviating the financial problems of the developing world.

In other words, all the proposals contained in the long memorandum issued in Washington in September 1984 by the Group of 24, which represents developing countries belonging to the Bank and Fund, have been roundly rejected. The memorandum of the Group of 24, entitled **The Revised Program of Action**, expressly requested a significant distribution of special drawing rights among needy countries, given the burden of their external debt. Furthermore, after a fundamental criticism of IMF practises in the renegotiation of underdeveloped countries' external obligations, practises which cause these countries to live in a succession of crises, the Group's document laid out a detailed programme for the reorganisation of the international financial and monetary system, including the Bretton Woods agreements which gave rise to the creation of both the World Bank and the IMF in 1945[13]. The document pointed out, **inter alia**, the basic asymmetry between the programmes of readjustment indicated to the poor countries by the Fund, on the one hand, and on the other, the policy of the United States which continues to increase in every way possible its own domestic and foreign debt.

The external financial situation of underdeveloped and indebted countries is becoming progressively more difficult as a result of the drastic reduction in the flow of private capital towards their part of the world economy during 1984, as confirmed by the statistics of the Bank of International Settlements in Basle, and the parallel, and no less severe, restrictions on the Third World's access to foreign public financial resources, both bilateral and multilateral, and to foreign private capital. This phenomenon, affecting particularly Latin America, has been reported in detail by the international financial press[14].

However, behind this sharp confrontation of the Group of Ten with the Group of 24 within the context of the World Bank and IMF, certain cracks seem to be appearing in the united front of the industrialised Northern countries. One can speak, in general terms, of a secondary confrontation between the hard-line coalition comprising the IMF and the US Government, and some West European countries sharing a more reasonable stance of the World Bank.

The literature on the international problem of foreign debt, both of developing countries and some industrialised, market-economy ones, including the United States, is so abundant that it will not be dealt with here[15]. One may merely mention that in debt renegotiations, both those which have been concluded and the much more numerous ones which are still underway, the basic problems have not been tackled - as is emphasised in the document prepared by the Group of 24 for the 1984 meeting of the World Bank and IMF. The current burden of servicing renegotiated debt - the major payments of the principal having been postponed to a large extent until the 1990s - involves the net transfers of financial resources to the creditor countries between 1984 and 1990 on account of accrued interest. Such transfers, almost equal to the debt itself, are a cause for serious doubt concerning the ability of indebted countries, not only to pay off their debt presumably before the year 2000, but even to keep up annual interest payments. It is not by chance that, in such circumstances, private banks, particularly those in the United States, keep reassessing constantly outstanding renegotiated debts and consider them to be progressively more uncertain.

In Latin America, the concrete cases of Argentina and Peru may be mentioned among others in this respect. Both the World Bank and independent specialists, as well as a growing number of private bankers, are coming to a simple conclusion, the discovery of the obvious: that perhaps the only way to solve the problem of international debt is to assure higher rates of growth in the Northern industrial economies for the rest of this century. But, as has already been seen, there is convincing evidence that such behaviour by the industrialised economies between 1985 and 2000 is highly improbable. Nor can solutions to the major economic and financial problems of the Third World be found in domestic development attempts, regional economic integration, or increased South-South economic relations. But while a world economic crisis seems inevitable, it is impossible to predict its date[16].

Conclusions

The global economic and financial negotiations within the UN between the industrial market-economy countries and the Third World have registered no progress at all for several years; there is no doubt that the United States does not want to make, nor will make during the rest of the 1980s, any concession to developing countries which does not reflect the philosophy of 'Reaganomics' incorporated in Reagan's project of 'aid' for Caribbean development, almost forgotten barely two years after being presented. In such conditions, a short summary of the 1983-85 negotiations between the EEC and the 66 countries of Africa, the Caribbean and the Pacific (ACP) in relation to the Third Lomé Convention will give a very clear idea as to what the peripheries of world economy can expect from the industrialised North during the next five to ten years.

When the first Lomé Convention was signed in 1975, European sources considered it a unique example of **cooperation between equals** in the field of trade and finance in mutually acceptable conditions. In practice, however, as a prestigious British daily newspaper noted: 'the EEC has continued in its historical role as dominant participant because of the growing gap in levels of wealth between the developing and the industrialised countries which signed the agreement'[17].

In fact, the share of Lomé Convention countries in EEC imports dropped between 1975 and 1982 from 7 to 5.5 per cent. Even calculations based on the percentage of Community imports coming from the Third World indicate that the ACP countries' share fell during the same period from 15.7 to 13.8 per cent. This relative decrease took place despite the fact that the EEC allows duty-free access to its market for 98 per cent of ACP countries' exports.

Growth or diversification of exports from the 66 under-developed countries of Africa, the Pacific and the Caribbean which signed the Lomé Convention has failed for reasons inherent to the Convention itself. Among them are the safeguard clauses and the ground rules which, as has been proved, are much more effective commercial barriers than tariffs. While safeguard clauses have not been applied in the Lomé Convention in the strict sense of the word, their presence has led countries in the ACP group to **voluntarily** restrict their exports of numerous manufactured goods considered to be **sensitive**, such as textile products and clothes. With respect to agricultural products, which constitute the great majority of exports from the ACP countries the quantitative controls and price mechanisms of the Community are the major obstacles. The EEC has imposed very strict quotas on meat exports from the Lomé Convention member countries, while sugar sales have felt the strong effect of the need to compete in world markets against the subsidised Community sugar production[18].

These difficulties in the commercial sector have been complicated even further by others in the use of financing coming from the EEC. The EEC Commission is complaining that these resources have been applied to 'projects of Pharaonic prestige', rather than to broaden and improve the production capacity of the receiving nations. The relationship between trade and financial aid (which amounted to nearly $6000 million in 1984) is at the core of the conflict, both between the EEC and the member countries and within the EEC itself. The ACP countries consider the financial aid to be inade-quate, and complain at the same time about the restrictions on access to the market of the EEC imposed on their products. During the negotiations for the third Lomé Convention, which began in late 1983 and finished in early 1985, even before the expiry date of the second Lomé Convention (February 1985), Great Britain, West Germany and the Netherlands proposed a reduction of financial aid in favour of freer trade. France and Italy, which have an interest in per-petuating the post-colonial link between Africa and the EEC, took the opposite position, given that the ACP group countries spend most of the funds received from the Community in these two countries. When the new Lomé agreement has finally been signed, it will not satisfy any of the major groups and its impact on the economic development of the 66 recipients will be negligible at best.

The tortuous and long negotiations were not peculiar to the third Lomé Convention; similar examples can be found also in wider international circles, even if in more complicated form. The debates of the meeting of EEC finance ministers, held in Ennis, Ireland, on the eve of the 1984 annual meeting of the Bank and the IMF, constitutes a fascinating example of the growing internal conflicts in the North Atlantic region over the matter of aid to developing countries.

The EEC ministers decided to support to a certain degree some of the demands of the Third World by dissociating themselves from the **hard line** preached by the United States and the IMF against **development aid**, criticising at the same time the US policy of high-cost money. France proposed a distribution of special drawing rights by the IMF among underdeveloped debtors to increase international solvency. Along with other continental members of the EEC, France also supported the proposal to increase emergency aid to Africa. Both initiatives were vetoed by the United States, with a resulting postponement of a common front among the industrialised North Atlantic countries until the final closed-door talks in Washington, shortly before the World Bank/IMF meeting. A last-minute desire for compromise resulted in the British initiative to hold a meeting of ministers in 1985 to **study** the long-term problems of foreign debt, international monetary policy and its repercussions and complications. In this way open division between **liberals** and **conservatives** in the industrial- ised North was averted at the last minute. All important decisions were postponed in view of the threat of a US veto, and in the spring of 1985 at the ministerial meeting nothing happened.

Given that the position of the IMF and the United States **vis-a-vis** the nature of the acute international problems continues without any change, both will be to blame for the world economic crisis which seems to be drawing slowly and inexorably nearer every day.

References

1. J. Fuerbringer, 'Economic Scene - Arms Outlays and the Upturn', The New York Times, 7 November 1984.
2. The Economist, 14 July 1984.
3. The New York Times, 2 November 1984.

4. The New York Times, 24 July 1985.
5. A.C. Wallace, 'The Experts Look at the Roaring 80s', The New York Times, 14 July 1985.
6. E.S. Hyman, economist with Cyrus J. Lawrence Inc. in New York, as quoted by Wallace.
7. Various OECD studies, the 1985 Annual Report of the Bank for International Settlements and a new report by the Centre for European Policy Studies, as reported in The Economist, 15 June 1985.
8. A. Kaletsky, 'Why Germany and Japan are reluctant to take up the slack', The Financial Times, 15 May 1985.
9. Economist Intelligence Unit, The Major European Economies, 1984-1990, (Special Report no. 173, London: 1984).
10. The summary of the document International Trade 1983-1984 appeared in GATT-Focus Information Bulletin, 31, September-October 1984.
11. S. Greenhouse, 'The Making of Fortress America', The New York Times, 5 August 1984.
12. M. Wilkinson, 'Group of Ten Ends Third World Hopes', The Financial Times, 22 September 1984.
13. M. Wilkinson, 'Third World Agrees Debt Charter', The Financial Times, 24 September 1984.
14. See, for example, E.E. Martin, 'US Business Firms Don't Care to Provide What Latins Need Most: Private Capital', The Wall Street Journal, 25 June 1985.
15. Examples include W.R. Cline, International Debt: Systemic Risk and Policy Response, (Washington: Institute for International Economics, 1984); and M.S. Wionczek and L. Tomassini (eds.), Politics and Economics of External Debt: the Case of Latin America, (Boulder, Col.: Westview Press, 1984).
16. This topic is dealt with by W. Clark, (Vice President of the World Bank during the presidency of R. McNamara), in a volume which may be put in the category of very convincing 'science-fiction': Cataclysm: The North-South Conflict of 1987, (London: Sidgwick and Jackson, 1984).
17. The Financial Times, 15 October 1984.
18. For a detailed critical analysis of the Lomé Conventions see Adrian Hewitt, 'The Lomé Conventions: Entering a Second Decade', Journal of Common Market Studies, vol. XXIII, no.2, December 1984.

20 Some Implications of the International Debt Crisis

David Carlton

William Clark, prominent for his work for the World Bank and for his sympathies with developing countries, recently wrote a semi-fictional book that offers a chilling insight into the possible consequences of the international debt crisis[1]. Following somewhat in the footsteps of John Hackett (who presented a plausible scenario for a superpower conflict[2]), Clark holds that unless wiser counsels prevail in the developed countries the present crisis could culminate in developing countries repudiating their astronomical debts. This in turn could cause a collapse of the world banking and financial system and could thus trigger a world depression as formidable as that occasioned in 1929 by the Wall Street Crash. In such sombre circumstances major wars would become much more probable. However, an East-West conflict, so much feared in the past, might come to seem less likely than a North-South polarisation culminating in desperate 'kamikaze' style assaults on the developed countries by some of the less fortunate countries whose social fabric would be at risk of complete disintegration in a World Depression.

Many leaders of the Third World evidently believe (in common with Clark) that only the developed countries (and the United States in particular) have the financial muscle to prevent some such scenario becoming a possibility. Moreover, some friends of the Third World hint from time to time at the possible creation of a debtor's cartel, somewhat along the lines of the Organisation of Petroleum Exporting Countries (OPEC), to try to force through, by threats of collective debt repudiation, the adoption of a more generous attitude on the part of the International Monetary Fund (IMF) which is of course controlled and financed by the countries belonging to the Organisation for Economic Co-operation and Development (OECD).

Certainly such a threat has credibility if it is aimed at preventing the IMF simply dictating in a high-handed way the economic policies of all debtor nations; or in the unlikely contingency that the OECD nations were to insist on all debt payments (principal as well as interest) being met strictly on schedule. For in that case the IMF and the OECD would be requiring the politically impossible of many Third World governments.

On the other hand, any attempt by a debtors' cartel to seek to obtain by threats of repudiation vast amount of **new money** in the form of further loans along the lines that occurred in the 1970s would be likely to be self-defeating. For in such a case it would be OECD countries that would be being asked to undertake the politically impossible. Moreover, the threat to repudiate existing debts **for the purpose of extorting new money** (as distinct from merely rescheduling existing obligations concerning principal and interest) is probably not quite powerful enough to be likely to be really credible and hence stand any chance of being effective. The difficulty is that it is simply not open to a debtors' cartel to ensure the total collapse of the world banking system dominated by the OECD countries. To be sure, numerous banks, particularly in the United States, could be rendered technically bankrupt. But the US Federal Government (and most other OECD governments) simply could not and would not allow these major banks to go under. They would in the final analysis print the money needed to keep them afloat.

The consequences of their having to do this, however, might be quite serious - and particularly so for Third World countries. A global economic collapse as severe as 1929 seems to me to be improbable. But within the OECD higher inflation, higher real interest rates, lower growth rates and increasing protectionist measures could well result from governments having to invest large sums to prop up insolvent banks. Some OECD countries would be able to cope with such results more comfortably than others. For example, a country like Great Britain, heavily dependent on world trade and on high oil prices, would be in greater difficulties than a near-self-sufficient one like the United States. Similarly, the effect on the Third World debtors would be uneven. Oil-rich Mexico might suffer more than oil-importing Brazil. All the same, the OECD countries taken as a group would be infinitely better placed than the Third World countries taken as a group to endure the consequences of a severe global inflationary recession. That is why a threat by a debtors' cartel to try to bring about a global disaster would lack credibility if its purpose was to extract vast new loans. For the debtors' cartel itself would have the most to lose. Hence such a threat would probably be treated as a bluff by the OECD countries - at least until it was too late.

In any case nobody in Washington or Wall Street is unaware

that a debtors' cartel, like certain kinds of bees, could only use its sting once. Formal repudiation of debt would not in the nature of things be repeatable for at least a generation. And any apparent gains conceivably attainable by such a threat would surely seem small on any comparison with the long-term consequences if the threat did not work. Such consequences would presumably include having to have trade relations with OECD countries only on the basis of barter.

Some observers may argue, however, that even in the light of all the foregoing logic a debtors' cartel might nevertheless succeed in extorting vast new loans from the OECD countries, if only they could impress upon the latter their utter desperation and hence their essentially irrational resolve. In my view there is a further reason why this could not work: new money is simply not available. The world's banker of last resort - the United States - would not in practice be able, even if it so desired, to perform again the conjuring tricks which kept the world economy afloat in the immediate aftermath of the last Third World bid to force through a rapid redistribution of global wealth, namely the OPEC price rises in the 1970s.

The OPEC shocks threatened to cause great strains to some OECD states and to bring total ruin to some non-oil-producing countries of the Third World. OECD governments responded to their own internal problems by stepping up their domestic inflation - and this was kept within bounds only by the fact that in a one-off operation millions of small savers were effectively locked into low and fixed interest rates, and were thus for a period systematically robbed of their assets. But OECD governments could only keep many non-oil-producing Third World countries afloat by arranging for them to borrow vast amounts of money at low real interest rates - money they cannot realistically have expected to see repaid. The honest course would have been to have lent this money on a government-to-government basis. For it was surely in the interest of OECD governments to prevent the reduction in world trade that would have resulted, had much of the Third World not been cushioned from the effect of the oil shocks. But the government-to-government lending on the vast scale required was held to be politically impossible; electors in OECD countries would soon have turned out any government that greatly increased taxes for such a purpose. So the short term and rather dishonourable solution was to lean on the private Western banks to recycle the greatly increased revenues flowing into their coffers from those OPEC countries which had no immediate means of spending their newly-acquired wealth. Hence much Saudi money was in effect spent in the 1970s by Latin American governments (some of which enjoyed remarkable growth rates exceeding anything seen in OECD states). On balance, such Latin American governments cannot be blamed for accepting this once for all windfall - though whether it was invariably wisely spent or invested is another question which will not be be addressed here.

The important point, however, is that this was an operation that cannot be repeated. The US banks, in particular, are now in no condition to continue to on-lend assets they do not even appear to possess. Moreover, OPEC countries have now found new ways to spend their revenues (which are in any case shrinking). In short, any new money will in future have to come from OECD taxpayers or be added to the national debts of their governments (and in the US case that would now really amount to the same thing). Such new money is thus unlikely to be available in any abundance in the near future. The party would thus appear to be over.

The main question now is whether frustration at this harsh reality will lead to mutually self-defeating North-South recriminations and worse. Let us hope not. For grim as are the prospects for many Third World countries, it would be folly for them to take steps that risk worsening the recession in the OECD countries. All concerned need to pull together to try to achieve the kind of non-inflationary global growth and a rejection of protectionism that was the achievement of the statesmen of the period immediately following the Second World War. In such conditions would lie the best hope of the Third World that OECD governments would be able to appeal successfully to their populations for constructive support for the ideas enshrined, in say, the Brandt Commission Report[3]. Debt repudiation would be likely to have exactly the opposite result.

References

1. W. Clark, Cataclysm: The North South Conflict (London: Sidgwick and Jackson, 1984).
2. J. Hackett, Third World War: A Future History (London: Sidgwick and Jackson, 1978).
3. W. Brandt, 'North-South: A Programme for Survival' Report of the Independent Commission on International Development Issues, (London: Pan Books, 1980).

21 Security Expenditure and Economic Growth in Developing Countries

Nicole Ball

Introduction

In a survey of the state of the world economy in the early 1980s, the United Nations Department of International Economic and Social Affairs painted a sombre picture of conditions in the Third World. It states[1] that, in 1982,

> output failed to increase for the first time in the postwar period. During the year, the recessionary conditions in fact spread to embrace a number of the energy-exporting developing countries which, in preceding years, had been centers of growth in the world economy ... For the least developed countries and food deficit countries in general, the situation became particlarly precarious ... Despite the prospects of a mild recovery in the main industrial countries, the outlook for developing countries is bleak. A number of forces are at work that are at present restraining growth in developing countries, so that the slight improvement in the prospects for the developed market economies does not translate into a significantly better outlook for developing countries. In fact, a further decline in **per capita** output appears to be in store for a considerable number of individual countries in 1983 as well as for the group as a whole.

This situation was confirmed by the World Bank in its 1984 **World Development Report.** The Bank noted that while the recession of the early 1980s appeared to be ending for the industrialised countries, growth prospects for the Third World remained poor. Despite increases, prices for raw materials were lower in 1983 than they had been in 1979, and 'almost all developing countries faced worse terms of trade by 1983 than they had in 1980'[2].

Although the situation confronting developing countries at the end of the 1970s and in the early 1980s was particularly

213

serious, it had been evident for many years that most Third
World governments had failed to set their countries on a path
of self-sustaining economic growth. A number of reasons for
this failure have been advanced. One set of explanations
is centred around the inequality within and among countries
which prevents resources from being used in such a way that
will promote the economic well-being of all people. A second
set of explanations focus on global economic conditions:
adverse terms of trade facing many developing countries,
declining official development assistance, and increasingly
heavy debt burdens. A third set of explanations concentrates
on the ways in which governments waste resources, for example
through systematised corruption, inefficient state sectors
and military expenditure.

In determining which factors cause and perpetuate underdevelopment in the Third World, it is clearly necessary to
consider both internal and external conditions. No one factor
or group of factors can be considered a sufficient explan-
ation of the current situation facing most developing
countries. This chapter examines the role played by security
expenditure in the economic development of countries in the
Third World, and describes some of the difficulties encountered when attempting to evaluate the relative importance of
security spending in promoting and hindering economic growth
and development. The term 'security expenditure' rather than
military expenditure is used here for two reasons. First, it
includes outlays on both the armed forces and police/
paramilitary forces. Secondly, it reflects the fact that
Third World governments frequently use their military forces
to maintain themselves in power, that is to promote regime
security.

The Data Problem

The first step in accurately evaluating the relationship
between security expenditure and economic growth is to obtain
reliable data. It is well known that it can be difficult to
obtain satisfactory data for a wide variety of economic
indicators for Third World countries, and security expenditure is no exception.

A report by a group of West German researchers, presented
to the United Nations' Special Expert Group on Disarmament
and Development in 1980, pointed out that 'although there is
a general suspicion in the public and the scientific
community that, because of its political and military
sensitivity, data on the military sector might be rather
misleading if put out by governments, there is also a feeling
that 'experts' can and do produce 'good' data on the

military'[3]. In fact the 'experts' rely very heavily on data 'put out by governments' in one form or another. The main sources of security expenditure data are the International Monetary Fund (IMF), the Stockholm International Peace Research Institute (SIPRI), the US Arms Control and Disarmament Agency (ACDA) and the International Institute for Strategic Studies (IISS). Of these, the IISS is the least reliable, while SIPRI and ACDA rely increasingly on the IMF. Unlike the other sources, the IMF has devised a common definition of security expenditure to which all countries are supposed to adhere when reporting to the IMF. The IMF requests information on a broad range of expenditure from countries, defining closely what each category should include. Governments then supply the IMF with a single figure for each category which is reproduced in IMF publications.

Some of the problems associated with the statistics produced by the major sources of security-expenditure data are illustrated in Table 1 where ACDA, IMF, SIPRI, and Guyanese government figures are compared. With the exceptions of 1978 and 1979, the Guyanese government states that its figures represent actual outlays. ACDA figures are clearly the operating costs for the military forces rounded to the nearest million. Between 1967 and 1973, the IMF appears to have reported total outlays on military forces; after 1973 there is rather little similarity between IMF figures and those published by the Guyanese government with the exception of 1978. Between 1967 and 1972, SIPRI seems to have reported total spending on military forces, in some years reproducing the IMF's figures. In 1973 SIPRI appears to have reported total security expenditure.

There are two points to be made here. One is the considerable variation that exists among these four sets of expenditure data. The second is that IMF figures are supposed to include expenditure on paramilitary forces. According to the US **Area Handbook for Guyana**, the Guyanese Police Force 'is an armed semi-military unit charged with the prevention and detection of crime, the represssion of internal disturbances, protection against fire, defense of the country against external aggression, and other duties as required by the government'[4]. A large portion, if not all, of the outlays on the Police Force should therefore be included in the IMF estimates but, for most of the years surveyed here, these estimates would seem to exclude such expenditure. What this shows is that while it may be correct to be suspicious of national statistics, it is wrong to assume that the major sources of military expenditure **necessarily** portrays the situation more accurately.

It is also incorrect to assume that all Third World

Table 1. Comparison of USAID/ACDA, IMF, SIPRI and Guyanese Security Expenditure Data
(million Guyanese dollars)

Year	USAID/ACDA	IMF	SIPRI	Guyana								
				Total Security			Military Forces			Police/Paramilitary		
				Total	a	b	Total	a	b	Total	a	b
1967	na	4.1	4.8	11.2	9.6	1.6	4.3	3.1	1.2	6.9	6.5	0.4
1968	na	4.0	4.0	11.1	10.2	0.9	4.1	3.4	0.7	7.0	6.8	0.2
1969	na	4.5	4.5	12.8	12.5	0.3	4.7	4.5	0.2	8.1	8.0	0.1
1970	na	6.7	6.7	15.5	15.2	0.3	6.7	6.5	0.2	8.8	8.6	0.2
1971	na	6.2	6.1	15.3	14.7	0.6	6.1	6.0	0.1	9.2	8.7	0.5
1972	7.0	7.5	7.5	17.4	17.0	0.4	7.1	7.0	0.1	10.3	10.0	0.3
1973	9.0	10.6	22.5	22.7	21.0	1.7	10.1	8.8	1.3	12.6	12.3	0.3
1974	16.0	24.8	38.1	32.9	30.0	2.9	17.9	15.9	2.0	15.0	14.1	0.9
1975	25.0	76.4	78.9	49.6	40.3	9.3	32.7	24.5	8.2	16.9	15.8	1.1
1976	48.0	86.7	120.0	99.9	76.3	23.6	70.0	48.3	21.7	29.9	28.0	1.9
1977	39.0	61.9	77.5	67.0	58.0	9.0	47.5	38.7	8.8	19.5	19.3	0.2
1978c	43.0	44.2	65.0d	67.0	65.8	1.2	43.8	42.8	1.0	23.2	23.0	0.2
1979e	44.0	na	95.0d	67.1	65.4	1.7	40.7	39.7	1.0	26.4	25.7	0.7

a = Operating costs (personnel and operations & maintenance).
b = Capital costs (procurement and construction).
c = The figures provided by the Guyanese government are for revised estimates.
d = SIPRI estimate.
e = The figures provided by the Guyanese government are for first estimates.

For sources to the Table see p.234.

governments attempt to conceal portions of their security expenditures at all times. There can be genuine differences of opinion as to whether a given item of expenditure should be categorised as security-related. The way in which budgets are organised also frequently produces problems. Military-related construction is sometimes listed under department of public works, military pensions can be listed with state pensions for civilian personnel, loans incurred to purchase weapons are often listed under debt repayment, and so on.

It is nonetheless true that many governments do consciously understate the extent of their security expenditures. There are essentially five main mechanisms used by governments to obscure these outlays[5].

The first is double bookkeeping. It has been suggested that many governments keep two sets of budget accounts. One is to be used as the basis of published accounts and the other is solely for internal, governmental use. This allegation is, of course, extremely difficult to substantiate but should by no means be rejected out of hand.

The second mechanism is extra-budgetary accounts which involves the creation of sources of funding within a country which do not appear in the national budget. The best known example of this is Indonesia, where as much as 50-60 per cent of security spending may be financed by the earnings of military-linked enterprises[6].

The third mechanism is highly aggregated budget categories. Many developing countries, for example, Pakistan (from 1966), Bangladesh and even Botswana, provide no more than a single figure for expenditure on the armed forces. For these countries, it would be quite easy to supply a number which would represent only a fraction of the actual security spending.

The fourth mechanism is foreign-exchange manipulation whereby some portion of foreign exchange earned abroad is not entered into any government accounting system and is not repatriated. These funds are available for extra-budgetary purchases, including - but by no means exclusively devoted to - military equipment. The only occasion on which a government official has been known to state publicly that this sort of system was in operation came in May 1983 when Indian Commerce Minister V.P. Singh stated before the Indian Parliament that purchases of Soviet weapons were paid for by exporting unspecified 'special goods' which were not entered into official Indian trade statistics. Other countries suspected of using export earnings to create special accounts (now or in the past) are Iran, Ecuador, Pakistan, Chile, and Ethiopia[7].

The fifth mechanism involves military assistance. Third

World governments have received considerable inflows of resources designed to support their military efforts since the end of the Second World War. The amounts received from Western governments, and whether these transfers have taken the form of grants or loans, are reasonably well known, although repayment schedules are not. Military assistance provided by Warsaw Treaty countries or oil-exporting Third World governments is surrounded by considerable uncertainty. Saudi Arabia, Libya, Iraq, Algeria, Kuwait and possibly the United Arab Emirates have given sizeable subsidies to the military budgets of other developing countries. It is not known how much of this money has taken the form of grants and therefore should be charged to the defence budgets of the donor countries, and how much has been in the form of loans and will have to be repaid by the recipients. As mentioned above, military-related loans tend not to be listed in the specifically military portions of recipients' budgets (categories such as 'Ministry of Defence', 'Armed Forces') but in the category 'External Debt'. It is generally the case that military related loans cannot be distinguished from loans for other purposes.

The combined effect of these concealment mechanisms is that considerable uncertainty surrounds the measurement of security expenditure. The one category which is probably most consistently understated is procurement, although the presentation of highly aggregated expenditure figures allows any category of expenditure to be manipulated. In addition, military assistance can take the form of general budgetary support or be used to purchase operating and maintenance material, not just weapons. Based as they are on national government data, the figures produced by the major sources of security expenditure must therefore be treated with considerable caution.

The Effect of Security Expenditure on Economic Growth

Econometric Analyses

Many researchers have sought to produce a general theory describing the interaction between military expenditure and economic growth and development in the Third World and have turned to econometric analysis for assistance. The earliest such study[8] concluded that military spending could have growth-enhancing effects, but this study was seriously flawed and most of its conclusions must be re-evaluated. More recent and more careful econometric analyses suggest that security expenditure is inversely related to economic growth, primarily because it competes with savings and investment[9].

The usefulness of the econometric approach is actually quite limited when considering a question as complex as the relationship between security spending and growth. To understand the role played by security expenditure in individual countries, in-depth case studies are the most satisfactory approach. If, however, the intention is to produce a general theory, one case study is an insufficient base on which to build. The production of the number of case studies necessary to provide an adequate basis would involve many researcher-years of work. In addition, a researcher could easily be overwhelmed by the variety of facts presented in these case studies and fail to identify important patterns of relationships. All statistical analyses, however, face certain constraints - such as quality of data, sample size, choice and definition of variables - which may seriously affect the validity of their results.

Statistical analyses should never be considered a substitute for a thorough-going historical examination of the economic and political systems of individual countries and the ways in which these are affected by security spending. This is very important because even valid results will not apply to each country in the sample. A team of researchers at the Massachusetts Institute of Technology (MIT), for example, discovered a negative association between the amount of Gross Domestic Product (GDP) devoted to the security sector and the amount of GDP devoted to investment for a sample of 46 developing countries between 1952 and 1970. Only seven of the 46 countries, however, showed a significant negative relationship between the two variables and another seven showed a marginally significant negative relationship. Three countries showed a significant positive relationship and one showed a marginally significant positive relationship. Of the remaining 28 countries, twelve had non-significant negative relationships and sixteen had non-significant positive relationships. The MIT researchers commented that 'for specific countries, the cross-national results carry over as strongly as might be expected in this type of regression'[10].

What statistical analyses can do is to suggest the types of relationships that should be investigated in more detail in case studies. In this instance, the finding that a higher security expenditure-GDP ratio is associated with lower growth rates because of competition between military expenditure, on the one hand, and savings and investment, on the other, is of considerable interest. Capital is an important component of growth; many have argued that it is the single most important element. If security expenditure absorbs capital that would otherwise have been used to increase productivity, to invest in production facilities or infrastructure, or to increase the quality of manpower, then security expenditure may occur at the expense of growth.

Composition of Security Expenditure

A first step in determining whether security spending competes with capital expenditure in the civil sector is to examine the composition of security expenditure. It is widely assumed that a large proportion of Third World military budgets is devoted to the purchase of weapons. This assumption has been fostered by the considerable increase in the volume and value of arms transfers to the Third World in the 1970s. It is also widely assumed that capital is allocated for the purchase of weapons from abroad at the expense of investment in the civil sector of the economy. The foreign-exchange requirements of weapons imports are particularly believed to compete with the purchase of machinery, spare parts and raw materials from abroad which are necessary to fuel the process of economic development.

In fact, operating costs (personnel plus operations and maintenance expenditures) have tended to absorb a very large share of Third World security outlays. A survey of the security budgets of 20 developing countries between 1951 and 1979 indicates that operating costs accounted for, on average, between 70 and 90 per cent of all security spending. Where it was possible to disaggregate operating costs satisfactorily, it was not uncommon to find personnel-related expenditure accounting for more than 50 per cent of the entire defence budget[5].

As mentioned above, it is the procurement portion of Third World security budgets that is most likely to be understated, but even if it were assumed that all countries under-reported their weapons purchases by 100 per cent each year, many countries would still devote less than 20 per cent of their total security budgets to capital expenditures of all kinds (procurement plus construction). The arms trade is also concentrated in a relatively few countries. Data prepared by ACDA indicated that nearly 60 per cent of all arms transferred between 1971 and 1980 went to just ten Third World countries, while the 20 major Third World importers accounted for nearly 75 per cent of total transfers. This means that about 90 countries imported the same amount (in terms of value) of weapons during the 1970s as the three largest Third World importers[11]. This should not be taken to indicate that even a relatively small amount of weapons imports cannot be a burden in terms of investment foregone. It does, however, make it less likely that security spending and productive investment are always in competition for the

same capital resources in all developing countries.
Furthermore, to the extent that civil-sector investments require outlays of foreign exchange, it is unlikely that reductions in military spending - which is so heavily orientated towards paying salaries and purchasing operating and maintenance material - would release a significant amount of resources which could be used for economic investment. There is, in fact, some evidence that military expenditure competes with other forms of recurrent expenditure for budgetary funds, and that both military and non-military recurrent expenditures crowd out capital spending of all kinds[12].

Beyond Savings and Investment

Much of the work on the relationship between security expenditure and economic growth and development has focussed on the availability of financial resources, specifically the association between security-related spending, on the one hand, and savings and investment rates and the availability of foreign exchange, on the other hand. This orientation has derived in part from the fact that the efficiency with which resources are used can be improved only if the resources are available in the first place, and that Third World countries tend to operate under severe financial constraints. At the same time, the need to look beyond savings and investment rates has become increasingly clear. As Keith Griffin has written[13]:

A second strand in Western thought on development has been the centrality of investment in determining the rate of growth. The key to faster growth was believed to be a rising capital-labour ratio. No matter that empirical studies show that capital formation could account for only a fraction of the rise in labour productivity, or that the effectiveness of investment (as measured by the incremental capital-output ratio) varied enormously from one country to another, if only a country could reduce consumption and raise saving and investment, growth would accelerate and all would be well. In practice, this view gave governments an excuse to squeeze the consumption of the poor and redistribute income in favour of the 'saving classes', that is the rich.

The Nature of Investment. It is not enough to ask how much investment takes place in an economy and whether security spending reduces the funds available for investment. It is also of importance to know what is being invested in and how security expenditure influences decisions of this kind. For many people involved in development since the end

of the Second World War, 'historical experience shows that a
structural transformation mainly based on industry is the
sine qua non of genuine development'[14]. This has had
several results. First, industry has been promoted at the
expense of agriculture which has severely handicapped
development in many countries. Secondly, the production
processes introduced into Third World economies have
frequently been heavily capital-intensive and have failed to
employ sufficient unskilled labour which is abundant in most
developing countries. Thirdly, the goods produced by these
countries have not necessarily been those most needed by the
majority of the people in the Third World and, in many cases,
have been destined for exports.

Given that the 'industrialisation-first' policy was
promoted by so many foreign development experts, it cannot be
claimed that the neglect of the Third World agricultural
sectors stemmed solely from the needs of Third World military
sectors. At the same time, certain Third World militaries
have strongly supported government efforts to industrialise
their countries, for example, the armed forces of Chile
and Argentina as early as the 1930s. Military-oriented
industrialisation frequently promotes the development of
industries which are heavily capital intensive and do not
produce the number of jobs or the kinds of goods required by
the majority of the population. A recent study of the effect
of military expenditure on Iranian development, for example,
demonstrated that state financing of industrial projects
shifted during the 1960s and 1970s from promotion of
traditional industries and the production of consumer foods
to heavy industry, and that to some degree this change
derived from the Shah's intention to turn Iran into a
regional power[15].

Military-oriented industrialisation need not always create
capital-intensive industries, however. In South Korea, the
textile industry received considerable impetus from orders
for military uniforms while the construction industry, an
important earner of foreign exchange at least until the late
1970s, came into being to build military installations for
South Korea and US troops, both in South Korea and in South
Vietnam. It is therefore important to evaluate the situation
for each country and industry individually, if an accurate
understanding is to be obtained of the influence of the
security sector on the kind of investment undertaken.

Efficiency of Capital Use. Just as the nature and not
merely the volume of investment is important in determining
how an economy grows, the efficiency with which invested
capital is employed must be considered. Factors such as the

lack of skilled labour, of efficient bureaucracies, or of industrial managers and the persistence of inequitable social systems, hamper efforts to use such capital resources as are available in a way which effectively promotes economic growth. In all too many cases available resources are not used efficiently, largely because of the existence of incompetent, corrupt political systems. These systems are frequently protected by military elites who gain both personally and professionally by their existence.

Consider, for example, the case of Honduras which has been ruled by the military for most of the last twenty years. The country lacks a professional civil service. This means that administrators at all levels are political appointees and that government jobs are regularly rotated in order to repay political supporters. It has been reported that the entire technical staff of the Honduras National Agrarian Institute was replaced three times in 1982 and 1983. In late 1983, 200 tonne of milk donated by the European Economic Community to Honduras for use in school nutrition programmes disappeared. The Honduran National Corporation for Investment was so riddled with corruption that it was forced to declare bankruptcy in the early 1980s[16]. Far from combatting these problems, members of the armed forces are busy ensuring that they and their families benefit from the system.

The fate of the NDC is strongly reminiscent of that of Thailand's National Economic Development Corporation (NEDCOL) in the late 1950s. NEDCOL was established in 1954 and was administratively subordinate to the Ministry of Defence. The Minister of Finance was closely affiliated with General Phao, the Director-General of the Police. When a **coup d'etat** ousted Phao's patron, in 1957, it was discovered that less than half the funds allocated to NEDCOL had actually been used for investment purposes. The remainder had disappeared. The belief is that these funds were used to keep Phao's political clique together[17]. This sort of activity has been repeated innumerable times since 1950. Widespread, institutionalised corruption is by no means limited to Thailand or Honduras. Nor is it limited to countries in which the military govern. It is nonetheless true that few military governments have done much to eliminate political and economic corruption (although many have come to power promising to do so) and most have done much to entrench it further. In countries suffering from capital shortages, the wastage engendered by the persistence of institutionalised corruption is a serious impediment to the attainment of self-sustaining growth.

It is frequently claimed that training received in the course of military service contributes to economic growth and development by increasing the amount of skilled manpower available in Third World countries. Where the actual experience of countries has been examined, it is clear that the anticipated positive effects of military training for the civil economy have thus far been largely illusory. Many of the jobs for which military personnel are trained do not have civil-sector counterparts. In South Korea, for example, 40 per cent of the 144 job specialities for enlisted men have no civil-sector equivalents[18]. Where civil counterparts exist, personnel are often unable to find jobs which enable them to use these skills upon leaving the military. Furthermore, the military can be a heavy consumer of skilled labour itself. Far from providing trained manpower for the civil economy, the Iranian armed forces, for example, had to import thousands of foreign tehnicians during the 1970s. The armed forces in countries such as Iran and India provide conscripts with special pre-release vocational training courses in skills such as carpentry, plumbing and welding, but these are not part of normal military training and reach very few people. In Iran prior to the revolution, some 250 000 men (equivalent to 2 per cent of the labour force) moved through the armed forces every two years. According to official Iranian statistics, only 3 per cent of them took part in the three-month elementary vocational training programmes offered by the armed forces[19]. Military training would thus seem to have a rather limited effect on the efficiency with which capital is used in developing countries.

Aggregate Demand. The one way in which it is generally agreed that security expenditure can stimulate economic growth is by increasing aggregate demand. Any item of public expenditure can be expected to increase aggregate demand irrespective of its military or non-military character, if the economy is operating at less than full capacity. Researchers at MIT have summarised the aggregate demand argument as follows[20]:

A military twist on the basic Keynesian model is the most cogent argument in support of a positive impact of increased arms spending on growth. In an economy with excess production capacity, increased aggregate demand from the military or any other source will drive up output, capacity utilisation and (under plausible assumptions) profit rates. Investments may respond to higher profits, increasing to put the economy on a faster long-term growth path.

If a large portion of security expenditure were to procure

equipment and services from abroad, the effects of aggregate demand would be minimised. In most developing countries, however, a substantial part of the defence budget is used to pay salaries and to purchase operating and maintenance material. To the extend that salaries are used to purchase domestically-produced goods and the operating and maintenance material is not imported, security expenditure will stimulate the domestic economy.

Not all salaries are used to consume locally-produced goods, however. In Iran during the 1970s, foreign technical personnel tended to command high salaries and to consume imported products. The same pattern of consumption might be expected for domestic military elites in many developing countries. Other expenditure categories show similar variations between the purchase of domestic goods and imports. The effect of military-related construction on aggregate demand in Iran during the 1970s, for example, was both positive and negative. Construction of facilities for Iranian troops employed local materials and construction skills. Construction of major bases and installations was contracted out to foreign companies and much of the funds was used to import materials and skills. Similarly in Nigeria large-scale military construction during the 1970s stimulated both investment in the domestic cement industry and massive imports of cement[21]. It should also be pointed out that Nigerian imports of cement involved considerable corruption. A satisfactory estimate of the aggregate-demand-inducing effects of security expenditure thus requires a detailed knowledge of what the armed forces buy with the money allocated to them.

Inflation. Although the relationship between security expenditure and inflation is the subject of continual debate, it is generally agreed that such expenditure can contribute to inflationary pressures in an economy. There are essentially three channels through which the inflationary tendency of security spending can make itself felt. To the extent that security outlays are used to make purchases from the domestic economy, they may combine with civil-sector demand to create shortages of particular industrial inputs. The costs of production are thus raised and, with them, the general level of prices. If wages and salaries in the security sector tend to be higher than those in the civil sector, they may also contribute to inflationary pressures by helping to push up wages in the latter faster than productivity. Finally, it has been suggested that security expenditure has historically contributed to inflation by leading to a growth in the money supply without a corresponding increase in output. Where it increases budget deficits, security spending promotes inflation because deficits which are financed by means other than borrowing from the non-bank public expand the money supply[22].

Security expenditure is, of course, not the only portion of the government budget which can have inflationary effects. Non-military government outlays which cause bottlenecks in the manufacturing sector, allow wages to rise faster than productivity, and resulting uncompensated budget deficits can contribute to inflation. Various corrective measures can be applied to mitigate the inflationary effects of any portion of government spending, for example reductions in expenditure in other sectors of the economy. But these are not always applied or do not always succeed.

When examining the experience of individual countries, it is frequently possible to conclude both that security-related expenditure contributes to inflation and that such expenditure is only one of several inflation-inducing factors. It is often difficult to determine which element or elements are most important in this respect. The effect of inflation on economic growth depends, in turn, on still other factors, such as the rate of inflation or the existence/non-existence of demand constraints on growth. In Peru, for example, inflation is caused by the interaction of numerous internal and external factors. The domestic ones appear to have been most important in the 1970s, particularly high government spending to which military expenditure contributed. The rapid increases in Peruvian military spending between 1971 and 1975 are said to have been very important in producing the relatively high (for Peru) rates of inflation experienced in 1977-1980. Nonetheless, there are so many other potential contributory factors to Peruvian inflation that it is difficult to determine to what **degree** security expenditure has stimulated inflation[23].

Balance of Payments: Trade and Indebtedness. Foreign exchange is often in short supply in developing countries, and that which is available frequently must be apportioned among competing requirements. Over the last decade, the non-oil exporting developing countries have faced an increasingly difficult external payments situation. Deficits on current account increased six-fold between 1970 and 1980 for these countries as a group. For most of them, the largest increases occurred following the oil-price rises of 1973-1974 and 1979. Third World indebtedness grew rapidly during the 1970s and early 1980s and the debt-servicing burden has accordingly grown more onerous for a greater proportion of the developing countries over the last decade. This combination of negative trade balances and heavy debt-servicing charges has produced an external payments crisis which has affected the growth potential of many developing economies.

Many countries are currently unable to import machinery, spare parts and raw materials necessary to keep their industrial sectors functioning at full capacity. It has been estimated, for example, that in early 1984 industry in Mozambique was operating at approximately 15-20 per cent of capacity, while Tanzanian industry was believed to be operating at about 20 per cent of capacity. Other countries in Asia and Latin America suffer similar problems[24].

In view of the rise in the security expenditure of developing countries over the last two decades, especially the sharp increases in arms imports for some of them, and the decline in security-related grants, it is sensible to ask whether there might not be some link between outlays on the security sector and the external payments problems in specific countries. Raju Thomas believes, for example, that the major constraint imposed by India's defence spending (particularly on modern weapons and the development of an indigenous defence industry) is the reduction of foreign exchange available to the civil sector of the economy[25].

Unfortunately, shortcomings in available arms-transfer statistics make it difficult, although not impossible, to address this question in an entirely satisfactory manner. One problem is that it is not clear if arms transfers are included in international trade statistics. Another problem is that the prices assigned to weapons in arms-transfer statistics (for example, those of ACDA and SIPRI) do not reflect the actual cost of the weapons to the purchaser. In addition, the estimated value of a transaction is recorded for the year in which the weapons are delivered, not when payments are in fact made and payments are frequently spread over a period of many years[26].

Increased military expenditure and arms procurement can be reflected in a country's trade balance in a variety of ways. On the import side, increased security-related imports could reduce civil-sector imports but allow the overall import level to remain stable, reduce civil-sector imports but cause the overall import level to rise, or stimulate civil-sector imports and cause even larger increases in the overall import level. In order to evaluate the effect of rising security-sector imports on economic growth, it is also important to know what kinds of goods are not imported when demand from the armed forces increases.

There are two main ways in which security expenditure and arms imports might interact with a country's exports. The most frequently mentioned relationship is that increased arms imports cause exports to rise, since money must be earned to pay for the weapons. A second possibility is that export capacity is reduced by previous arms imports or military expenditure which reduced state-financed investment. Most attention has been focussed on the first relationship, and there is some evidence that higher levels of security expenditure and arms imports are associated with increased exports over the long term. This is particularly true for the 1970s[27].

It is difficult, however, to disentangle the effects of rises in security-related imports and security spending from general economic trends which affect the capacity of developing countries to import and their need to export. For example, a deterioration in developing country terms of trade means that civil-sector imports will decline irrespective of the level of security-related imports. If commodity prices rise, the export earnings of the Third World will rise as well, regardless of the level of weapon imports.

It is likely that for most countries, at most times, these general economic conditions are more influential in determining the volume and value of Third-World imports and exports than are security-expenditure and arms imports. Nonetheless, for particular countries during specific periods, the desire to increase expenditure in the security sector has influenced import and export policies. In Iran, for example, the emphasis in foreign economic policy changed from import substitution to export promotion in the late 1960s. Iranian economic planners have claimed that this shift was the direct result of Iran's rising arms imports[28].

The most commonly discussed causes of the sharp rise in the debt burden carried by developing countries which occurred in the late 1970s are negative trade balances and deficits on current account, declining official development assistance, rising interest rates, the strength of the US dollar, and the hardening of terms for new loans contracted to cover debt-servicing. Despite the growth of the arms trade with the Third World and the decline in security-related grants (which parallels the decline in official development assistance) during the 1970s, no detailed analysis has been made of the role played by the security sector in the debt problems facing developing countries. While the vast majority of the major weapons transferred to the Third World during the 1970s went to a relatively small number of countries, it stands to reason that the security-related portion of debt has increased and will continue to do so in the foreseeable future.

A serious impediment to an accurate evaluation of the

effect of the arms trade on Third World indebtedness is the absence of valid data on the cost of weapon imports to individual countries. Although Western countries may have well-established rules governing the terms under which sales are made, exceptions to these rules are not unknown and security-related debts are sometimes written off. The value of East-bloc arms transfers can only be estimated roughly. Furthermore, while military assistance has been curtailed by many major donors in recent years, it has by no means disappeared. To take but one example, Morocco bought a large amount of weapons in the latter half of the 1970s for its war against the Polisario guerrillas in the Western Sahara. According to the US Agency for International Development, 'Middle Eastern countries' have paid for many of these weapons[29]. The terms of this financing are completely unknown.

Although security-related purchases may engender increased borrowing on the part of Third World countries, there are many other reasons why these countries have contracted the debts they currently hold. Between 1974 and 1978, for example, Peru imported some $1 billion worth of arms ($650 million of which came from the Soviet Union). The effect of these purchases on the distribution of Peruvian public-sector borrowing was to increase substantially the category 'other', which includes debt related to weapons-procurement during the 1970s. Nonetheless, for the 1968-1980 period, these 'other' debts accounted for only 25 per cent of Peru's total public debt. Nearly half of its public indebtedness had been incurred to finance investment[30].

It stands to reason that as the terms for weapons sales become harder, and the more weapons a country buys, the more it has to ensure financing out of its own pocket. If export earnings are not sufficient to cover the costs of imports, military and civil-sector, and if grants or low-interest subsidies are unavailable for financing other categories of imports, then arms purchases will necessitate increased borrowing and will burden the economy with additional debt-servicing requirements. That this is one legacy of the 1970s is clear, even if detailed data are still unavailable. At the same time, it is clear that even with major arms, buyers have not borrowed simply or even primarily to cover purchases of weapons. Weapons-related borrowing will come to play an increasingly important role in the debt profile of many Third World countries, but it cannot be blamed for the totality of the debt crisis which emerged in the late 1970s.

Security Expenditure and Political Development

There is sufficient evidence from both case studies and

macrostatistical analyses to support the contention that expenditure on the security sector is more likely to hinder than to promote economic growth in the Third World. At the same time, in view of the large number of factors which determine the success with which a country develops, security expenditure cannot be seen as the sole cause of underdevelopment. Nor does it only affect growth prospects negatively. Its exact effect varies from country to country and over time within countries. For most countries, at most times, security expenditure is more the symptom of a deepseated malaise than the illness itself.

The primary cause of underdevelopment remains inequalities among and within countries. Throughout the Third World, armed forces have become important both as mediators between different élite groups and as guarantors of élite-dominated political systems. The developmental effects of the concentration of political and economic power in the hands of a small élite - be it composed of wealthy landowners, industrialists, transnational corporations, state bureaucrats, military officers or communist parties - are more likely to be negative than not. Geoffrey Barraclough has commented[31]:

> There is now agreement across a wide political spectrum that the 'central development problems for most LDCs are internal', or, as the Algerian minister of industry and energy has put it, that 'the real solution of the development problem lies in the capacity of each of the developing countries to mobilize its resources and energies'.

That the concentration of economic and political power in the hands of a few is not the best recipe for the mobilisation of a country's 'resources and energies' for self-sustaining socio-economic development is evident from the experiences of most Third World countries over the last 30 years. Rather, it is an open invitation for the few - distinguished by characteristics such as class, ethnicity, religion, occupation - to exploit the many. (Most Latin American countries, of course, offer a 150-year example of these points).

In a situation such as this, the single most important effect of security expenditure is to strengthen the armed forces at the expense of civilian groups within society. The greater the political power of the armed forces, the more difficult it is to effect change not approved by them. Most armed forces support the continuation of élite-dominated political systems rather than their replacement by more participatory forms of government, because they believe they stand to gain more, both personally and professionally, from the former. The perpetuation of élite-dominated systems reduces the likelihood that a participatory political system, responsive to the needs of all citizens and not just a small proportion of them, will ever be created. The lesson taught by élite-dominated systems is that government exists primarily to fulfil the needs of those in power. Such attitudes can be changed with sufficient pressure from the mass of the population, but only over the long term and not if the armed forces constantly intervene.

If security expenditure were to decline sharply, the security sector to be substantially reduced in size, and the armed forces to leave the political arena, this would in no way guarantee that development prospects would improve immediately for most Third World countries. There are too many examples of inefficient and corrupt civilian governments to warrant such an optimistic conclusion. Yet, the removal of the armed forces from politics is a necessary first step for the initiation of genuine development which will benefit all members of society.

References

1. United Nations, Department of International Economic and Social Affairs, World Economic Survey, 1983: Current Trends and Policies in the World Economy, E/1983/42, ST/ESA/131 (New York, 1983) pp.1,4,8.
2. World Bank, World Development Report, 1984, (New York: Oxford University Press, 1984) p.26.
3. M. Brzoska, P. Lock, R. Peters, M. Reichel, and H. Wulf, 'An Assessment of Sources and Statistics of Military Expenditure and Arms Transfer Data', IFSH-Study Group on Armaments and Underdevelopment, (University of Hamburg, mimeo, 1980) p.1. The portion of this report dealing with military expenditure is summarised in M. Brzoska, 'The Reporting of Military Expenditures', Journal of Peace Research 18:3 (1981) pp.261-75.
4. W.B. Mitchell et al, 'Area Handbook for Guyana' (Washington D.C: US Govt. Printing Office, November 1969) pp.338-9.
5. For a more detailed discussion see Nicole Ball, 'Measuring Third World Security Expenditure: A Research Note', World Development 12:2 (February 1984) pp.157-64, or Nicole Ball, 'Third World Security Expenditure: A Statistical Compendium', FOA Report C 10250-M5 (Stockholm: National Defence Research Institute, 1984) pp.15-19.

6. H. Crouch, 'Generals and Business in Indonesia', Pacific Affairs 48 (Winter 1975-76): pp.519-40; D. Jenkins, 'The Military, Secret Cache', Far Eastern Economic Review (8 February 1980) pp.70-2; and A. Rieffel and A.S. Wirjasuputra, 'Military Enterprises', Bulletin of Indonesian Economic Studies (July 1972) pp.104-9.
7. On India, see 'To Buy or Not to Buy', Far Eastern Economic Review (2 June 1983) p.30. On Iran, see Ann Schulz, 'Military Expenditures and Economic Performance in Iran, 1950-1980', (Worcester, Mass: Clark University 1982, mimeo) pp.40-1,43.
8. E. Benoit, Defense and Economic Growth in Developing Countries, (Lexington, Mass: Lexington Books, 1973). For a critique of the Benoit study, see Nicole Ball, 'Defense and Development: A Critique of the Benoit Study', Economic Development and Cultural Change 31 (April 1983) pp.507-24.
9. R. Faini, Patricia Arnez and L. Taylor, 'Defense Spending, Economic Structure & Growth: Evidence Among Countries and Over Time" (Cambridge, Mass: Massachusetts Institute for Technology, mimeo, October 1980), and S. Deger and R. Smith, 'Military Expenditure and Growth in Less Developed Countries', The Journal of Conflict Resolution 27:2 (1983) pp.335-53.
10. R. Faini, Patricia Arnez and L. Taylor, op. cit and personal communication from L. Taylor to Nicole Ball, 23 March 1984.
11. US Arms Control and Disarmament Agency, World Military Expenditure and Arms Transfers 1971-1980, Publication 115 (Washington, DC: March 1983) Table II. ACDA data are used here in preference to SIPRI data because the former are more inclusive. SIPRI figures are limited to transfers of major weapons. Both SIPRI and ACDA data show similar levels of concentration.
12. For a survey of 32 countries, see N. Hicks and Anne Kubisch, 'Cutting Government Expenditures in LDCs', Finance & Development (September 1984) pp.37-9. For the specific case of Upper Volta, see R. Vengroff, 'Soldiers and Civilians in the Third Republic', Africa Report, 25 (January-February 1980) pp.7-8.
13. K. Griffin, 'Economic Development in a Changing World', World Development 9 (March 1982) p.224.
14. A.F. Ewing, 'Some Recent Contributions to the Literature on Economic Development', Journal of Modern African Studies 4:3 (1966) p.341.
15. Schulz, op.cit., especially p.133.
16. A. Pine, 'Diminishing Returns: Can Central America Absorb More Aid? Lots of Experts Say No', Wall Street Journal,

(8 February 1984). See also J.A. Morris, Honduras: Caudillo Politics and Military Rulers, (Boulder, Colorado: Westview Press, 1984), esp. pp.86-105.
17. J.C. Scott, Comparative Political Corruption (Englewood Cliffs, NJ: Prentice Hall, 1972) p.71; D. Elliott, Thailand: Origins of Military Rule (London: Zed, 1978) pp.116-7; and C. Noranitpadung Korn, 'Thailand's National Economic Development Corporation Limited: An Evaluation with Special Emphasis on the Political Implications', Thai Journal of Development Administration 9 (October 1969) pp.732-45.
18. Korea University, Labor Education and Research Institute, Economic Development and Military Technical Manpower of Korea, Seoul (Korea University Press, 1976) p.36.
19. Schulz, op.cit. pp.175-6.
20. Faini, Arnez and Taylor, op.cit. p.2.
21. On Iran, see Schulz, op.cit, pp.78-9, 125-6, and 138. On Nigeria, see J. 'Bayo Adekanye, 'The Role of Military Expenditure in the Development Process: Nigeria' (Ibadan: University of Ibadan, 1983.
22. United Nations, Study on the Relationship Between Disarmament and Development. Report of the Secretary-General. A/36/356 (New York: 1981) pp.84-5.
23. J. Encinas del Pando, Economic, Military and Socio-Political Variables in Argentina, Chile and Peru (Lima: University of Lima, mimeo, 1983), pp.109, 115-16.
24. A. Singh, 'The Interrupted Industrial Revolution of the Third World: Prospects and Policies for Resumption', forthcoming in Industry and Development. The ILO report referred to by Singh is JASPA/ILO, Tanzania: Basic Needs in Danger (Addis Ababa, 1982). On Mozambique, see M. Holman, 'Why Machel is Wooing the West', Financial Times (24 April 1984). See also R. Green, 'African Economies in the Mid-1980s', pp.173-203, in J. Carlsson (ed.), Recession in Africa (Uppsala, Sweden: Scandinavian Institute of African Studies, 1983).
25. R.G.C. Thomas, The Defence of India: A Budgetary Perspective of Strategy and Politics (Delhi: The Macmillan Company of India, 1978) pp.124-35. The foreign-exchange requirements of Nigerian security expenditure are discussed in Adekanye, op.cit.
26. See for example US Arms Control and Disarmament Agency, World Military Expenditures and Arms Transfers, 1971-1980. Publication 115 (Washington, DC: March 1983) pp.127-8.
27. M. Brzoska, 'External Trade, Indebtedness, Foreign Direct Investment and the Military Sector in LDCs: A Study of the Effects of Militarization on External Economic

Relations, Working Group on Armament and Undervelopment (Hamburg: IFSH, November 1982, mimeo) pp.73-6 and 94-8.
28. Schulz, op.cit., p.138.
29. US Agency for International Development, Implementation of Section 620(s) of the Foreign Assistance Act of 1961, as Amended. A Report to Congress (Washington, DC: 1980) p.6.
30. J. Encinas del Pando, op.cit., Table 2.43.
31. G. Barraclough, 'The Struggle for the Third World", The New York Review of Books, (9 November 1979) p.53. The first quotation cited by Barraclough is part of a statement by C. Dias-Alejandro in A. Fishlow, C. Diaz-Alejandro, R.B. Fagen and R.D. Hansen, Rich and Poor Nations in the World Economy, (New York: McGraw-Hill, 1978) p.156. A Second is from Towards a New International Order: An Appraisal of Prospects, Report on the Joint Meeting of the Club of Rome and of the International Ocean Institute, Algiers, 25-28 October 1976 (Algiers, 1977) p.21.

Sources to Table 1

USAID, International Development Cooperation Agency, Implementation of Section 620(s) of the Foreign Assistance Act of 1961, as Amended, A Report to Congress, Washington, DC: various years (for ACDA data). World Bank, World Tables, 1976, (Baltimore, Md.: Johns Hopkins University Press, 1976) (for IMF data 1967-1972). International Monetary Fund, Government Finance Statistics Yearbook, vol. 5, (Washington, DC: 1981), p.336 (for IMF data 1973-1979. Stockholm International Peace Research Institute, World Armament and Disarmament, SIPRI Yearbook, (London: Taylor & Francis, 1979 1983, 1984). Guyana, Estimates, Current and Capital of Guyana as Passed by the National Assembly, various years.

22 The Emergence of Military Industry in the Third World

Renato Dagnino

Introduction

The importance of the study of the technical and economic aspects of armaments has been emphasised by M.S. Wionczek[1], who also pointed out the absence of detailed studies of the subject. Sharing his stand, the intention of this paper is to analyse the technological and economic aspects of the emergence of military industries in the Third World.

Many authors[2] have stressed the appearance, since the end of the 1970s, of three fundamental trends in the world armaments trade and production. The first is the high percentage of conventional expenditure in the world military burden, roughly 80 per cent of its total. The second is the increasing importance of military technology trade in the context of the arms trade in general. The third is that Third World countries no longer are the main buying market but increasingly are, both qualitatively and quantitatively, manufacturers and exporters.

The political consequences of this last trend on the international level have been repeatedly stressed by many authors and international organisations. Of particular importance are the risks of disrupting regional balances, the virtual impossibility of controlling the arms trade, and the social impact, associated with the misutilisation of the scarce resources available in the Third World to satisfy the real necessities of populations.

Although greatly concerned with the above general consequences, the main aim of this chapter is to call attention to the technological aspects of the emergence of military industries in the Third World. It is not my intention to present an all-encompassing approach, but only to point out some of the issues that are considered fundamental to the comprehension of the current process. An attempt will also be made to clarify some controversial or obscure topics and to offer some reflections on their possible evolution.

Main Products and Manufacturers

Many of the studies on the subject are concerned with an effective characterisation of the arms industries of the newly industrialised countries (AINICs)[3].

Table 1 gives the rank order of arms producing countries grouped according to the range and magnitude of their involvement in twelve weapon catagories namely: fighters, jets, trainers, engines; light planes, transporters; helicopters; guided missiles, rockets; major fighting ships, fast patrol boats; small fighting ships; submarines; tanks; artillery cannons; light tanks, armoured personnel carriers (APC), trucks, jeeps; electronics, avionics, optronics; small arms, mortars, bombs.

Some studies of this subject, apart from identifying AINICs structures, attempt to establish a typology that tries to obtain a set of common characteristics for them. In some cases, the appearance of these characteristics in more than two of the important countries leads them to incorrect generalisations. For example, it is being said that the largest armaments-exporting newly industrialised countries (NIC) are also the biggest importers[4]. We understand this to mean that in the process of developing AINICs, there would be a sequence of 'logical and natural' steps in a technological learning ladder: maintenance and repair would be followed by components manufacturing, licensing, and finally arriving at an indigenous technological development[5]. This may be correct as far as Israel is concerned, but in the case of Brazil, one of the main producers and the biggest major weapons exporter, it does not apply. In fact, in the 1977–81 period, Brazil was responsible for 45.6 per cent of the total Third World exports, although it is not even in the twentieth rank of the major importing countries of the region[6]. On the other hand, the constant and meticulous care shown in the Brazilian aeronautic strategy planning and implementation since 1950s (through many different governments and historical periods), striving to create a scientific and technological capability that would allow further autonomy, seems to make it doubtful that such a sequence would be generally expected[7].

Similar doubts can be expressed about other statements. It is said that the arms production costs in the Third World are almost invariably higher than those of the developed countries[8]. Although this might be true about India, it would not appear to apply to Israel[9] or Brazil. The existence of an almost absolute control by transnational corporations over the AINICs could be similarly challenged. It is difficult to view the AINICs as a homogeneous lot.

Table 1. **Rank Order of Major Arms Producing Countries**

Group	Rank Order	Country	Arms Production
I	1	Israel	diversified and
	2	India	sizeable production
	3	Brazil	
	4	Yugoslavia	
II	5	South Africa	production in most
	6	Argentina	of the twelve weapon
	7	Taiwan	categories
	8	Korea (South)	
III	9	Philippines	production in several
	10	Turkey	weapon categories,
	11	Indonesia	without substantial
	12	Egypt	capacity for indigen-
	13	Korea (North)	ous development.
	14	Pakistan	
	15	Singapore	
IV	16	Iran	isolated projects
	17	Colombia	
	18	Portugal	
	19	Greece	
	20	Peru	
	21	Thailand	
	22	Venezuela	
	23	Dominica	
	24	Nigeria	
	25	Mexico	
	26	Malaysia	
	27	Burma	
	28	Chile	
	29	Saudi Arabia	
	30	Sudan	
	31	Zimbabwe	
	32	Libya	

Source: IFSH Study Group on Armaments and Underdevelopment, Transnational Transfer of Arms Production Technology, IFSH Forschungsbericht 19. Hamburg: 1980. appendix.

But for the fact of having emergent arms industries, the relevant NICs have different development processes and experiences in both external and internal political fields. It seems correct to state that there were always political reasons behind their creation, even though, in some cases, there has been great economic influence in their growth, connected either with foreign trade gains or with some internal priority in industrial development. Even in these cases, the political backing is evident. Israel in establishing its aircraft factory in 1953, South Africa reacting to the threat of a general boycott, and Brazil asserting itself as a 'major power', with the creation of its main aircraft plant in 1969, each presents a different case. In short, differences that exist between AINICs render invalid the superficially attractive common approach.

The Evolution of the International Framework of the Arms Trade and Production: The Common Determinant Factors

Perhaps one of the few common characteristics of the AINICs is that they are all conditioned by factors that are really external to them: the evolution of the international framework of the arms trade and production, and the transfer of military technology. Although there are specific political constraints for each country, the role of the main international actor, the United States, has been an extremely important factor in the creation of AINICs. This is so because it was the ambiguous position of the United States as a competitor and an ally of West European countries that led to the establishment of one of the main channels for the creation and strengthening of the AINICs, namely the military technology transfer. Given that the performance and opportunities of AINIC expansion will tend in the future to be subordinated to this common external constraint, it is appropriate to analyse briefly the process of evolution of the international framework in the last decades.

From the 1950s, the United States began to export military technology to European countries in order to fortify the Western bloc in the Cold War context. In the case of Great Britain, and to a lesser extent France, where arms industries had not been greatly affected by World War II, this technological transfer was such that, in a very short span of time, they were able to take part in the international arms trade themselves. By the 1960s the contribution of the West European countries (mainly Great Britain, France and Italy) to the arms export to the Third World had risen to between 20 and 30 per cent, thus breaking the virtual monopoly of the two superpowers. Undoubtedly, the US need to allocate a major part of its arms production to the Vietnam war effort was also an important factor in expanding European participation in the world arms market.

In the middle of the 1970s, the United States sponsored a policy of standardisation of military equipment within NATO, which aimed at an improvement of efficiency (a 40 per cent increase was expected) and reduction of expenses (up to $10 billion was expected)[10]. In order to achieve this aim the West European countries had to produce equipment based on technology transferred from the United States. The ensuing development of the arms industry of these countries opened up the possibility of selling armaments to other regions, especially those items in which the standardisation policy gave them the biggest advantages. Although they kept importing arms from the United States, their share in the international trade grew substantially, especially in the Third World. Another opportunity resulted from President Carter's Human Rights policy and the evolution of US policy on arms transfers to the Third World. During the 1950s and 1960s, the principal instrument of US policy was the Military Assistance Programme. Subsidised supply of armaments allowed the US administration a considerable amount of control over the type of equipment, and the effective imposition on recipients of obsolescent material. From the end of the 1960s onwards - in the face of pressure from the US Congress, alienated by the Vietnam experience - military assistance policy was replaced by the Foreign Military Sales policy, and this reduced the direct US control over Third World armies. This change of policy allowed Third World countries to behave as normal buyers in a market and hence to diversify sources. They turned mainly towards France, Italy and Great Britain.

Influenced by liberal forces, the US Government stuck to its intention of trying to establish control over the flow of armaments to the Third World. This culminated in 1976 in the International Security Assistance and Arms Control Act which prohibited transfers to any country 'which engaged in a consistent pattern of gross violation of internationally recognised Human Rights'. As a consequence, Argentina and Uruguay announced that they wanted no American assistance at all. Brazil, which has been cited in the Human Rights Evaluation Report for torture of political prisoners, as well as for arbitrary arrest and detention, cancelled a 25 year old military assistance treaty, and rejected US military credits.

A direct result of this situation was that the Third World countries which favour a greater degree of autonomy in arms supply through internal production gained in strength. Arms trade contracts with countries which had less rigid policies towards arms technology transfer and co-production, created a real possibility of starting internal production.

The policy of the Reagan administration has changed the fundamental position relating to Third World countries and eliminated the main obstacles to the production of indigenous arms that existed until then[11]. Although the most immediate result may have been an increase in arms export to these countries, without any regard to human rights or regional military balances, the greater degree of freedom in technological transfers, has caused an increase in co-production of sophisticated armaments. In fact, to judge by the current evolution of US cooperation and licensing contracts, one may expect a gradual shift away from the previous predominance of the West European producers.

Future Trends

Any attempt to investigate the future development of AINICs has to be related to possible scenarios of economic and political reorganisation at the international level. The issue of technology, as it affects the dynamics of the arms sector, has to focus on the deep changes that are taking place in current developments and diffusion mechanisms. The basis of my discussion is that the conditions that have induced the creation of the AINICs will remain. Among these it is important to single out the increasing tendency of the superpowers to expand their intervention capability in the Third World through the world-wide control of arms production and trade. Even so, regional power balances in the Middle East or Latin America, for instance, could result in different impacts on the AINICs.

The recent past: the trend towards arms super-sophistication

During the 1960s and the 1970s, arms production in the United States and Great Britain was characterised by an increasing level of complexity and sophistication which brought about undesirable cost and performance consequences. According to Mary Kaldor[12], this trend led to equipment of decreasing reliability and service life, and yet demanded increasing levels of spare parts, fuel consumption, specialised manpower for operation and maintenance involving escalating costs.

In order to understand the dynamics of this trend towards super-sophistication it is necessary to consider some aspects of the arms market, and the intrinsic logic of the military as applied to the characteristics of the arms in use[13].

Consider the case of the United States, one of the biggest arms producers. Its armaments market is controlled by huge oligopolistic companies that frequently specialise in the development and production of weapon systems on order from the armed forces. There is a single buyer, the government, which buys on a budget and not on what is **necessary** to fulfil defence requirements. The development of a given weapon system in contracted through the cost plus system, that is, the profit of this activity is calculated as a proportion of the actual final cost. This kind of project usually has a span of years which gives the producers a measure of security in their operations once they have obtained the contract. The competition is not through prices, but through the product performance. The companies specialise in a given type of weapon and - with almost non-existent external competition - this makes the behaviour of the market even more atypical. These elements constitute an environment favourable to the practice of administered prices, in which the R&D component is the most likely to be increased, which in turn leads to super-sophistication.

It is understandable that there exists among the military a somewhat obsessive worry about the performance of the weapons they use. Besides security, their prestige is involved. Their professional competence is as highly valued as their equipment is sophisticated.

The basic configuration of armaments did not suffer radical changes during the 1960s or the 1970s. Those changes that did take place were marginal and yet were expected to produce considerable improvements in performance (which did not actually happen). Sophisticated microelectronic-based emergent technologies were introduced in land, naval and air platforms, leading to a range of products that combined considerable conservatism in design with an enormous nominal (expected) destructive potential.

The current situation: the trend to exploitation of a microelectronics base

There are two trends in the arms production of the major countries that are related to different conceptions of future war. This section will address the first of them, namely the 'exploitation of the microelectronics base'. On the surface, this trend would appear to be a continuation of the super-sophistication of previous decades, since it is also centred on the joint use of traditional weapon platforms and microelectronics-based equipment. Actually, however, it should be understood as the counter-trend to super-sophistication. This is because, instead of producing low-efficiency high-cost equipment, it allows the building of intelligent weapons, which are more suitable to actual conflict situations. The reversal of the previous trend was possibly due to the maturation of the technologies earlier introduced into arms production. Having originated in the R&D military sector as a result of massive concentration of resources, they failed in their immediate applications. After the transfer to the civilian sector, and further research, the technologies had the opportunity to mature, and be successful upon the return to arms production. It seems that the improvement of the set of innovations centred on microelectronics technology - from the middle 1960s - was the main element in this reversal. The appearance of the microprocessor, just over ten years go, which allowed the degree of miniaturisation and reliability indispensable to the generalised use of microelectronics in weapons, illustrates the situation. It is also well known that many of the hardware improvements gain full use only as time goes by, and as more adequate software is conceived for military purposes. This indicates that the main US military R&D effort is concentrated on six major areas, all of which involve development of electronic equipment and data processing, as well as its correspponding software. These areas are: search and surveillance; target acquisition and fire control; communications; navigation; command and control; and electronic warfare.

It remains to be seen how far the large quantity of resources allocated to the R&D activities and procurement of this new generation of smart weapons will be capable of causing a reversal in the super-sophisticiation trend.

Prospects: the trend towards the exploitation of new technological frontiers

The second trend is characterised by the design of entirely new weapons. In contrast to the first trend, the many innovations in telematics are not being incorporated into the pre-existent weapon systems. For instance, while the first trend keeps the basic configuration of the current weapons platforms, the second trend assumes and demands considerably different technical solutions. According to experts' opinion, there are some weapons in their initial development stages whose innovative conception, if turned into reality, could significantly modify the characteristics of future conventional warfare.

Using the jargon of the theory of technological innovation diffusion, we could characterise this second trend as a set of technological leaps, as opposed to the first one which ould be more properly described by the concept of incremental innovations on an already consolidated technological paradigm. Beyond microelectronics and its connected areas, bio-technology - another major technological revolution whose impact is already felt in many sectors - should play a central role in this trend.

The realisation that nuclear war means the complete destruction of mankind, and the belief that it would be impossible to limit it to a given geographical area, have lead to the development of conventional weapons of near-nuclear efficiency, that 'would be more controllable than nuclear devices'.

The Implications of the Future Trends

The trends so far discussed support the new international division of labour in the military area. The role of major states is that of growing specialisation on the frontier of R&D and its applications, while the peripheral countries are restricted to the production of less technologically intensive items. This is made possible through importation (or adaptation) of these technologies by the peripheral countries. This situation could lead to a self-regenerating process of technological dependence in the military area. This would further harm the relative position of NICs, making it impossible for them to achieve real autonomy in this area, and defeating one of the very purposes that led to the creation of AINICs.

Although other authors have reached the same conclusions[14], I believe that a more accurate analysis will identify trends pointing in another direction. One of these is related to the growing scientific, technological and industrial capability of NICs, which enables them to explore the quick technological shifts, typical of the process of formation of a new paradigm. The evident need of foreign technology by the AINICs may be satisifed through the import of parts, especially those which are more technologically intensive, through licensing or co-production. In the armaments sector, in contrast to the civilian sector, the role of those companies which control technological know-how - the major transnational corporations (TNC) - is not so striking. This is so because, in this specific case, the ownership of technology is not a near-sufficient condition for market control, since the relevant issues, connected as they are to 'national security' needs, force it into a restrictive and atypical behaviour - the curtailment of the market and requisites of national control over the corporations' capital. The differentiated posture of the state leads, on the other hand, to a stronger concern about the issues of technological autonomy, and allows a much more intelligent and efficient attitude towards such matters as local R&D, import decisions, what to license and what to develop, and suppliers diversification.

The bargaining power of the TNCs which have these technologies is further limited by the increasing level of competition involved in the search for new markets, by the opportunities of paying back part of their increasing R&D costs, by co-producing at cheaper production costs, and by the current financial situation, which discourages new investments. In fact, even though the West European companies seem to be - judging by their higher ratio of exports to total production - more fragile than US companies, the growing need for export sales on the part of the latter will tend to increase the level of competition.

So one can expect from the major countries and their TNCs a more flexible posture - in the matter of technological transfer - although compatible with the new international division of labour. This is especially true about technologies connected with the 'exploitation of the microelectronics base' trend. The practice of extending the work life of the old weapon platforms, and the introduction of improved equipment such as 'precision guided munitions', is compatible with the NICs' attitude in this context. On the other hand, we can also expect a concentration of effort in R&D of the 'exploitation of the new technological frontier' trend. Even though the arms industries of the major countries will tend to maintain their super-sophistication and conservatism, they have obvious advantages vis-a-vis the NICs when it comes to incorporating microelectronics. So one can expect the major countries to maintain a good edge over the NICs, even if the latter should be the first to turn towards de-sophistication.

If we further take into account that it is exactly in the area of microelectronics that the technological bottleneck of the AINICs is situated, it becomes easy to imagine the effects of such a decomplexisation strategy upon the arms industry of such a country as Brazil, which depends for more than 80 per cent of its sales on the external market. Even though the share of AINICs in the world market is small, pressures have already been applied in respect of both technological supply and arms trade. Traditional producers try to maintain their hegemony through a number of practices. In any case, and without resorting to retaliation, a whole series of measures, such as the 'export only systems', aim at the curtailment of arms trade within the Third World. The United States, for instance, will attempt to compensate for the decrease in its share in the world arms market and its effects on the balance of payments and levels of employment. It will attempt to reinforce its position as exporter of such components as avionics and aircraft engines or their production technology.

In order to compensate for the trend towards technological sources diversification and bilateral arms trade between Third World countries, a number of arrangements tend to become established in major weapon co-production, manufacture of parts and components, either for internal use or export, as well as barter of equipment or technology for oil and other strategic raw materials.

On the other hand, the NICs can be expected to play a more aggressive role in their search for new opportunities for the acquisition of technology and co-production of equipment. This is especially the case in critical areas, such as electronics components, composite materials, computers and their software, engines, simulators and scientific equipment. We can expect thus a strategy of autonomously filling out the industrial sector linked to the arms industry, with everything that this implies for the technological, scientific and industrial capacity of certain NICs. This is contrary to what was done in those NICs, where the arms industry could be considered more properly as an enclave. Overall, this is a strategy qualitatively different from past experience, when export sales results were based mainly on exploitation of the internal preconditions and the market niche of the comparatively simpler equipment brought into existence by the super-sophistication trend[15].

Deriving from this strategy are the well-known 'national security' reasons, which can barely disguise the ambitions for regional power, the fear of political boycotts, the manipulation of public opinion, or even internal political repression.

There is also the pursuit of the technological spin-off 'mirage', or the presumed positive Keynesian effects ensuing from arms production - both currently contested by the experience of the major countries[16] - which would reinforce the adoption of that strategy.

Lastly, there is the exemplary case of some NICs. For example, Brazil was able in a short period to reduce its imports and increase substantially its arms exports, entering into a growing market apparently left untouched by the crisis.

In spite of the stimuli that this situation may provide to other Third World countries, it is improbable that horizontal spread of arms production will take place. The present trend, if it continued, would mean that, concurrently with a worldwide accelerated industrial growth some peripherical countries would change from repair and small weapons production, into weapon systems manufacturers. From now on, however, it seems more probable that the restricted number of countries that can produce some sophisticated equipment will increase the variety and volume of their production. This process of vertical diversification - possibly associated with the generalised world crisis - is much more probable.

A forecast on the trends of the AINICs would not be complete if it did not take into account future arms demands by the Third World. The absence of reliable information makes it in fact difficult to project the potential major weapons market in the Third World. Additionally, the Middle East arms escalation of recent years, coupled with the availability of resources and the maintenance of potential conflicts, renders it almost impossible to make an aggregate estimate.

However, the analysis of a region such as Latin America, which is far from experiencing an arms race[17], gives us an insight into the dimension of the potential Third World market. According to estimates made in 1980 by international consultants of US arms producers, the calculated demand for the 1980-85 period was over $25 billion worth of armaments; this seems to me to be an over-estimate. This market would break down as follows: $5 billion for almost 1000 combat aircraft; $1.4 billion for around 1400 aircraft of other types; $900 million for 800 helicopters; $600 million for 40 000 missiles; $600 million for 90 tanks; $400 million for 1300 armoured vehicles; plus 70 ships of various kinds for $14 billion. It is obvious that potential markets of this order attract arms dealers. The struggle for the markets would be conditioned by the aforementioned factors and also, perhaps decisively, by the eventual concentration of the two main exporters on the trends towards the 'exploitation of the new technological frontiers'. A qualitative change in the nature of the conventional arms race initially restricted to the R&D effort would, in fact, open the opportunities for AINICs expansion.

Conclusions

The above considerations seem to indicate that a new pattern is being established in the international arms trade and production system. This would be compatible with current and expected technological changes and the new international division of labour. The AINICs will tend to become **integrated** into it and specialised in weapon systems different from those produced by major countries. The NICs could, then, obtain some advantages in their struggle for technological autonomy in the arms sector.

Following neither a model of 'import substitution' - which would aim at a utopian independence - nor that of 'export substitution' - which would purely seek, through the diversification of its export profile, to obtain external gains - the most important Third World arms producers seem to be moving to a logic of production decisions, very similar to those of the major countries.

This process of integration presents, however, yet another heavy burden to the Third World arms producers. It adds to the ethical, social and economic restriction on it: the construction of a military infrastructure which is not adapted to actual necessities. When arms industries are built along the lines of those of the major countries, military conceptions are being moulded to respond to issues that confront the major countries. NICs thus renounce an independent and responsible approach to their defence necessitites. More than that, they refuse to face their actual economic, political and social problems[18].

References

1. M.S. Wionczek,'Economics of the Armaments Race', In J. Rotblat and A. Pascolini (eds), The Arms Race at a Time of Decision (London: Macmillan, 1984) p.295.
2. See A. Pierre, The Global Politics of Arms Sales. (Princeton University Press, 1982); and S. Neuman, 'International Stratification and the Third World Military Industries', International Organization vol.38 (Winter 1984).
3. See H. Wulf, 'Developing Countries' (Chapter 10), in Nicole Ball and M. Leiteberg, (eds), The Structure of Defense Industry. (New York: St. Martin's Press, 1983); M. Moodie, 'Defence Industries in the Third World: problems and promises', in S. Neuman and Harkavy (eds), Arms Transfers in the Modern World. (New York: Praeger, 1979); S. Neuman op. cit.; T. Ohlson, 'Third World Arms Exporters - a new facet of the global arms race', Bulletin of Peace Proposals, vol.13(3) (1982).
4. H. Tuomi and R Vayrynen, Transnational Corporations, Armaments and Development (New York: St Martin's Press, 1982).
5. M. Moodie, op. cit. S. Landgren-Bäckström, 'The Transfer of Military Technology to Third World Countries', in H. Tuomi and R. Vayrynen (eds), Militarization and Arms Production in the Third World, (London: Croom Helm, 1983).

6. SIPRI Yearbook, World Armaments and Disarmament. (London and Philadelphia: Taylor and Francis, 1982).
7. R. Dagnino, 'A Industria de Armamentos O Estado e a Tecnologia', Revista Brasiliera de Tecnologia. vol.14(3) May-June (1983).
8. H. Tuomi and R. Vayrynen - op. cit. (1982).
9. G. Steinberg, 'Israel' (Chapter 9), in Nicole Ball and M. Leitenberg, op. cit.
10. A. Pierre, op. cit.
11. M. Klare, Unnoticed Arms Trade. International Security vol.8(12) (Fall 1983).
   Mary Kaldor, The Baroque Arsenal, (London: Andre Deutsh, 1981).
13. R. Dagnino, 'A Industria de Armamentos Brasileira: desenvolvimento e perspectivas', in R. Arnt (ed.), O Armamentismo e o Brasil, (Brasiliense, SP., 1985).
   See H. Tuomi and R. Vayrynen, op. cit. (1982); S. Landgren-Bäckström, op. cit.; H. Wulf, op. cit.
15. R. Dagnino, 'R&D Militar e desenvolvimento na America Latina', Politica e Estrategia, vol.2(3) July-September, (1984).
16. Mary Kaldor, op.cit.; and S. Melman, The Permanent War Economy (New York: Simon and Schuster, 1974).
17. S. Newman, op. cit.
18. E. Mercado, 'Armamentismo en America Latina y reduccion de gastos militares', Nueva Sociedad no.59 March/April (1982)

Appendix
Statement from the Pugwash Council 'East–West Conflicts and the Third World: Interrelationships and Implications for Peace'

The 35th Pugwash Conference on Science and World Affairs met in Campinas, Sao Paulo, Brazil on 3-8 July 1985. The participants comprised 89 scientists, other scholars, and public figures - as well as twelve students - from four international organisations and 33 countries (including China, whose high-level scientist participants were especially welcome after many years of absence from Pugwash Conferences).

The Conference was hosted by the State University of Campinas (UNICAMP) with helpful support from the City of Campinas, the Carlos Gomes School, the Secretary of Planning and the Secretary of Education of the State of Sao Paulo, Centrais Eletricas de Sao Paulo (CESP), and the Ministry of Science and Technology and the Ministry of Foreign Affairs of the Federal Government of Brazil. To all of these organisations - and especially to UNICAMP Rector José Aristodemo Pinotti and the Conference organiser Professor Ubiratan D'Ambrosio - we express our sincere appreciation.

The opening session of the Conference heard addresses from Lieutenant Governor Orestes Quercia of the State of Sao Paulo, and Federal Minister of Science and Technology Renato Archer. A message of welcome and encouragement by President José Sarney was also conveyed.

This 35th Pugwash Conference coincided with the 30th anniversary of the Russell-Einstein Manifesto - drafted by Bertrand Russell, signed in addition by Albert Einstein and nine more of the world's most eminent scientists, and announced on 9 July 1955 - which called on scientists to assemble to 'appraise the perils that have arisen as a result of the development of weapons of mass destruction' and thus gave rise to the first such Conference in Pugwash, Nova Scotia in 1957.

This year's Conference in Campinas also derived special significance from several other important anniversaries: 1985 marks the 40th anniversary of the creation of the atomic bomb, the destruction of the cities Hiroshima and Nagasaki by two such weapons, the Allied victory, and the signing of the

United Nations Charter: and it marks the 10th anniversary of the Helsinki Final Act stemming from the Conference on Security and Cooperation in Europe.

Of the 35 Pugwash Conferences held since 1957, the Campinas meeting was only the second to take place in Latin America. (The 1979 Conference was held in Mexico City). This venue underlined the increasing prominence of issues related to development, Third World conflict, and North-South relations on the agenda of scientists concerned with world affairs. The attention traditionally given by Pugwash to the nuclear arms race in the North and to the East-West confrontation in Europe was continued in Campinas - including coverage of such issues as new technological developments in nuclear and non-nuclear weaponry, avoidance of the weaponisation of space, and the prospects for tightening restraints on chemical weapons - but added to these focuses was a wide-ranging programme of topics of special relevance to the South. These latter topics included: proliferation of nuclear weapons, the arms trade, emergence of military industries in the South, the current situation in Central America and its global implications, external indebtedness problems of developing countries, the Malvinas-Falklands issue, maintenance of Antarctica as a zone free of military activities, and the problems of Southern Africa.

The participants at Pugwash Conferences take part as individuals and not as representatives of their governments or institutions. The following statement on some of the topics treated at the 35th Conference was prepared by the Pugwash Council. It is not a summary of all the discussions that took place at the Conference, and it should not be interpreted as a consensus of all the participants, among whom a wide range of views was represented. Summaries of the discussions in the individual Working Groups of the Conference have been prepared by rapporteurs for those Groups and will become part of the published Proceedings of the Conference, which are circulated to heads of state, a variety of other decision makers, and past Pugwash participants around the world.

Nuclear and Other Weapons in the Context of the East-West Confrontation

In the 40 years since the destruction of Hiroshima and Nagasaki, no further nuclear weapons have been exploded in warfare. This success in the primary goal of avoiding nuclear war should be a source of satisfaction (and relief) to Pugwash scientists, as well as to all the other scientists and citizens around the world who have worked during this period to communicate the great dangers of nuclear weapons to decision makers and to the public.

Yet there are no grounds for complacency. The confrontation between East and West has contributed to a nuclear arms race that has produced a global arsenal of perhaps 50 000 nuclear weapons, most of them in the possession of the United States and the Soviet Union. The explosion of even a small fraction of these weapons could destroy most of industrial civilisation, with incalculable consequences for developing countries as well (even assuming the latter were not targetted directly). Not even the most pessimistic of the concerned scientists of 1945 or 1955 could foresee the tremendous expansion in the numbers and types of nuclear weapons that has now taken place, leaving the builders of these arsenals as well as the rest of the citizens of the world both poorer and less safe than we would be without them.

Now, in 1985, a combination of trends in the continuation of the nuclear arms competition is creating even greater dangers. Both sides continue to deploy new nuclear weapons with characteristics suited for pre-emptive attacks on the retaliatory capacity of the adversary, building fear and mistrust and generating an action-reaction spiral in which the arsenals grow without limit. The pursuit of technologies for defending populations against attack by nuclear missiles, the futility of which is recognised by an overwhelming majority of professional opinion, threatens to extend the nuclear arms race into space and to provoke further build-ups of offensive nuclear weapons. And the continuing failure of the United States and the Soviet Union to stop and reverse their own nuclear arms race is adding to the temptations for other nuclear powers to expand their nuclear arsenals and for additional countries to acquire such weapons for themselves.

The fragile web of arms-control agreements that until now has provided at least some measure of restraint on the foregoing tendencies is in danger of disintegration. The centrepieces of this web of restraints are the Anti-Ballistic Missile Treaty of 1972 and the SALT II Agreements of 1979 (never ratified but so far observed by both sides). The collapse of either of these treaties would inevitably lead to collapse of the other, and that would lead in turn to grave threats to the Partial Test Ban Treaty, the Non-Proliferation Treaty (which comes up for review in September of this year), and others.

The comprehensive nature of the threats to the arms-control regime means that only a comprehensive approach can prevent disaster. That approach must include:

(1) Preservation of the ABM Treaty and - if possible - its

strengthening by clarification, in the Standing Consultative Commission, of ambiguities.
(2) Other measures to prevent the weaponisation of space,
including independent moratoria on testing anti-satellite
weapons, followed by a permanent negotiated ban.
(3) Continued observance of SALT II restraints, as a precursor to deep cuts in nuclear forces. (The cuts should
give priority to those forces that most contribute to
mutual fears of first strike).
(4) A comprehensive ban on the testing of nuclear explosives
(CTB). (A CTB would terminate a key part of the futile
and dangerous pursuit of ways to make nuclear weapons
usable and would strengthen the Non-Proliferation
Treaty).

The illusory concept of controlled and limited use of
nuclear weapons for 'war fighting' has had a particularly
perverse influence on the nuclear arms race, and the dangerous idea that it is sensible to try to deter conventional
attack by threatening the first use of nuclear weapons has
been an important part of this problem. NATO has been
reluctant to match the pledges of 'no first use' of nuclear
weapons that have been made by China and the   Soviet Union,
for fear that such a posture would reduce the barriers to
conventional conflict; but the risks of the present policy of
'first use if necessary' seem intolerable in the long run.
NATO should re-examine its position and make any changes in
its posture needed to permit reliance on non-provocative
conventional deterrence of conventional threats. The
effectiveness of mutual declarations of a policy of no first
use can and should be reinforced by actual changes in nuclear
force postures, such as withdrawal of 'battlefield' nuclear
weapons from forward positions, and by a restructuring of
conventional forces to increase the ratio of defensive over
offensive capabilities.
The use of chemical weapons is prohibited by the Geneva
Protocol of 1925; but this agreement does not prohibit their
production and stockpiling, and some of its signatories
reserved the right to use chemical weapons in retaliation
against first use of such weapons by others. The much more
comprehensive Convention on Chemical Weapons being explored
in the Geneva Conference on Disarmament represents an
appropriate and needed addition to the restraints in the
Geneva Protocol. The difficulty of reaching accord on
verification procedures has proved to be an obstacle to
concluding an agreement. Progress in verification technology
and in clarification of the types of verification procedures
that would be acceptable to all parties has now reached the

point, however, where the issues that remain unsolved are not
so important as to stand in the way of concluding the Convention.

The meeting of President Reagan and General Secretary
Gorbachev scheduled for Geneva in November 1985 will provide
an important opportunity for reaching a general agreement on
principles between the two leaders, which, if accomplished,
would open the way to early achievement of the specific
measures described here for strengthening restraints on
nuclear, conventional, and chemical weapons. We respectfully
urge the two leaders to seize this crucial opportunity.

Problems in the South and North-South Interactions

Pugwash participants have long recognised that improving the
prospects for a sustainable peace not only will require halt-
ing and reversing the nuclear arms race and improving the
management of East-West relations more generally, but also
will require much more systematic attention to the problems
inherent in conditions in the South and in North-South interactions. These problems include: the widespread prevalence in
the South of crushing poverty, manifested in absolute shortages of the material ingredients of a decent existence; low
economic growth rates that in some regions do not even keep
pace with population growth; punishing rates of inflation;
debilitating burdens of external debt; the accelerating
destruction in many areas of the environmental   basis of
human well-being in the form of soils, forests, and water
supplies; the diversion of desperately needed productive
resources and foreign exchange into regional arms races; and
the devastating human and economic costs of internal and
regional armed conflicts.

While these problems are in part manifestations of
conditions indigenous in the South, they often have been
aggravated and sometimes have been caused by the actions (or
inactions) of countries in the North. Examples include:
maintenance of economic relationships inequitable to and
exploitative of the South; the tiny proportions of the
economic output of the North devoted to concessional economic
assistance for the South; the embarrassing inadequacy of
programmes of North-South technological cooperation and
assistance; the export from North to South of particularly
unsafe and environmentally disruptive industrial activities
in the name of 'development'; the export from North to South
of sophisticated weaponry that has fuelled regional arms
races and increased the tendency of major powers in the North
to interpret their international 'interests' as justifying
extensive military and political intervention in the South.

These patterns of action and inaction by the North need urgently to be changed, most importantly because such change is essential to realisation of the fundamental rights of peoples in the South to self determination and attainment of a decent standard of living. Even beyond this most basic consideration, however, people and governments in the North should recognise that the necessary changes are also in their own direct self interest: in a world increasingly inter-connected by flows of people, money, information, resources, pollutants, and sophisticated armaments, it is an illusion to think that the countries of the North can isolate themselves from the catrastrophic consequences of continued poverty, oppression, environmental deterioration, and conflict in the South.

The location of this Conference in Latin America led to special focus on the problems of this region as represent-ative of the difficulties in the South more generally. The most immediately threatening of such problems on our agenda is the crisis in Central America, which has social, politi-cal, economic, and military dimensions and which poses the threat of escalation into major war. Mindful of the principles of non-intervention and national integrity inscribed in the charters of the United Nations and the Organisation of American States, and emphasising the approach of conflict resolution through negotiation consistently advocated by Pugwash, we strongly urge:

(1) that the United States should accept the efforts of the Contadora countries in their search for a peaceful solution to the Central American crisis;
(2) that all the Central American countries accept the September 1984 Condatora draft proposals, as amended by those of the October proposals from El Salvador, Honduras, and Costa Rica that are acceptable to Contadora;
(3) that the Contadora process be strengthened through more direct support by Brazil, Argentina, Uruguay, and other South American countries;
(4) that the United States return to bilateral talks with the Nicaraguan government and cease its attempts to undermine that government through funding of the contras and imposition of an economic embargo;
(5) that the Soviet Union should exercise restraint from encouraging or undertaking any actions that might aggravate this fragile situation.

Another problem of great potential impact on the linked security concerns of North and South is the proliferation of nuclear weapons to additional countries. In this connection, we reiterate our strong belief that countries that acquire nuclear weapons decrease rather than increase their security by doing so. This is so not only because acquiring such weapons may stimulate regional rivals to acquire them, and because possession of nuclear weapons may make a country the target of nuclear weapons possessed by others, but also because diversion of scarce technical and economic resources into nuclear weaponry reduces the **real** bases of security, which are economic, technological, social, and political.

In Latin America in particular, we are concerned that both Argentina and Brazil, which are neither parties to the Non-Proliferation Treaty nor **full** parties to the Treaty of Tlatelolco, are close to possessing the technological capability for producing nuclear weapons. It is in the interest of both countries, of the other countries in Latin America, and of the rest of the world, that Latin America remain a nuclear-weapon-free zone. (Today it is the only such zone in a major, populated geographic region. We of course support the preservation of Antarctica as a region free of **any** military activities). We therefore urge Argentina and Brazil to refrain from exercising the option, which their state of development in nuclear technology may provide them, to acquire nuclear weapons, and we hope that both countries will certify such a commitment by becoming full parties to the Treaty of Tlatelolco and parties to the Non-Proliferation Treaty at an early date. We emphasise also the commitment by the extra-regional nuclear-weapons states that are parties to the Treaty of Tlatelolco not to introduce nuclear weapons into the region.

Among other topics related to security in the South and its linkages to global security, we single out for comment here the situation in Southern Africa. The system of apartheid has resulted in internal unrest in the Republic of South Africa, where the politically, economically, and socially deprived majority has begun to resist the long-standing injustices. In neighbouring countries, economic and military pressures being exerted by South Africa have been compounded by droughts and floods, with disastrous consequences for agriculture. South Africa's technical capability to build nuclear weapons - an option some analysts think she has already exercised - adds a further frightening complication to the situation.

Solutions to these problems will be difficult. We have several recommendations:

(1) Every pressure should be brought to bear on South Africa not to produce and/or test nuclear weapons, and to sign and adhere to the provisions of the Non-Proliferation

Treaty.
(2) The international community should support anti-apartheid forces in South Africa in working to bring about political, economic, and social change.
(3) Efforts should be intensified to bring about Namibian independence.

*   *   *

In the Russell-Einstein Manifesto that gave birth to the Pugwash Movement, and whose thirtieth anniversary we celebrate today, there appear these words:

> Most of us are not neutral in feeling, but, as human beings, we have to remember that, if the issues between East and West are to be decided in any manner that can give any possible satisfaction to anybody, whether Communist or anti-Communist, whether Asian or European or American, whether White or Black, then these issues must not be decided by war. We should wish this to be understood, both in the East and in the West.

> There lies before us, if we choose, continual progress in happiness, knowledge, and wisdom. Shall we, instead, choose death, because we cannot forget our quarrels? We appeal, as human beings, to human beings: Remember your humanity, and forget the rest.

It is obvious to us - as surely it would be to Russell and Einstein if they were alive today - that this appeal is not less applicable and compelling in the context of the growing problems of a South-South and North-South nature than it is in the context of the East-West confrontation. Indeed, the problems along these various geographic axes have now become so complexly and tightly linked that, although reducing the danger of global nuclear war must remain the first priority of Pugwash, we see that this goal cannot be accomplished without attention to the **interaction** of problems of North and South with those of East and West. That has been the insight and theme underlying this 35th Pugwash Conference on Science and World Affairs, and we expect it to infuse our efforts for the next thirty years and beyond.

Index

SOCIAL SCIENCE LIBRARY

Oxford University Library Services
Manor Road
Oxford OX1 3UQ
Tel: (2)71093 (enquiries and renewals)
http://www.ssl.ox.ac.uk

This is a NORMAL LOAN item.

We will email you a reminder before this item is due.

Please see http://www.ssl.ox.ac.uk/lending.html
for details on:

- loan policies; these are also displayed on the notice boards and in our library guide.

- how to check when your books are due back.

- how to renew your books, including information on the maximum number of renewals. Items may be renewed if not reserved by another reader. Items must be renewed before the library closes on the due date.

- level of fines; fines are charged on overdue books.

Please note that this item may be recalled during Term.